Building Contractor's Exam Preparation Guide

By John E. Traister & C. Keeler Chapman

Craftsman Book Company
6058 Corte del Cedro/ P.O. Box 6500 / Carlsbad, CA 92018

Acknowledgments

We are indebted to several individuals and organizations who helped in the preparation of this book. One group is the electrical examining boards throughout the United States. A list of these organizations appears in Appendix I.

Especially helpful in the production of this book was:

Ruby Updike, typist and organizer

Library of Congress Cataloging-in-Publication Data

Traister, John E.
   Building contractor's exam preparation guide / by John F. Traister
   & C. Keeler Chapman
      p.   c.m
   Includes index.
   ISBN 1-57218-030-7
   1. Building--Examinations, questions, etc. 2. Building-
   Examinations--Study guides. I. Chapman, C. Keeler. II. Title.
TH166.T73   1996
690'.076--dc20   96-22868
                              CIP

©1996 Craftsman Book Company
Eighth printing 2008

Contents

Introduction

The primary reason that states, counties, and cities license building contractors is to protect public health, safety, and welfare. State laws accomplish these goals by preventing unqualified people from practicing a given profession or occupation. To become licensed, potential building contractors must meet minimum standards of experience and sometimes education. Licensing is also a formal and legal way of defining a trade or profession and assuring that those who meet the predetermined standards necessary for licensing can provide the public with competent and knowledgeable services and/or work. Licensing bodies serve society in a positive way and provide the following benefits:

- Screening applicants to ensure that they possess those minimum qualifications necessary for safe practice.
- Providing a mechanism for investigating charges of incompetence or faulty installations.
- Setting standards of practice and codes of conduct. These standards give the public a basis for determining acceptable quality in workmanship, service, and conduct.

A governmental agency which will first investigate charges of a contractor licensee's incompetence or failure to perform work and then will take the appropriate disciplinary action, helps to protect the profession from incompetent, unethical, or dishonest practitioners. It also serves notice on others that the regulatory agency will not tolerate practitioners whose activities may not be in the public interest.

Licensing in the United States

Standards for licensure are set forth by law or regulations. State, county, or city professional and occupational boards have the responsibility for filling in specific details through the rule-making process. Such boards have responsibility for determining the content of the licensing examination and for interpreting certain other requirements. Furthermore, these same boards are responsible for determining who is qualified to be licensed.

In most areas, applicants apply to the appropriate agency by filing a form supplied by the board, paying the appropriate fee, being approved, and taking a written examination.

Most first-time applicants for a building contractor's license have been working in the building construction industry for a long time, accumulating much on-the-job experience. Yet many of them do poorly on a written examinations because the thought of taking exams worries them, or they do not know how to prepare for such exams.

This book shows how to properly take examinations, how to build the confidence you deserve, and how to keep exam anxiety from getting in the way of your knowledge.

What better way to prepare for your building contractor's examination than to study sample questions from actual state, county, and city examinations — in the privacy of your own home?

Building Contractor's Exam Preparation Guide will also help you:

- Familiarize yourself with state, county, and city testing procedures.
- Eliminate any pre-exam anxiety.
- Better understand the subjects appearing on contractor's examinations.

Building Contractor's Exam Preparation Guide covers all the topics that will appear on any contractor's examination. Once you have reviewed the basic subject matter (using the hundreds of sample questions in this book), you can take the full-length practice examination that is included at the end of this book. This practice exam covers the same subject areas and types of questions that appear on actual contractor's examinations throughout the United States.

State Building Construction Requirements

States frequently change their requirements for licensing. We recommend that you call your state's licensing office or check their Web site to make sure these requirements haven't changed. See page 305 for a listing of state contractor's licensing offices.

Alabama

Any person, firm or corporation engaged in contracting building projects in Alabama costing over $10,000 shall be required to be licensed. A license is also required for any type of swimming pool construction or repair costing more than $5,000.

Alaska

General contractors may not submit bids or do work until they are registered by the Alaska Department of Commerce and Economic Development. Bids from subcontractors may not be used unless that subcontractor is also registered.

Alaska has not adopted any state-wide building codes. However, most localities hav adopted the Uniform Building Code (UBC), as published by the International Conference of Building Officials (ICBO).

Arizona

Any person, firm or corporation must submit evidence of qualifications to engage in contracting in Arizona, and shall be licensed as described in the Arizona State Contracting Licensing Laws and Regulations.

Arkansas

Any construction work in excess of $20,000 is regulated at the state level. Residential construction work, however, may be regulated at the local level.

California

Licensing is required for all building construction involving projects of $500 or more. First time applicants are subject to a business law examination and a trade examination. Exam results are good for 5 years.

Colorado

Most building construction work, other than electrical and plumbing, is regulated in varying degrees by cities or counties.

Connecticut

To safeguard life, health and property, no person is allowed to engage in or offer to practice as a general contractor or major subcontractor in the state unless such person has secured a license as provided by the Connecticut General Statutes and the Regulations of Connecticut State Agencies Statute.

Building codes used in Connecticut include: BOCA National Building Code, BOCA Supplement, State of Connecticut Code Supplement, and OSHA Standards for the Construction Industry.

Delaware

A license is required for any type of building construction in Delaware. Contractor licenses are issued for a one-year period, expiring on December 31st. The average processing time for a first-time applicant is approximately 6 weeks.

District of Columbia

Licenses are required only for home improvement contractors in the District of Columbia. Other contractors may be required to demonstrate their ability to handle a project before contracts are awarded.

Florida

Building construction in the state of Florida, depending upon the circumstances, is regulated by either the local/municipal level or by certification at the state level.

Georgia

Only specialty building construction trades are handled at the state level in Georgia. Some municipalities and counties, however, may require building contractors to be licensed.

Hawaii

Every aspect of building construction is regulated at the state level in Hawaii. At the present time, no written examination is required for building contractors; only a performance bond for each project.

Idaho

Building construction is not regulated at the state level; only electrical construction work is regulated. However, local cities and counties may require licensing.

Illinois

Except for public works, building construction is not regulated at the state level. Some cities and counties, however, do have licensing requirements.

Indiana

State licensing requirements exist for plumbing contractors only. Some cities and counties, however, may require licensing for building construction.

Iowa

All building construction may require state registration. All work performed for the state or a state agency definitely requires registration.

Kansas

Licensing for building construction is not handled on the state level in Kansas. Many cities and counties, however, have licensing requirements and a bond is required for all contracts. In lieu of local examinations, code exams given by the International Congress of Building Officials and Block & Associates are recognized by the local licensing authorities. The examinations recognized are the ICBO's General Contractor exam (4 hours, open book) and Block's Kansas UBC exam (6 hours, open book).

Kentucky

Licensing for building construction is not handled on the state level in Kentucky. Many cities and counties, however, have licensing requirements.

Louisiana

Licensing is required for all building construction exceeding $50,000 in cost. Building contractors must pass a written examination dealing with the specific trade as well as business law.

Maine

Licensing for building construction is not handled on the state level in Maine. Many cities and counties, however, have licensing requirements.

Maryland

Home improvement contractors are licensed at the state level. Other construction work requires registration by the state.

Massachusetts

Building construction up to 35,000 cu. ft. requires a licensed contractor supervisor. Many cities and counties in Massachusetts have their own examinations and prequalification requirements.

Michigan

Residential building construction requires licensing at the state level. All other building contractors are regulated at a local city or county level.

Minnesota

Residential building and remodeling contractors are licensed at the state level. All other building contractors are regulated at a local city or county level.

Mississippi

Any person contracting or undertaking projects as a prime contractor, subcontractor or sub-subcontractor in the state of Mississippi must have a Certificate of Responsibility or a Residential Builder's License, depending upon the size and type of project.

The Southern Building Code Congress International (SBCCI) is the standard building code in Mississippi. The state also uses OSHA Standards for the Construction Industry.

Missouri

Construction is not regulated at the state level in Missouri. Some municipalities and counties, however, may require building contractors to be licensed.

Montana

All construction work over $500 requires registration, but licensing of contractors is not held at the state level. Some municipalities and counties, however, may require building contractors to be licensed.

Nebraska

Contracts exceeding $2,500 by out-of-state contractors are regulated at the state level in Nebraska. Some municipalities and counties, however, may require building contractors to be licensed.

Nevada

All building construction in the state of Nevada is regulated at the state level. A license is not required when a contractor performs work for the federal government on federal land.

New Hampshire

General building construction is not regulated at the state level. Many cities and counties, however, have licensing requirements.

New Jersey

New residential building construction, maintenance, and repair is regulated at the state level. Many cities and counties have licensing requirements for other building construction projects.

New Mexico

All building construction is regulated at the state level in New Mexico.

New York

Building construction is not handled on the state level in New York. Many cities and counties, however, have licensing requirements.

North Carolina

All building construction is regulated at the state level in North Carolina. Applicants for a general contractor's license must pass trade and law examinations before a license will be issued.

North Dakota

All construction work exceeding $2,000 per project is handled at the state level in North Dakota. Some cities and counties may also have licensing requirements.

Ohio

Licensing for building contractors is not handled on the state level in Ohio. Some municipalities and counties, however, may require building contractors to be licensed.

Oklahoma

Building construction is not regulated at the state level in Oklahoma. Many cities and counties have licensing requirements for building construction projects.

Oregon

All building construction costing over $500 is regulated at the state level in Oregon. One responsible individual per new contracting business must complete 16 hours of business and law classes before an application can be made. General contractors are further required to post a bond to bid on construction work.

Pennsylvania

Building construction is not handled on the state level in Pennsylvania. Many cities and counties have licensing requirements for building construction projects.

Rhode Island

Residential building construction of 4 dwelling units or less is regulated at the state level through registration. Many cities and counties have licensing requirements for other building construction projects.

South Carolina

General building construction projects costing over $30,000 are regulated at the state level in South Carolina. Residential general work over $5,000, and residential specialty work over $200, also requires a state license.

South Dakota

General building construction projects, and licensing thereof, are not handled at the state level. Many cities and counties have licensing requirements for building construction projects.

Tennessee

Any person, firm or corporation engaged in contracting in Tennessee shall be required to submit evidence of qualifications to engage in contracting, and shall be licensed as described in the State of Tennessee Contractors' License Law.

The Southern Building Code Congress International (SBCCI) is the standard building code in Tennessee. The state also uses OSHA Standards for the Construction Industry.

Texas

Building construction is not handled on the state level in Texas. Many cities and counties have licensing requirements for building construction projects.

Utah

All building construction work costing over $500 is regulated at the state level in Utah. The size of each construction project is limited, based on the financial statement of each individual contractor.

Vermont

Building construction is not handled on the state level in Vermont. Many cities and counties have licensing requirements for building construction projects.

Virginia

Building construction work in excess of $1,000 is regulated at the state level. Applicants for a building or general contractor's license must pass an open book examination on regulations and statutes of the Contractor's Board and business management practices.

Washington

Construction work of all kinds is regulated at the state level in Washington. However, building contractors are not required to take any examination at the present.

West Virginia

All construction work costing over $1,000 (including materials and labor) is regulated at the state level. Applicants for a building contractor's license must pass an open book examination on business and law, and a trade specific test, with a minimum score of 70%. Furthermore, before undertaking a construction project, the contractor must show proof of Worker's Compensation and Employment Security coverage.

Wisconsin

Building construction is not regulated at the state level in Wisconsin. Many cities and counties, however, have licensing requirements for building construction projects.

Wyoming

Building construction is not regulated at the state level in Wyoming. Many cities and counties, however, have licensing requirements for building construction projects.

How to Prepare for the Contractor's Exam

This book is a guide to preparing for building contractor's examinations throughout the United States. It is not, however, a substitute for studying the recommended references. It will not teach you all about the building construction industry; you need some prior knowledge and experience first. But this book will give you a complete knowledge of the type of questions asked in any contractor's exam. It will also give you a "feel" for the examination and provide some of the confidence you need to pass.

The emphasis is on multiple-choice questions because that's the style that nearly all tests utilize. Questions are grouped into chapters, each chapter covering a single subject. This will help you discover your strengths and weaknesses. Then when you take the final exam in the back of this book, you can analyze the questions you miss. You will probably notice you are weaker in some subjects than others. When you learn where your weak-nesses are, you will know what areas need further study.

The preparatory questions in the front part of this book have the answer after each question. When reading a question, cover the answer with a card or a ruler of an appropriate size. Read the question carefully. Mark your answer on a separate sheet of paper before moving the card or ruler that covers the correct answer. Then slide the card or ruler away and check to see if your answer is correct. If it isn't, read the responses under the answer to find out why it is wrong.

How to Study

Set aside a definite time to study, following a schedule that meets your needs. Studying a couple of hours two or three nights each week is better than studying all day on, say, Saturdays. The average mind can only concentrate for approximately 4 hours without taking a break. There is no point in studying if you don't retain much of the information. Study alone most of the time, but spend a few hours reviewing with another person before exam day. If you have a buddy that is also going to take the building contractor's exam, work together. You can help each other dig out the facts and concepts you will need to pass the exam.

Try to study in a quiet, well-lighted room that is respected as your study space by family members and friends. If it's hard to find a spot like that in your home, go to the local library where others are reading and studying.

Before you begin to study, spend a few minutes getting into the right frame of mind. That's important. You don't have to be a genius to pass the builder's exam, but good motivation will nearly always guarantee your success. No one can provide that motivation but *you*. Getting your contractor's license is a goal you set for yourself; it's your key to the future and a satisfying career in the building construction industry.

The Examination

Questions on state and local city and county examinations are usually compiled by members of the Contractor's Examination Board or by a private company that provides examination services.

Although the exact content will vary from state to state, and from one examination to another, all will contain questions relative to the building construction industry. Most of these questions are covered in this preparation guide.

The format of the actual examination, the time allowed, and the reference material which the applicant may be allowed to take into the examination room vary with each locality. The following is typical of the examination given in many areas:

BUILDING CONTRACTOR'S EXAM	
Subject	**Percentage of Total Exam**
Carpentry	20%
Concrete	14%
Masonry	14%
Structural Steel and Rebar	12%
Roofing	10%
Associated Trades	10%
Excavation and Site Work	7%
Drywall	5%
Insulation	4%
Safety	4%

In many localities, a business and law examination is also required of all contractors; this business and law examination is in addition to the trade examination. Again, the content of the business and law exam will vary from state to state, but the following is typical:

BUSINESS AND LAW EXAMINATION	
Subject	**Percentage of Total Exam**
Project Management	20%
Contract Management	20%
Licensing Law and Rules	10%
Financial Management	10%
Safety Requirements	10%
Employment Laws	8%
Payroll Taxes	6%
Risk Management	6%
Mechanics' Lien Law	6%
Business Organization	4%

The Answer Sheet

Most answer sheets used today are designed for computer grading. Each question on the exam is numbered. Usually there will be 4 or 5 possible responses for each question. You will be required to mark the best answer on the answer sheet. The following is a sample of a multiple-choice question:

1) Richmond is the capitol city of what state?

(A) Texas   (C) Virginia

(B) Maryland   (D) Alabama

You should mark answer C for question 1 on the answer sheet.

Answer sheets will vary slightly for each examining agency, so be sure to follow any instructions on that sheet. Putting the right answer on the wrong section will almost certainly cause you to fail.

The Night Before

Give your mind a rest! If you have not prepared correctly for the exam by this time, then you can't cram it all into your brain in one night. So take it easy. If the place of the examination is more than an hour's drive from your home, you might want to stay at a motel in the city where the examination is being held. Getting up at, say, 4 a.m. and driving a couple of hours in heavy traffic will not help you to pass the exam. On the other hand, a drive to the location the afternoon before the exam, a good dinner, and a relaxing evening watching TV will help your possibilities of passing. Just don't stay up too late.

There are, however, exceptions to this rule. Some people find it difficult to sleep comfortably the first night at a strange location. If this is the case with you, you would be better off getting a good night's sleep at home and driving to the location the next morning.

Just be sure to have all of your reference material with you, and get a good night's sleep before the day of the exam. If you have prepared yourself correctly, you will pass with flying colors!

Examination Day

On the day of your examination, listen carefully to any oral instructions given and read the printed directions. Failing to follow instructions will probably disqualify you.

You will seldom find any trick questions, but many will require careful reading. Certain words like *shall*, *should*, *always*, and *never* can make a big difference in your answer.

Sometimes several of the answers may seem possible, but only one will be correct. If you are not sure of the answer, use the process of elimination.

There are several ways to take an exam, but the following is the method I used to pass the Virginia State Electrical Contractor's Exam a few years ago. This method should apply equally well to building contractor's examinations.

When the exam booklets were passed out for my exam and we were given permission to open them, I spent the first 2 or 3 minutes going over the entire exam booklet, noting the total number of questions. This knowledge allowed me to pace myself. I noted a total of 100 questions on the morning exam, which allowed me less than 3 minutes to spend on each one.

I then started with question number 1 and continued in sequence through the test booklet. When a tough question was encountered or I found one that I was not sure of, I merely skipped it and went on to one that I definitely knew. This way, I went through the entire test booklet one time and answered about 50% of the questions in a little over an hour. I was quite sure that I had answered all of these questions correctly. However, 70% is usually the minimum passing grade, and at this point, I had only 50% of the questions answered. However, I still had about 3 hours to spend on the tougher questions.

I started back at the beginning of the exam and went down the list of questions until I found one that was left, and answered it. This process continued until I had answered all the questions to the best of my ability. I spent the remaining time reviewing all answers, making changes as necessary.

After lunch, the "afternoon" portion of the exam was handed out, and I used the same procedure as before. I found out a few days later that I had scored 94% on the examination. This method is merely a suggestion; if another way suits you better, by all means use it.

Chapter 1

Print Reading

A standard set of building construction documents consists of working drawings and written specifications. The drawings are usually divided into the following categories:

- A plot plan showing the location of the building on the property, streets, sidewalks, outside electrical wiring, plumbing pipes, and similar facilities. The plot plan is drawn to scale with the exception of some symbols, which must be enlarged to be readable.
- Floor plans showing the walls and partitions for each floor level.
- Elevations of all exterior faces of the building.
- A number of cross sections to indicate clearly the various floor levels and details of the footings, foundation, walls, floors, ceilings, and roof construction.
- Schedules, notes, and large-scale details as may be required.

For projects of any consequence, architects usually commission consulting engineers to prepare structural, electrical, plumbing, and heating, ventilating and air-conditioning (HVAC) drawings. A brief description of each follows:

Structural drawings are most often prepared by structural engineers on the basis of proper allowances for all vertical loads and lateral stresses. Such drawings are included with the architectural drawings for all long-span, wood-truss construction and all reinforced concrete and structural steel construction.

Electrical drawings for a building project generally cover the complete electrical design for lighting, power, alarm and communication systems, special electrical systems, and related electrical equipment. These drawings sometimes include a plot plan or site plan showing the location of the building on the property and the interconnecting electrical systems; floor plans showing the location of all outlets, lighting fixtures, panelboards, and other components and equipment; power-riser diagrams; a symbol list or legend; schematic diagrams; and large-scale details where necessary.

Mechanical drawings cover the installation of the plumbing, heating, ventilating, and air-conditioning systems within a building and on the premises. They cover the complete design and layout of these systems and show floor-plan layouts, cross sections of the building, and necessary detailed drawings. Control wiring for various heating and air-conditioning controls may also be included on the mechanical drawings.

To be able to "read" all types of building construction drawings, you must become familiar with the meanings of the symbols, lines, and abbreviations used on the drawings and learn how to interpret the message conveyed by the drawings.

Specifications

Specifications go hand in hand with the working drawings by giving a written description of the work and the duties required by the owner, architect, and engineer. Together with the working drawings, the written specifications form the basis of the contract requirements for the construction of the building.

Chapter Objectives

The questions in this chapter are designed to review working drawings and written specifications to give you an idea of the type of questions that might appear on builder's and general contractor's exams.

In reviewing these questions, please be aware that drawing symbols may vary on different drawings, but in actual practice there is usually a symbol list or legend giving the exact meaning of each. It is recommended that you review several books on the subject, as well as actual working drawings, if you find that print reading is one of your weak areas.

1-1   A "section" or "cross section" of an object or a building is what could be seen if the object were:

A) Sliced into two parts with one part removed

B) Sliced into six parts with three parts removed

C) Sawed into four parts

D) Left solid

Answer: A

A section of an object is what could be seen if the object were cut or sliced into two parts at the point where the section is taken; then the portion between the viewer and the cutting plane is removed to reveal the interior details of the object.

1-2   A supplemental drawing used with conventional working drawings that gives a complete and more exact description of the item's use is called:

A) Title block

B) Detail drawing

C) Schedule

D) Riser diagram

Answer: B

A detail drawing is a drawing of a single item or a portion of a building or system; it gives all the necessary details, and a complete description of its use, to show workers exactly what is required for the installation.

1-3   A site plan is a plan view (as if viewed from an airplane) that shows:

A) Each floor level of the building

B) Power-riser diagrams

C) Cross sections of the building

D) Property boundaries and buildings

Answer: D

A site plan shows the property boundaries and the building(s) drawn to scale and in its (their) proper location on the lot. Such plans will also include sidewalks, drives, streets, and similar details. Utilities, such as water lines, sanitary sewer lines, telephone lines, and electrical power lines, also appear on site plans.

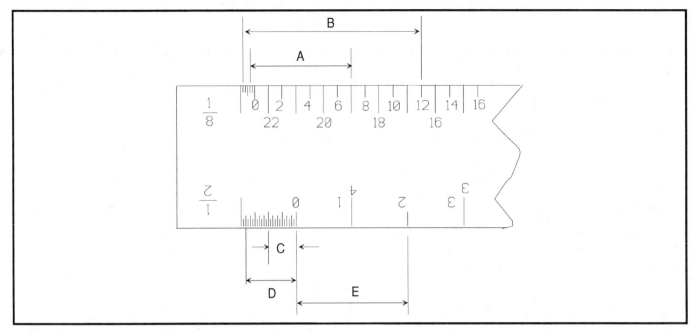

Figure 1-1: The ⅛-inch architect's scale used to measure building dimensions.

1-4   Using the ⅛-inch architect's scale in Figure 1-1, what is dimension A?

A) 12 feet 8 inches

B) 7 feet 4 inches

C) 12 feet 6 inches

D) 11 feet

Answer: B

Reading the ⅛-inch scale from left to right, the inch scale shows a dimension of 4 inches. Continue from the zero mark on the foot scale to the right to 7; thus, the reading is 7 feet 4 inches.

1-5   Using the ⅛-inch architect's scale in Figure 1-1, what is dimension B?

A) 12 feet 10 inches

B) 7 feet 4 inches

C) 12 feet 6 inches

D) 11 feet

Answer: A

Reading the ⅛-inch scale from left to right, the inch scale shows a dimension of 10 inches. Continue from the zero mark on the foot scale to the right to 12; thus, the reading is 12 feet 10 inches.

1-6   Look at the architect's scale in Figure 1-1. What is dimension C on the ½-inch scale?

A) 6 inches

B) 8 inches

C) 10 inches

D) 14 inches

Answer: A

Each mark on the inch scale represents ½ inch. Since 12 marks are covered, this is 6 inches.

1-7   Look at the architect's scale in Figure 1-1. What is dimension D on the ½-inch scale?

A) 6 inches

B) 8 inches

C) 10 inches

D) 11 inches

Answer: D

Each mark on the inch scale represents ½ inch. Since 22 marks are covered, this is 11 inches.

1-8   Look at the architect's scale in Figure 1-1. What is dimension E on the ½-inch scale?

A) 1 foot

B) 2 feet

C) 3 feet

D) 4 feet

Answer: B

Each mark on the foot scale represents 1 foot. Since 2 marks are covered, this represents 2 feet.

1-9   What is dimension A on the ¼-inch scale in Figure 1-2 on the next page?

A) 4 feet 9 inches

B) 1 foot 9 inches

C) 1 foot 6 inches

D) 37 feet 0 inches

Answer: A

Each mark on the inch scale represents 1 inch; each mark on the foot scale represents 2 feet. Consequently, the measurement of A is 4 feet 9 inches.

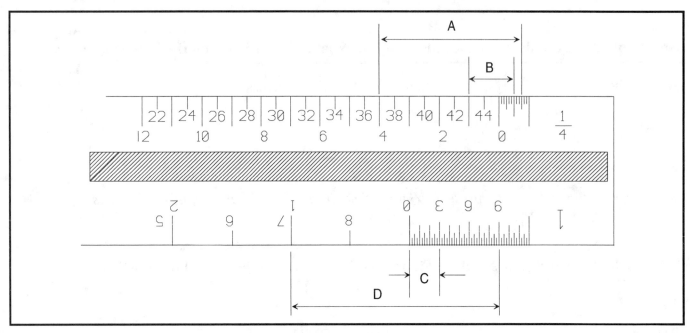

Figure 1-2: Typical architect's scale.

1-10   What is dimension B on the ¼-inch scale in Figure 1-2?

A) 1 foot 6 inches

B) 4 feet 6 inches

C) 43 feet 6 inches

D) 6 feet 4 inches

Answer: A

This scale is read from right to left; each mark in the inch section of the scale represents 1 inch. Therefore, 6 inches are shown in the inch section and 1 foot is shown in the foot section. Thus, 1 foot 6 inches is correct.

1-11   What is dimension C on the 1-inch scale in Figure 1-2?

A) 6 inches

B) 3 inches

C) 2 inches

D) 1 inch

Answer: B

Each of the longer marks on the inch scale represents 1 inch. Since there are 3 long marks, the measurement is 3 inches.

1-12   What is dimension D on the 1-inch scale in Figure 1-2?

A) 1 foot 6 inches

B) 12 inches

C) 1 foot 9 inches

D) 12 feet

Answer: C

This inch section of the 1-inch scale is read from left to right; each long mark represents 1 inch. The reading is 9 inches. The foot scale is read from right to left, indicating 1 foot. Therefore, the measurement is 1 foot 9 inches.

1-13   Which of the following best describes a sectional drawing?

A) A cutaway view of a building or object

B) A drawing as if the object were viewed from above

C) A drawing of an object as if viewed directly from the front

D) A drawing of an object as if viewed from one side

Answer: A

A section is as if an object were sliced in two portions with one portion removed to reveal the interior area of the object. For example, a vertical slice through a building drawing will reveal the interior structure.

1-14   At which of the following drawing locations is the drawing scale most likely to be shown?

A) In the symbol list

B) In the written specifications

C) Door and window schedule

D) Title block

Answer: D

The drawing scale is usually indicated in the drawing title block, but scale markings may also be encountered under other supplemental views found on the drawing sheet. A scale marking under a particular view on a drawing sheet supersedes the scale indicated in the title block for that particular view only.

1-15   A legend or symbol list is shown on building construction working drawings to:

A) Describe materials and installation methods

B) Show the outline of the architect's floor plan

C) Identify all symbols used to indicate materials and finishes

D) Enable the electric service size to be calculated

Answer: C

Drawing symbols vary, so a legend or symbol list usually appears on drawings to show the meaning of each symbol. Where a symbol is used to identify a single component, sometimes a note is used adjacent to the symbol to describe it.

1-16   Elevations shown on a site plan refer to:

A) The side view of the building

B) Horizontal distances between utility poles

C) Vertical height above or below a given reference point or "bench mark"

D) The dimensions of the parking lots

Answer: C

Site elevations are vertical heights above or below a given reference point. The reference point is called a bench mark. Sometimes the bench mark reference is sea level.

1-17   Site contours are:

A) Locations of buried utility lines

B) Continuous grade lines that show the height above or below a given reference point

C) Dimensions that are used to locate a building on a given site

D) Dimensions that define site boundaries

Answer: B

Site contours are represented by continuous lines sometimes called "grades." They are not dimension lines, but are used to calculate vertical dimensions similarly to site elevations.

1-18 If the fire hydrant in Figure 1-3 protrudes above the ground 2½ feet, what is the elevation at the base of the hydrant?

A) 102.50 feet

C) 97.50 feet

B) 0.00 feet

D) Cannot be determined

Answer: C

The top of the hydrant is bench mark elevation 100.00 feet. The base of the hydrant is 2½ feet below bench mark or 97.50 feet.

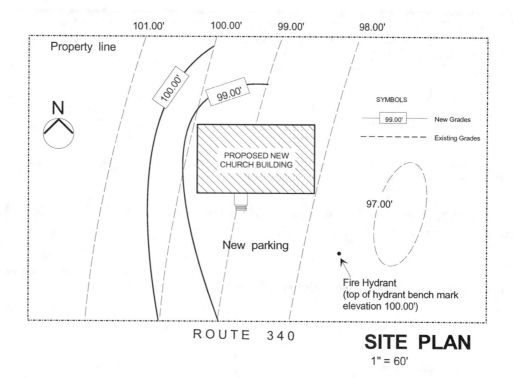

Figure 1-3: Site plan.

1-19 Proposed finished grade lines (contours) are:

A) Grades at the site before construction

C) Grade marks given by the building inspector on how well the contractor has done his job

B) Site grades at the completion of construction

D) Imaginary lines used only for bidding

Answer: B

Finished grade lines indicate how the land is to be reshaped and regraded at the end of all construction activities.

1-20   What is the proposed finished grade elevation at the northwest corner of the proposed building in Figure 1-3?

A) 99.00 feet

B) 98.00 feet

C) 97.50 feet

D) 1 foot below floor line

Answer: A

Existing contour 99.00 feet intersects the proposed building at about midpoint. This contour is shown to be moved to the NW corner and extends to the SE corner.

1-21   Does the structural joist framing shown on a floor plan normally indicate the floor framing of that level or the floor/ceiling framing above?

A) The floor framing of the plan level shown

B) The floor/ceiling framing above

C) The roof framing

D) Floor framing is shown only in a building section

Answer: B

Normally, framing shown on a plan is the framing of the floor/ceiling above. If structural framing is shown on the main or ground floor plan, then the framing shown is for the second floor (above).

1-22   To what scale is the floor plan of the residence in Figure 1-4 drawn?

A) $\frac{1}{8}$" = 1'0"

B) $\frac{1}{16}$" = 1'0"

C) 1" = 1'0"

D) $\frac{1}{4}$" = 1'0"

Answer: A

The floor plan is drawn to a scale of $\frac{1}{8}$" = 1'0" as indicated by note on the drawing.

1-23   Which best describes the size of the screened porch in Figure 1-4?

A) 9 × 9 feet

B) Screened porch size is not shown

C) 15 × 15 feet

D) 18 × 15 feet

Answer: D

The width of the porch is 11 feet 8 inches + 6 feet 4 inches or 18 feet. The length is shown as 15 feet.

1-24   What is the slope of the front porch roof shown in Figure 1-5 on the next page?

A) 4:12

B) 12:4

C) 20 degrees

D) 2 inches per foot

Answer: A

A 4 in 12 slope (4:12) indicates that for every 12 horizontal dimension units, the roof pitch elevates 4 vertical dimension units.

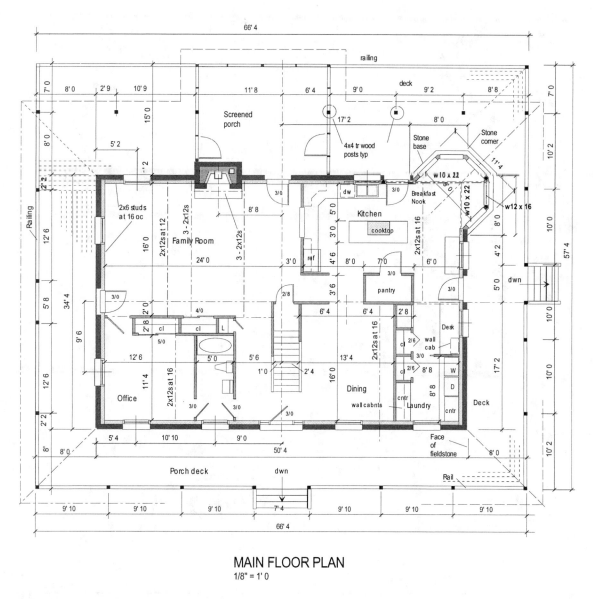

MAIN FLOOR PLAN
1/8" = 1' 0

Figure 1-4: Main floor plan.

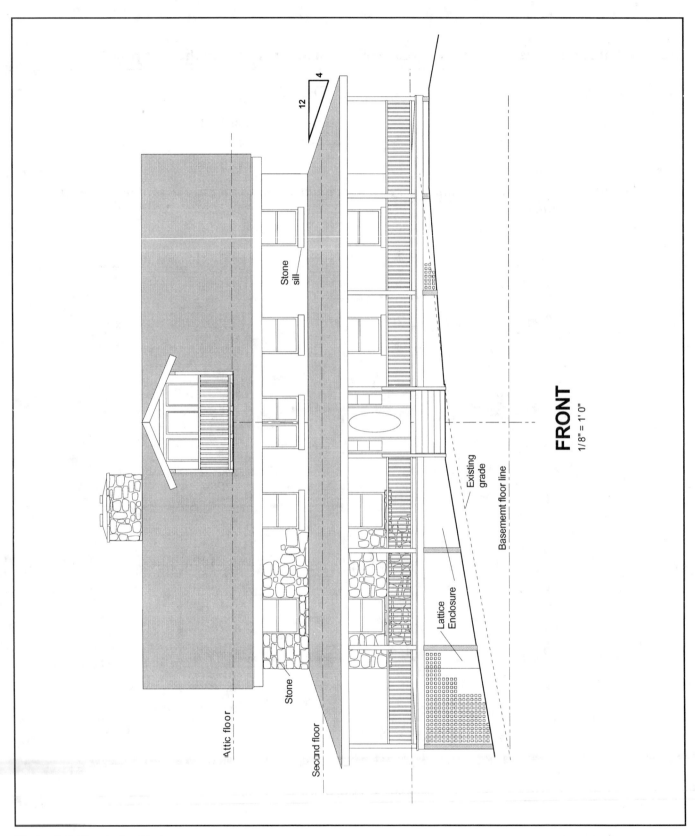

Figure 1-5: Front elevation.

1-25   **The front elevation shown in Figure 1-5 faces east. It can be renamed:**

A) The west elevation

C) The east elevation

B) The south elevation

D) The building front facade

Answer: C

The east elevation. The viewer is looking westward, but the front of the building faces east, therefore the front is the east elevation.

1-26   **What is the clear inside width of the stairs (located adjacent to the dining room) in Figure 1-6?**

A) 2 feet 4 inches

C) 3 feet 4 inches

B) 5 feet 6 inches

D) The dimension is not shown

Answer: C

The dimension shown on the drawing is 2'4" + 1'0" = 3'4" (3 feet 4 inches).

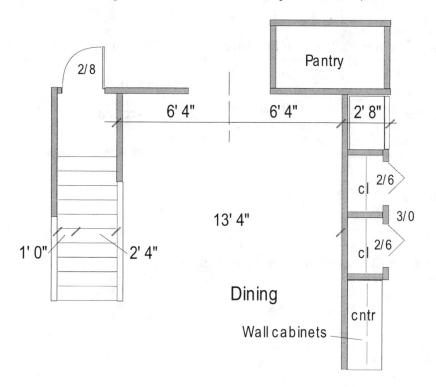

Figure 1-6: Enlarged drawing of the dining area in Figure 1-4.

1-27   Figure 1-7 shows another view of the house in Figure 1-5. Figure 1-7 could also be called:

A) The north elevation

B) The south elevation

C) The southeast elevation

D) The west elevation

Answer: B

One can tell that this elevation is the left side of the house primarily because of the location of the chimney. This side of the house faces south because the front of the house faces east.

1-28   How many exterior doors are shown on the main floor plan in Figure 1-4 on page 23?

A) 3 doors

B) 5 (not including screen doors)

C) 4 (not including screen doors)

D) 8

Answer: B

The floor plan shows 5 exterior doors.

1-29   Window sizes are normally given in which of the following tables?

A) Finish schedule

B) Window schedule

C) Door schedule

D) Wall sections

Answer: B

The window schedule.

1-30   The scale of a detail drawing drawn $\frac{1}{4}$ full size is:

A) $\frac{1}{4}" = 1'0"$

B) $\frac{3}{4}" = 1'0"$

C) $\frac{1}{2}" = 1'0"$

D) $3" = 1'0"$

Answer: D

$3" = 1'0"$ because $\frac{1}{4}$ of 12 (inches) is 3 (inches).

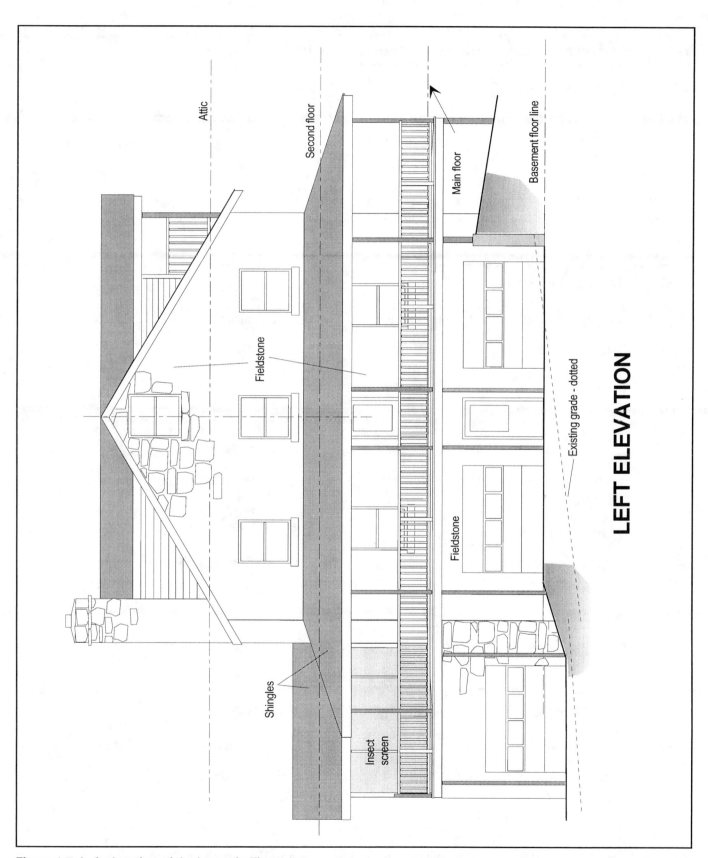

Figure 1-7: Left elevation of the house in Figure 1-5.

1-31 If a dimension is not shown, the contractor should:

A) Scale the drawings

B) Calculate sizes by the dimensions given

C) Redesign the drawing

D) Ask the building inspector

Answer: B

It is not a good idea to depend on scaling the drawings if an exact dimension is needed. By adding or subtracting the dimensions given, an exact dimension can usually be determined.

1-32 Match lines shown on a drawing:

A) Show alignment position of separate drawings

B) Are dimension lines

C) Show alignment of 1st and 2nd floors

D) Are utility lines

Answer: A

Match lines are used to align separate drawings that are too large to be shown as one drawing.

1-33 A symbol list is:

A) A list of imaginary lines

B) Always shown to scale

C) A listing of different window types

D) A description of drawing symbols

Answer: D

A symbol list illustrates each one of the symbol representations used on the drawings.

1-34 A building perspective (three-dimensional view of a building):

A) Can be scaled for pricing estimation

B) Cannot be scaled

C) Can be substituted for the building elevations

D) Can be measured for quantity take-offs

Answer: B

Perspectives, if included in a set of drawings, are not drawn to scale and should not be used as substitutions for building elevations or any other scaled drawing.

1-35   A sidewalk drawing scale is shown as ⅜" = 1'0". The walk is represented, on paper, by a line 3 inches long. What is the actual length of the constructed sidewalk?

A) 5 feet

B) 24 feet

C) 8 feet

D) 5 feet 6 inches

Answer: C

The fraction ⅜ inch converts to 0.375 inch (3 ÷ 8 = 0.375). Therefore, 3 inches ÷ 0.375 inch = 8 feet.

1-36   What is the best reason for not drawings trees and shrubs on building elevations?

A) They distract from the technical construction information

B) They are too hard to draw

C) They could not be scaled

D) They would interfere with window placement

Answer: A

Building elevations on a working set of drawings should stick to describing finish materials and other materials needed for construction.

1-37   A good reason for electrical circuit lines to be drawn curved rather than straight is:

A) This is how conduit is installed in buildings

B) To enable the drafters to route the lines around partitions

C) So as not to confuse the circuit lines with building lines

D) Curved lines are easier to draw on CAD systems than straight lines

Answer: C

When circuit lines are drawn straight, they are sometimes confused with the building lines. Thus, Answer C is one good reason for drawing curved circuit lines.

1-38   If the blueprints show a brick exterior finish, why can't the contractor pick the cheapest brick he or she can find for bidding the project?

A) This is exactly what the contractor should do

B) The written specifications may demand a specific brick or give a cost allowance

C) This would be a contract violation

D) If the blueprints do not show the cheapest brick then that brick is not allowed

Answer: B

The point to be remembered here is that the blueprints and written specifications work hand in hand. The contractor must review each very thoroughly before making decisions concerning the project.

1-39   Which is potentially a clearer detail drawing to understand, one drawn at a scale of $\frac{1}{16}$" = 1'0" or one drawn at a scale of $\frac{3}{8}$" = 1'0"?

A) Both scales are generally inappropriate

B) $\frac{1}{16}$" = 1'0" because it is smaller and allows more to be drawn on the sheet

C) There is very little difference between the two scales

D) $\frac{3}{8}$" = 1'0"

Answer: D

A scale of $\frac{3}{8}$ " = 1'0" is potentially better because its component parts are larger and easier to see.

1-40   Where are room ceiling heights normally noted?

A) In the finish schedule

B) In the schedule of values

C) In the specifications

D) On the architectural plans

Answer: A

The finish schedule lists ceiling finishes. This is also the traditional place to find the ceiling heights of each room.

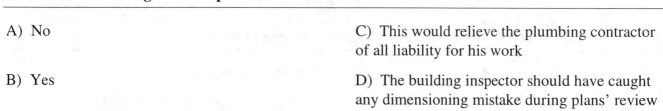

CHAPMAN & CHAPMAN
ARCHITECTS

New Church Building

ELECTRICAL

DATE:

REVISED:

SHEET No

E-1

Figure 1-8: A typical title block for architectural drawings.

1-41 From the title block in Figure 1-8, what does this drawing sheet entail; that is, which of the trades?

A) HVAC

B) Electrical

C) Plumbing

D) Interior decorating

Answer: B

The main sheet title is "Electrical."

1-42 There may not be any building dimensions on the plumbing floor plans. Would this be considered an oversight on the part of the architect?

A) No

B) Yes

C) This would relieve the plumbing contractor of all liability for his work

D) The building inspector should have caught any dimensioning mistake during plans' review

Answer: A

The floor plans are dimensioned on the architectural plan drawings. Special dimensions for the plumber should be on the plumbing plans, but these would normally be of limited scope.

1-43   Figure 1-5 on page 24 shows an exterior house finish of stone. Individual stones are shown. Must the stone mason conform to the individual stone pattern shown?

A) Yes

B) No

C) The stone mason needs only to see the floor plans to understand his or her portion of the work

D) Yes, if a pattern is not indicated in the written specifications

Answer: B

Only a typical random pattern is represented on the drawing in Figure 1-5. The specifications should clarify this somewhat and give a typical range of sizes for the stone and a stone pattern, but individual stones do not have to be shaped and spaced to match the elevations.

1-44   Again refer to Figure 1-5. Is it possible to tell what the house wall finish requirements are below the porch?

A) The wall finish is shown as lattice

B) It is assumed that stonework is required from grade up to roof eaves

C) No

D) Yes

Answer: C

It is not possible to know the wall finish requirements below the porch by looking at this elevation. The wall sections would be the best source for this information.

1-45   Does the subfloor sheathing shown in Figure 1-9 extend under the stud wall?

A) No

B) Yes

C) Cannot be determined

D) Subflooring never extends under walls

Answer: B

Subflooring is shown under the wall. This is a standard framing detail.

1-46   In Figure 1-9, what are the characteristics of the ceiling insulation?

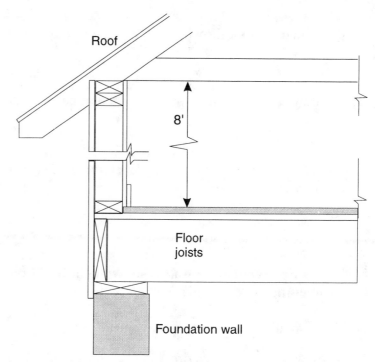

Figure 1-9: Wall section of a building.

A) It has an R-factor of 30

B) No specifications are shown

C) This insulation is to be blown in

D) The insulation has an R-factor of 20

Answer: B

Ceiling insulation is not shown in this drawing. The characteristics of the ceiling insulation must therefore be found on other drawings, or else described in the written specifications for the project.

1-47   The floor joists in Figure 1-9:

A) Are to be spaced at 16 inches on centers

B) Are to be 2- x 10-inch joists

C) Are to be floor trusses

D) Are to bear on a foundation wall plate

Answer: D

In this standard wall section, the floor joists are to bear on a foundation wall plate.

1-48   The floor-to-ceiling height in Figure 1-9:

A) Is incorrectly shown

B) Would be clearer if shown only on the floor plan

C) Cannot be measured by scale

D) Cannot be determined

Answer: C

The ceiling height is clearly marked as 8 feet but the section has a horizontal cut line which makes it impossible to scale the vertical floor to ceiling height.

1-49   Which of the following best describes a detail drawing?

A) A cross-sectional view

B) A drawing clarifying a specific item or area

C) An enlarged cross-sectional drawing

D) An enlarged floor-plan view

Answer: B

A detail clarifies information. It explains any item or specific area of the project that may otherwise be left to chance.

1-50   If a fire-separation wall is shown on a building's floor plan, which of the following applies to any openings in the wall?

A) They should be left completely open

B) They will need to have fire doors, dampers, or shutters

C) They are not allowed

D) They must have smoke detectors

Answer: B

A wall that is used to prevent the spread of smoke or fire must have opening closures. The exact type depends on the building type and the local fire marshall or building inspector.

Chapter 2

Building Calculations

Calculations are required for all types of building construction, from design to installations. Consequently, anyone involved in building contracting — in any capacity — will frequently be called upon to make certain mathematical calculations. Most contractor's examinations have some layout problems involving the knowledge of equations and mathematical calculations. The following examples were taken from actual county and state examinations. They are typical of those you will find on many trade examinations and also state contractor's examinations.

The basic math operations are *multiplication*, *division*, *addition*, and *subtraction*. My high school algebra teacher would frequently remind her students of this by using the phase, "**M**y **D**ear **A**unt **S**ally." She would also remind us that regardless of how complicated the equation, you could solve it using these four operations. Building contractors, and also workers anticipating taking any of the trade examinations, should be able to use these operations in solving whole number problems, decimal number problems, and problems dealing with fractions. With these four basic math operations, along with squares, square roots, and percents, the contractor will have all the basic tools necessary for solving most building construction calculations.

It is beyond the scope of this book to review mathematical functions, other than the examples given. Therefore, if you feel that your knowledge of mathematics is lacking, it is highly recommended that you take some means to improve your knowledge before taking the examination.

Fractions

Fractions result when one whole number is divided by another whole number, such as $\frac{3}{4}$. The top number, 3, is called the *numerator*, and the bottom number, 4, is called the *denominator*. Fractions come in three types:

- Regular fractions ($\frac{3}{4}$)
- Improper fractions ($\frac{5}{4}$)
- Mixed-number fractions ($2\frac{1}{4}$)

Regular, improper, and mixed numbers can all be added or subtracted by following a few simple steps. For example, if $2\frac{3}{5}$ is to be added to $1\frac{1}{2}$, the denominators of the fractions must be converted to the same number (called the *common denominator*). A number must be chosen that both 5 and 2 will divide into. Ten is the smallest number that 5 and 2 will both go into. There are larger numbers, such as 20 and 40, that will also work as common denominators, but the smallest is always chosen. If difficulties arise in finding a common denominator, multiply all the denominators together and it will produce a number that will always work.

$$2\frac{3}{5} = 2\frac{}{10}$$

$$+1\frac{1}{2} = 1\frac{}{10}$$

To determine what number is to be used for the numerator of each new fraction, multiply the numerator in the problem by the same number that the denominator is multiplied by to form the new denominator.

$$2\frac{3 \times 2}{5 \times 2} = 2\frac{6}{10}$$

$$1\frac{1 \times 5}{2 \times 5} = 1\frac{5}{10}$$

Next, add the whole numbers together and add the numerators together, leaving the denominators the same.

$$2\frac{3}{5} = 2\frac{6}{10}$$

$$+1\frac{1}{2} = 1\frac{5}{10}$$

$$3\frac{11}{10}$$

If the answer is an improper fraction (top number larger than the bottom number), divide the bottom number into the top number, in this case 10 into 11, with the result being $1\frac{1}{10}$. Add the 1 to the whole number 3 in the answer, and you get $4\frac{1}{10}$ as the answer to the problem.

Subtraction of fractions is solved in a similar way as the addition of fractions. First, obtain a common denominator.

$$4\frac{4}{5} = 4\frac{8}{10}$$

$$-2\frac{1}{10} - 2\frac{1}{10}$$

$$2\frac{7}{10}$$

Thus, the answer to this problem is $2\frac{7}{10}$. However, if the top fraction is smaller than the bottom fraction, another method must be used to solve the problem. For example:

$$5\frac{1}{3} = 5\frac{4}{12}$$

$$-2\frac{3}{4} = 2\frac{9}{12}$$

It becomes obvious that $\frac{9}{12}$ cannot be subtracted from $\frac{4}{12}$. A 1 must be borrowed from the whole number and made into a fraction. Thus, 5 and $\frac{4}{12}$ becomes 4 and 1, or $\frac{12}{12}$, and $\frac{4}{12}$. More simply, $4 + \frac{12}{12} + \frac{4}{12} = 4\frac{16}{12}$. The problem is then solved as follows:

$$4\frac{16}{12}$$

$$-2\frac{9}{12}$$

$$2\frac{7}{12}$$

You may recall that multiplication of fractions is usually the easiest operation with fractions. For example, to solve the problem $\frac{3}{4} \times \frac{2}{3}$, multiply the numerators together and then multiply the denominators together.

$$\frac{3}{4} \times \frac{2}{3} = \frac{6}{12}$$

Reduce your answer to the smallest fraction possible. This is achieved by dividing the numerator and denominator by the same number that achieves this goal. In this case, the number is 6, and the lowest fraction or answer to the problem is $\frac{1}{2}$.

To multiply mixed numbers, such as $3\frac{1}{2}$ by $\frac{1}{5}$, first change $3\frac{1}{2}$ to an improper fraction. To do this, multiply the whole number (3) by the denominator (2) and add the numerator (1). Thus, $3\frac{1}{2}$ becomes $\frac{7}{2}$. Then solve the problem.

$$3\frac{1}{2} \times \frac{1}{5} = \frac{7}{2} \times \frac{1}{5} = \frac{7}{10}$$

Division of fractions is accomplished in a similar manner to multiplication of fractions. However, the one rule to remember in the division of fractions is to invert (turn upside down) the divisor (number dividing by) before you multiply. For example, solve the problem $\frac{3}{4} \div \frac{2}{3}$. First, invert the divisor $\frac{2}{3}$, which becomes $\frac{3}{2}$, and then multiply.

$$\frac{3}{4} \div \frac{2}{3} = \frac{3}{4} \times \frac{3}{2} = \frac{9}{8} \text{ or } 1\frac{1}{8}$$

Percent

Percent problems can be solved very easily if the problem is turned word-for-word into a math equation. The math symbols that replace words are the following:

Word	Symbol
What	N
is	=
%	100
of	×

Thus the percent problem

What is 5% of 800?

becomes

$$N = \frac{5}{100} \times 800$$

Once a percent problem has been turned into an equation, it falls into one of two types:

- When the unknown N is by itself on one side of an equation
- When the unknown N has other numbers with it on the same side of the equation.

For the first type, refer again to the previous problem. What is 5% of 800? Substituting symbols for the words, we have:

$$N = \frac{5}{100} \times 800$$

This type is solved simply by multiplying the fractions on the right.

$$N = \frac{5}{100} \times \frac{800}{1}$$

$$N = \frac{4000}{100}$$

$$N = 40$$

To solve the second type of percentage equation, let's use the following problem:

What % of 500 is 250?

$$\frac{N}{100} \times 500 = 250$$

When solving this type of equation apply an "undoing" process to the problem. Undoing is the process of doing just the opposite of what is done to the problem. Untying shoestrings is an undoing process that is the reverse of tying. In this problem, $N/100 \times 500 = 250$. N is divided by 100 on the left side of the ×, and N is multiplied by 500 on the right side of the ×. Thus, to undo the problem, do just the opposite to both sides of the equation.

$$(100) \frac{N}{100} \times 500 = 250 \,(100)$$

Multiply both sides by 100

$$(100) \frac{N}{100} \times 500 = 250(100)$$

$$500N = 25,000$$

Now do the opposite to both sides; that is, divide both sides by 500.

$$\frac{500N}{500} = \frac{25,000}{500}$$

$$N = 50$$

Thus, the answer is 50%.

Proportions

Two ratios that are equal are known as a proportion. Proportions are one of the easiest types of problems to solve and this type of problem is frequently used in all building trades.

For example, if it takes 3 beam clamps to safely secure 10 feet of pipe, how many beam clamps are required for 50 feet of the same type of pipe?

$$\frac{3 \; beam \; clamps}{10 \; feet \; of \; pipe} = \frac{N \; beam \; clamps}{50 \; feet \; of \; pipe}$$

Multiply diagonally:

$$\frac{3}{10} \diagdown \frac{N}{50}$$

$$10N = 3 \times 50$$

$$\frac{10N}{10} = \frac{150}{10}$$

$$N = 15 \text{ beam clamps}$$

Let's reverse the unknown and put it on the bottom of the equation this time to solve a similar problem.

$$\frac{500 \; feet \; of \; pipe}{80 \; beam \; clamps} = \frac{100 \; feet \; of \; pipe}{N \; beam \; clamps}$$

$$\frac{500}{80} = \frac{100}{N}$$

$$500N = 80(100)$$

$$\frac{500N}{500} = \frac{8000}{500}$$

$$N = 16 \text{ beam clamps}$$

Powers and Roots

Problems involving powers and roots of numbers are best solved using a small electronic pocket calculator that has these functions. Most examining agencies allow nonprogrammable calculators to be used during examinations. Some agencies, however, may not; also, your calculator may become inoperative during the exam, and in most cases the applicants are not allowed to leave the room to obtain another one. In any event, powers may be calculated by repeat multiplication.

$$2^5 \text{ means } 2 \times 2 \times 2 \times 2 \times 2 = 32$$

Roots may be found using a chart, a calculator, slide rule, trial-and-error methods, and by using other mathematical techniques. The most accurate and easiest way is to use an electronic calculator.

2-1 The plan in Figure 2-1 shows a building foundation with outside dimensions measuring 24 feet and 36 feet. What is the volume of excavation in cubic yards (cu. yds.) if the foundation depth is uniformly 9 feet and the lines of excavation are 1 foot outside the building lines?

A) 400 cu. yds.

B) 329.3 cu. yds.

C) 200.6 cu. yds.

D) 882.9 cu. yds.

Answer: B

The foundation hole is 9 × 26 × 38 feet. Volume = 9 × 26 × 38 = 8892 cu. ft. Convert cu. ft. to cu. yds.: 8892 ÷ 27 = 329.3 cu. yds.

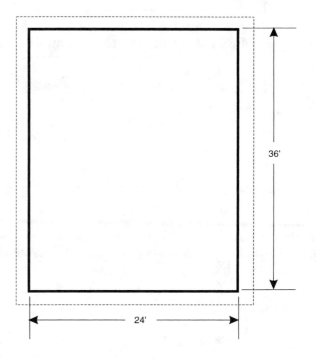

Figure 2-1: Dimensions of a foundation plan for a building.

2-2 Figure 2-2 gives the dimensions of an L-shaped building. What is the volume of excavation if the excavating line is 1 foot outside the building line and the depth is 8 feet?

A) 1589.3 cu. yds.

B) 2098.5 cu. yds.

C) 4589.6 cu. yds.

D) 5890.2 cu. yds.

Answer: A

The area of the excavation is more readily computed if the plan is divided into two rectangles, one 82 feet by 27 feet and the other 75 feet by 42 feet. The areas of these two rectangles are: 82 × 27 = 2214 sq. ft. and 75 × 42 = 3150 sq. ft., for a total of 5364 sq. ft. Multiply this total area by the 8 feet depth for a volume of 42,912 cu. ft. This figure is changed to cu. yds. by dividing the cu. ft. by 27 to get 1589.3 cu. yds.

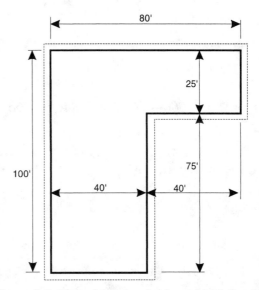

Figure 2-2: Plan view of an L-shaped building foundation.

2-3 **A building weighing 100 tons rests on a footing 18 inches wide and 10 inches deep, with a total length of 84 feet. What is the unit soil pressure?**

A) 0.6 ton per sq. ft.

B) 0.8 ton per sq. ft.

C) 1.0 ton per sq. ft.

D) 1.2 ton per sq. ft.

Answer: **B**

Bearing area = 1.5 × 84 = 126 sq. ft. Unit soil pressure = 100 ÷ 126 = 0.8 ton per sq. ft.

2-4 **If the safe bearing on coarse gravel has been determined to be 6 tons per sq. ft., what area of bearing is required to support a load of 72 tons on coarse gravel?**

A) 4 sq. ft.

B) 8 sq. ft.

C) 12 sq. ft.

D) 16 sq. ft.

Answer: **C**

72 ÷ 6 = 12 sq. ft.

2-5 **What area of bearing is required for a load of 536,000 pounds on firm clay if the safe-bearing factor has been determined to be 3 tons per sq. ft.?**

A) 8 sq. ft.

B) 10 sq. ft.

C) 89.33 sq. ft.

D) 98.33 sq. ft.

Answer: **C**

Convert pounds to tons: 536,000 ÷ 2000 = 268 tons; 268 ÷ 3 = 89.33 sq. ft.

2-6 **What is the pitch of a roof with a rise of 6 feet and a span of 18 feet?**

A) 0.666 or 2/3 pitch

B) 0.444

C) 0.5 or 1/2 pitch

D) 0.3333 or 1/3 pitch

Answer: **D**

Rise ÷ span = pitch; 6 ÷ 18 = 0.33333 or 1/3 pitch.

2-7   How many cu. yds. of concrete are required to pour a 12 foot × 24 foot × 6-inch deep patio?

A) 3.55 cu. yds.

B) 5.33 cu. yds.

C) 12 cu. yds.

D) 12.66 cu. yds.

Answer: B

Volume = length × width × depth; 24 × 12 × 0.5 = 144 cu. ft.; divide cu. ft. by 27 to obtain cu. yds; thus, 144 ÷ 27 = 5.33 cu. yds.

2-8   Reinforcing bars are to be lapped 24 bar diameters. How many inches are No. 4 bars lapped?

A) 6 inches

B) 12 inches

C) 18 inches

D) 2.4 inches

Answer: B

No. 4 bar diameter = .5 inches; 24 × .5 = 12 inches.

2-9   A stud wall is to be 40 feet long. How many vertical studs are required for this wall if they are to be spaced 16 inches on centers?

A) 31

B) 40

C) 30

D) 41

Answer: A

40 feet × 12 (to convert feet to inches) ÷ 16 inches = 30 spaces; 30 spaces + 1 = 31 studs required.

2-10   The 40-foot wall in Question 2-9 will have a double top plate and a single bottom plate. What is the total number of 8-foot studs (including top and bottom plates) required for this wall?

A) 31

B) 46

C) 41

D) 40

Answer: B

The 31 vertical studs + 10 studs (top plate) + 5 studs (bottom plate) = 46 8-foot studs.

2-11 A total length of 32 linear feet of No. 4 rebar is needed for one side of a footing. If the steel will be spliced with 12 inches of lap at two places, how many linear feet of steel must be laid?

A) 34 feet

B) 36 feet

C) 32 feet

D) 33 feet

Answer: A

One lap requires 12 inches of additional steel; 2 laps = 24 inches or 2 feet; total length = 32 feet + 2 feet = 34 feet.

2-12 How many steps (risers) will be required for a residential stair where the floor-to-floor distance is 9 feet 6 inches? The risers are to be approximately 7 inches each.

A) 16

B) 14

C) 18

D) 12

Answer: A

9 feet 6 inches ÷ 7 inches = 16.29; 16 risers will give a 7.125-inch riser. Therefore, the exact height of each riser will be 7.125 or 7¹/₈ inches.

2-13 The run (tread) of each step in Question 2-11 is 10 inches; what is the total run (length) of the stair?

A) 160 inches

B) 12 feet 6 inches

C) 13 feet 4 inches

D) 11 feet 8 inches

Answer: B

The stair will have 15 treads at 10 inches each. 15 × 10 inches = 150 inches or 12 feet 6 inches.

2-14 A 12-foot long laminated wood beam can support a uniform load of 420 pounds per linear foot; what total load can the beam support?

A) 4,200 pounds

B) 4,060 pounds

C) 5,040 pounds

D) 5,000 pounds

Answer: C

12 feet × 420 pounds per foot = 5,040 pounds.

2-15 The beam in Question 2-14 is to be used to support brick at 320 pounds per linear foot, plus a stud wall at 125 pounds per linear foot. What total load will the beam have to support? Is the beam safe to use?

A) 5,340 pounds; the beam is safe

C) 5,340 pounds; the beam is unsafe

B) 5,040 pounds; the beam is safe

D) 5,280 pounds; the beam is unsafe

Answer: C

320 pounds per foot + 125 pounds per foot = 445 total pounds per foot; 445 pounds per foot × 12 feet = 5,340 pounds; this more than its capacity of 5,040 pounds.

2-16 The building in Figure 2-3 is 24 feet × 40 feet; the pitch of the roof is 8/12; what is the area (in sq. ft.) of the roof?

A) 1153.6 sq. ft.

C) 1000 sq. ft.

B) 960 sq. ft.

D) 360 sq. ft.

Answer: A

The roof rise is 8/12 × 12 = 8 feet; hypotenuse = $\sqrt{8^2 + 12^2}$ =14.42 feet; 14.42 feet × 40 feet × 2 = 1153.6 sq. ft.

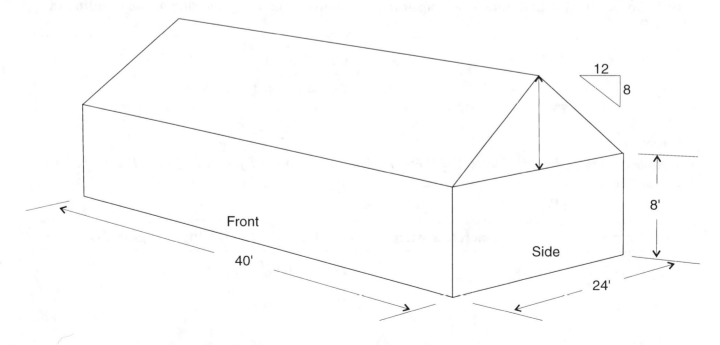

Figure 2-3: Building with an 8/12 roof pitch.

2-17   A brick is $2\frac{1}{4}$ inches high; mortar joints are $\frac{1}{2}$ inch. What is the height of 19 courses of brick?

A) 4 feet 6 inches

B) 8 feet

C) 4 feet $4\frac{1}{4}$ inches

D) 52 inches

Answer: C

$2\frac{1}{4}$ inches + $\frac{1}{2}$ inch = $2\frac{3}{4}$ inches (for one course); $2\frac{3}{4}$ inches × 19 courses = 4 feet $4\frac{1}{4}$ inches.

2-18   A board-foot measure (fbm) is the equivalent to a board 12 inches long × 12 inches wide × 1 inch thick. How many board feet are in a beam 12 feet long × 10 inches wide × 10 inches thick?

A) 1780 board feet

B) 100 board feet

C) 364 board feet

D) 104 board feet

Answer: B

Multiply the length in feet by the width in inches and the thickness in inches and divide the product by 12. Thus, 12 × 10 × 10 = 1200 ÷ 12 = 100 board feet.

2-19   How many finished square feet of siding are required for the gable side of the building in Figure 2-3?

A) 192 sq. ft.

B) 288 sq. ft.

C) 320 sq. ft.

D) 640 sq. ft.

Answer: B

The gable area = 24 feet × 8 feet × .5 = 96 sq. ft. Below the gable = 8 feet × 24 feet = 192 sq. ft. 96 + 192 = 288 sq. ft.

2-20   How many cu. yds. of concrete are needed for 35 linear feet of footing in Figure 2-4?

A) 4 cu yds.

B) 3 cu. yds.

C) 2 cu. yds.

D) 3.5 cu. yds.

Answer: B

12 inches × 28 inches = .26 sq. yds.; 35 feet = 11.67 yds.; .26 × 11.67 = 3 cu. yds.

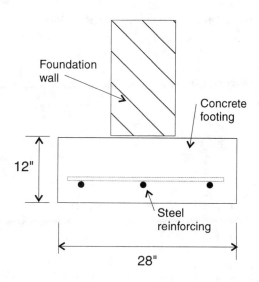

Figure 2-4: Cross-sectional view of a foundation wall.

2-21   How many cu. yds. of concrete are required to fill a hollow 10-inch (nominal thickness) concrete block wall 7 feet high × 70 feet long if the blocks are 53% solid?

A) 9.1 cu. yds.

B) 7.98 cu. yds.

C) 7.1 cu. yds.

D) 5 cu. yds.

Answer: C

A 10-inch block = .83 foot. Therefore, .83 feet × 7 feet × 70 feet × 47% hollow = 191.1 cu. ft.; 27 cu. ft. per cu. yd; 191.1 ÷ 27 = 7.1 cu. yds.

2-22   If each linear foot of foundation wall in Figure 2-4 supports 6,990 pounds, what is the unit soil pressure under the footing in pounds per sq. ft.?

A) 2,000 pounds per sq. ft.

B) 2,500 pounds per sq. ft.

C) 3,000 pounds per sq. ft.

D) 4,000 pounds per sq. ft.

Answer: C

The footing is 2.33 feet wide. 6,990 pounds per foot ÷ 2.33 feet = 3,000 pounds per sq. ft.

2-23   If a floor must support 50 pounds per sq. ft. and the joists are spaced at 19.2 inches on centers, how much load must a 12-foot joist carry?

A) 1,000 pounds

B) 960 pounds per sq. ft.

C) 960 pounds

D) 600 pounds

Answer: C

19.2 inches ÷ 12 inches = 1.6 feet; 1.6 feet × 12 feet × 50 pounds per sq. ft. = 960 pounds.

2-24   If ceiling joists with a span of 16 feet are allowed to have a mid-span deflection of L/240, what is the allowed deflection in inches?

A) .8 inch

B) .06 inch

C) .08 inch

D) 1.5 inches

Answer: A

L/240 = span in inches divided by 240; 16 feet × 12 = 192 inches ÷ 240 = .8 inch.

2-25   In Question 2-21, how much does one linear foot of wall weigh, if one 10- × 16- × 8-inch hollow block weighs 55 pounds, and concrete weighs 150 pounds per cu. ft.?

A) 475 pounds

B) 600 pounds

C) 1000 pounds

D) 844 pounds

Answer: D

A 10- × 16- × 8-inch block weighs 55 pounds; a 10- × 16- × 8-inch block = 1280 cu. in. Concrete weights 150 pounds per cu. ft. (1728 cu. in.); 1280 ÷ 1728 = .74; .74 × 150 pounds = 111 pounds. Since the block is 53% solid, concrete can only fill 47% of the area, so .47 × 111 = 52.17 pounds of concrete. One block with concrete = 55 + 52.17 = 107.17 pounds. A linear foot of block weighs (12 ÷ 16) × 107.17 or 80.38 pounds. There are 10.5 8-inch blocks in a 7-foot high wall, so one linear foot of wall weighs 10.5 × 80.38 = 844 pounds.

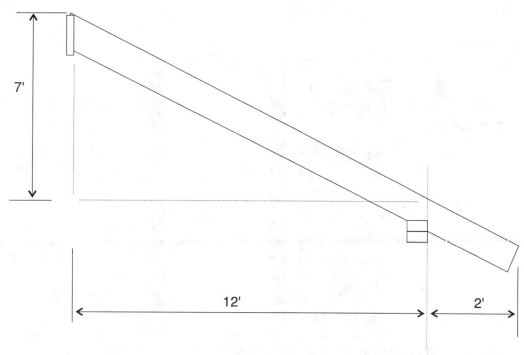

7'

12'

2'

Figure 2-5: Cross section of a gable roof.

2-26 A wood beam has a bearing area at each end of 5 × 5 inches. This species of wood can safely resist a unit bearing pressure of 250 pounds per sq. in. What is the maximum allowed bearing pressure?

A) 6,250 pounds

C) 12,500 pounds

B) 250 pounds

D) 8,000 pounds

Answer: C
5 inches × 5 inches × 250 pounds × 2 = 12,500 pounds.

2-27 The roof in Figure 2-5 has a rise of 7 feet and a run of 12 feet; eaves project 2 feet horizontally; what is the length of the rafters?

A) 13.89 feet

C) 16.20 feet

B) 12.5 feet

D) 17 feet

Answer: C
Solving for the hypotenuse of the 7/12 roof pitch = $\sqrt{7^2 + 12^2}$ = 13.89 feet; solving for the length of the eave rafter, 7/12 = $\frac{x}{2}$ is the ratio to use, where x = 1.17. Thus, $\sqrt{1.17^2 + 2^2}$ = 2.31; 13.89 + 2.31 = 16.20 feet of total rafter length.

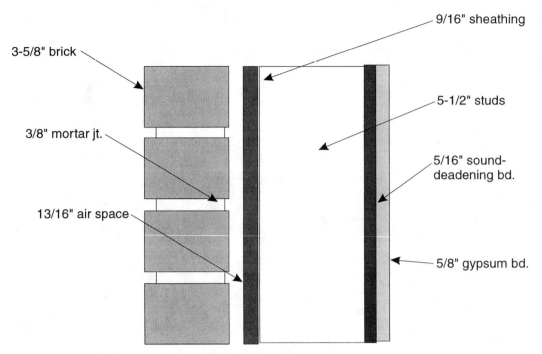

3-5/8" brick

9/16" sheathing

3/8" mortar jt.

5-1/2" studs

13/16" air space

5/16" sound-deadening bd.

5/8" gypsum bd.

Figure 2-6: Cross-sectional view of a stud wall with brick veneer.

2-28   How wide is the wall in Figure 2-6?

A) $3\frac{1}{4}$ inches

C) $9\frac{3}{16}$ inches

B) $6\frac{11}{16}$ inches

D) $11\frac{7}{16}$ inches

Answer: D

Adding the dimensions of the brick, air space, sheathing, stud, sound-deadening board, and gypsum board = $11\frac{7}{16}$ inches. The mortar joint is not included in the calculation.

2-29   An octagonal roof cupola has a width of 9 feet 8 inches (Figure 2-7), what is the dimension d of each side?

A) 2 feet 6 inches

C) 3 feet

B) 4 feet

D) 2 feet 10 inches

Answer: B

Dimension $d + 2a$ = 9 feet 8 inches. $\sqrt{2a^2} = d$; $1.414a = d$; $1.414a + 2a = 116$ inches. If $3.414a = 116$ inches; $a = 34$ inches; 1.414×34 inches = 48 inches, so d = 48 inches or 4 feet.

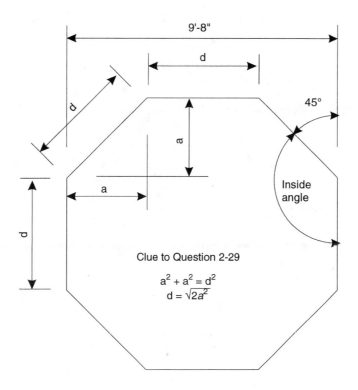

Figure 2-7: Plan view of an octagonal cupola.

2-30 What degree of angle is the inside angle shown in Figure 2-7?

A) 90 degrees

B) 120 degrees

C) 135 degrees

D) 45 degrees

Answer: C

Each side makes a 45-degree exterior angle with its adjacent side (Figure 2-7). 180 degrees – 45 degrees = 135 degrees.

2-31 The cupola in Figure 2-8 on the next page has an octagonal roof. The horizontal side measures 4 feet. The distance shown from the eave to the peak is 5 feet. How many sq. ft. of roof area is on the cupola?

A) 90 sq. ft.

B) 30 sq. ft.

C) 45 sq. ft.

D) 80 sq. ft.

Answer: D

Triangle areas = ½ base × height. ½ × 4 feet × 5 feet = 10 sq. ft. Therefore, 8 sides × 10 sq. ft. = 80 sq. ft.

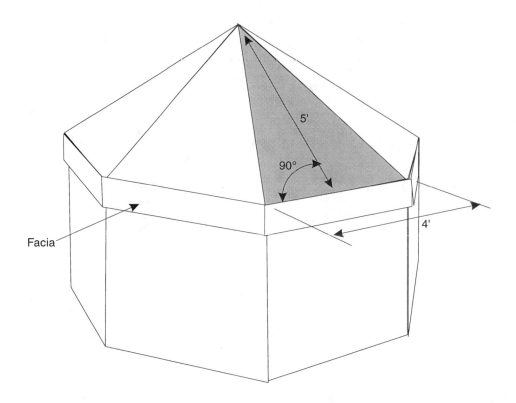

Figure 2-8: Perspective view of an octagonal cupola.

2-32   How many linear feet of fascia are required for the cupola of Figure 2-8?

A) 32 linear feet   C) 40 linear feet

B) 16 linear feet   D) 20 linear feet

Answer: A

The fascia on one side is 4 feet long. Therefore, 8 × 4 linear feet = 32 linear feet.

2-33   The hip roof in Figure 2-9 has a rise of 5 feet and a run of 12 feet. What is the vertical distance (rise) between the eave and the roof ridge?

A) 6 feet   C) 8 feet

B) 6 feet 8 inches   D) 8 feet 8 inches

Answer: B

Half the roof width is 16 feet. A pitch of 5/12 = x/16. Therefore x = 6 feet 8 inches.

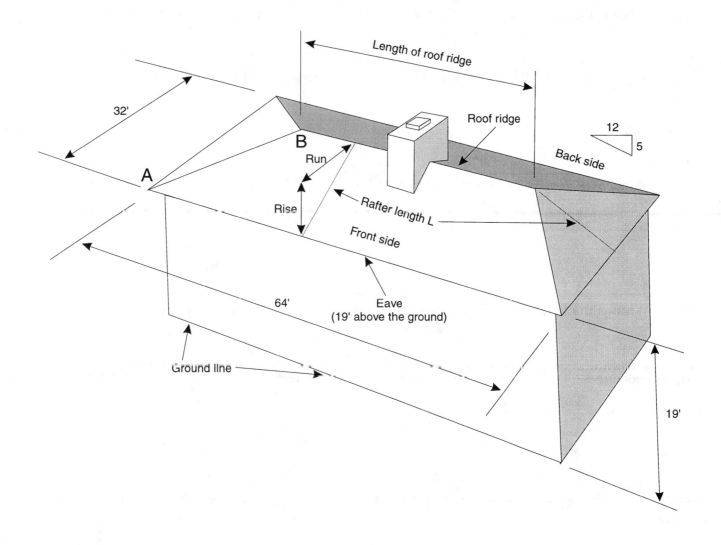

Figure 2-9: A dimensioned perspective view of a building with a hip roof.

2-34 **If the chimney in Figure 2-9 extends 2 feet above the roof ridge, what is the total height of the chimney above the ground line?**

A) 27 feet 8 inches

C) 28 feet 8 inches

B) 25 feet 8 inches

D) 28 feet 6 inches

Answer: A

19 feet + 6 feet 8 inches + 2 feet = 27 feet 8 inches.

2-35   What is the length of the roof ridge in Figure 2-9 on the preceding page?

A) 34 feet

B) 32 feet

C) 29 feet 4 inches

D) 16 feet

Answer: B

The total length of the roof is 64 feet. Therefore, 64 feet – (2 × 16) (twice the run or horizontal distance from the eave to the ridge) = 32 feet.

2-36   What is the length (L) of each rafter in Figure 2-9 on the preceding page?

A) 18 feet

B) 16 feet 4 inches

C) 17 feet 4 inches

D) 16 feet

Answer: C

Use the equation $a^2 + b^2 = c^2$. Therefore, $(6\ feet\ 8\ inches)^2 + (16\ feet)^2 = (length\ of\ rafter)^2$; 44.43 feet + 256 feet = 300.43 feet = $(length\ of\ rafter)^2$; The length of each rafter is $\sqrt{300.43}$ = 17 feet 4 inches.

2-37   What is the length of the corner ridge line A-B in Figure 2-9 on the preceding page?

A) 18 feet

B) 24 feet 7 inches

C) 23 feet

D) 23 feet 7 inches

Answer: D

Use the equation $a^2 + b^2 = c^2$ to find the unknown hypotenuse, AB — the length of the corner ridge line. $(17\ feet\ 4\ inches)^2 + (16\ feet)^2 = AB^2$; 300.43 + 256 = 556.43; 556.43 = AB^2; AB = $\sqrt{556.43}$; AB = 23 feet 7 inches.

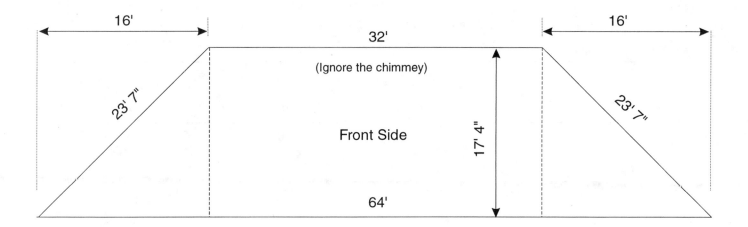

Figure 2-10: Cross-sectional view of the roof in Figure 2-9.

2-38 How many squares of shingles (rounded to the closest whole number) does it take to cover the front side of the roof in Figure 2-10 (a square = 100 sq. ft.)?

A) 8.32 squares

C) 832 squares

B) 8 squares

D) 10 squares

Answer: B

Ignoring the chimney area, the center section has an area of 32 feet × 17 feet 4 inches = 554.56 sq. ft. Each of the end triangles has an area of ½(base × height). Therefore, ½(16 × 17.33) = 138.64 sq.ft. The two triangles plus the center section = 2 × 138.64 sq. ft + 554.56 sq. ft. = 831.84 sq. ft. or 8 squares of shingles if rounded to the closest whole number.

2-39 A carpenter needs 4 pieces of plywood 24 × 50 inches each; the carpenter also needs 4 pieces of plywood 25 × 50 inches each. How many 4- × 8-foot sheets of plywood must be ordered?

A) 8 sheets of plywood

C) 6 sheets of plywood

B) 4 sheets of plywood

D) 2 sheets of plywood

Answer: C

Each 25- × 50-inch piece must be cut from a single sheet of plywood. The leftover portion is too small for any of the other pieces. Two 24- × 50-inch pieces, however, can be cut from one sheet (ignoring the width of the saw cut). The carpenter would need 6 sheets of plywood.

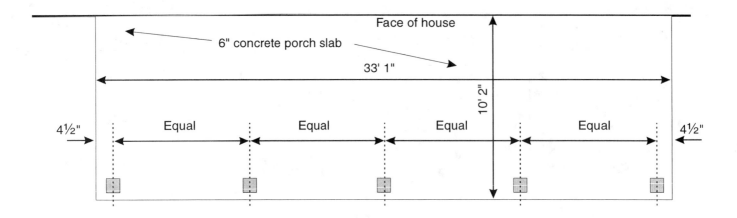

Figure 2-11: Floor plan of a residential porch.

2-40   The total length of the porch in Figure 2-11 is 33 feet 1 inch. What is the column spacing required for 4 equal spaces?

A) 8 feet 2 inches

B) 6 feet 1 inch

C) 8 feet

D) 8 feet 1inch

Answer: D

The total length is 33 feet 1 inch. Therefore, $\dfrac{(33\ feet\ 1\ inch) - (2 \times 4\frac{1}{2}\ inches)}{4} = 8\ feet\ 1\ inch.$

2-41   How many cu. yds. of concrete are required for the porch slab in Figure 2-11?

A) 6.23 cu. yds.

B) 8 cu. yds.

C) 632 cu. yds.

D) 10 cu. yds.

Answer: A

33.08 feet × 10.17 feet × .5 feet = 168.2 cu. ft. in the porch slab. At 27 cu. ft. per cu. yd., there are $\dfrac{168.2}{27} = 6.23$ *cu. yds. of concrete required for this slab.*

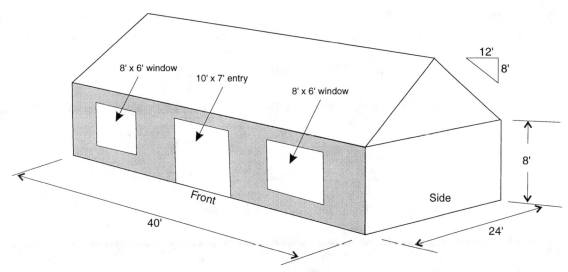

Figure 2-12: Perspective view of a simple structure with a gable roof.

2-42 **In Figure 2-12, what is the net front wall area — less the entry and windows — to be calculated for the application of wood siding?**

A) 400 sq. ft.

B) 320 sq. ft.

C) 154 sq. ft.

D) 155 sq. ft.

Answer: C

The front wall is 40 feet × 8 feet = 320 sq. ft. The entry is 70 sq. ft. The windows together are 96 sq. ft. The total wall area is 320 sq. ft. – (70 sq. ft. + 96 sq. ft.) = 154 sq. ft.

2-43 The front wall of Figure 2-12 is to have 1 × 6 wood bevel siding. How much siding must be ordered to cover the front wall? Use the chart in Figure 2-13 on the next page for help in answering this question.

A) 300 sq. ft.

B) 208.82 sq. ft.

C) 240 sq. ft.

D) 219.16 sq. ft.

Answer: D

The net wall area as figured previously is 154 sq. ft. Multiply this by the area factor for 1 × 6 siding, 1.33, to get 204.82 sq. ft. Add in trim and waste, 7% × 204.82 = 14.34 sq. ft. The total material necessary for the job is 204.82 sq. ft. + 14.34 sq. ft. = 219.16 sq. ft.

Wood Bevel Siding	Nominal Size	Dressed Width	Area Factor	Trim & Waste %
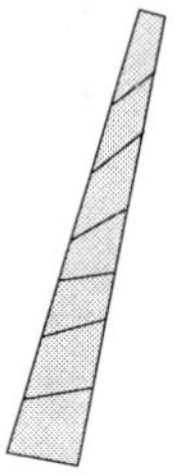	1 × 4	3½"	1.60	
	1 × 6	5½"	1.33	7%
	1 × 8	7¼"	1.30	
	1 × 10	9¼"	1.20	

Manufacturer's chart for estimating material amounts. Instructions for using the chart: (1) calculate the net area of the building that will have siding; (2) multiply the dressed width by the area factor to determine the siding required; (3) add 7% to the siding required in (2) to get the total quantity of siding that must be ordered for the job.

Note: the area factor takes into account the overlapping of the siding.

Figure 2-13: Dimensions and characteristics of wood bevel siding.

2-44 If 1 × 4 is used in Question 2-43, will the square footage required be more or less than using 1 × 6 siding?

A) More

B) Less

C) The same

D) There is insufficient data to determine an answer

Answer: A

The chart in Figure 2-12 shows an area factor of 1.60 for 1 × 4 siding. Since none of the other figures used in determining the answer change, we know that more material will be required to do the same job using 1 × 4 siding.

2-45 In the preceding question, what is the percentage of increase in material caused by switching from 1 x 6 siding to 1 x 4 siding?

A) 10%

B) 15%

C) 20%

D) 25%

Answer: C

The net wall area as previously calculated is 154 sq. ft. Multiply this amount by the area factor for 1 × 4 siding, 1.60, to get 246.4 sq. ft. Add in trim and waste, 7% × 246.4 = 17.25 sq. ft. The total material necessary for the job is 246.4 sq. ft. + 17.25 sq. ft. = 263.65 sq. ft. To find the percentage increase, (263.65 − 219.16) ÷ 219.16. 44.49 ÷ 219.16 = 20% increase.

2-46   If a carpenter can install 50 sq. ft. of siding in 1 hour, how long will it take to install the 1 × 6 siding on the front wall of the residence in Figure 2-12?

A) 4 hours and 15 minutes

C) 4 hours and 30 minutes

B) 4 hours and 10 minutes

D) 4 hours and 23 minutes

Answer: D

The material required for 1× 6 siding is 219.16 sq. ft. of siding. 219.16 ÷ 50 = 4.38 hours or 4 hours and 23 minutes.

Chapter 3

Law and Business Management

In addition to an examination covering the various building trades, many states now require all applicants for a contractor's license to take a business and law exam. Such exams are designed to test the applicant's knowledge of construction business activities.

Subject matter on law and business exams will vary from state to state. However, most will include types of business organizations, lien laws, workers' compensation law, unemployment compensation law, computation of payroll taxes and IRS filing procedures, labor laws, financial management, general bidding, and quantity survey procedures.

A typical law and business management examination will be open-book, last for approximately three hours, and consist of the following subjects:

EXAMINATION CONTENTS	
Subjects	**Number of Questions**
Contract Management	10
Project Management	6
Financial Management	4
Tax Laws	5
Insurance and Bonding	2

EXAMINATION CONTENTS *(Cont.)*	
Subjects	**Number of Questions**
Business Organization	2
Personnel Regulations	10
Lien Laws	3
Licensing	8
Total number of questions	50

When the state contractor's examinations are prepared and supervised by a private company like Experior or PSI, a Contractor's Reference Manual (your state's edition) is normally available for a fee directly from the company.

In any case, if a law and business management exam is required in your area or state, you should obtain a copy of your state contractor's licensing laws. See Appendix I of this book for addresses and phone numbers.

State law and business management exams are usually prepared by the state's Board of Contractors or equivalent, and in many cases the board works directly with a private company in compiling suitable exams. In doing so, all pertinent laws are reviewed to obtain an appropriate list of questions that the board feels the contractor should know to be in business. The following references are frequently used to prepare state law and business management exams:

Americans with Disabilities Act,
    Public Law 101-336
Superintendent of Documents
U.S. Government Printing Office
Washington, DC 20402

Builder's Guide to Accounting
Craftsman Book Company
6058 Corte del Cedro
Box 6500
Carlsbad, CA 92018

Code of Federal Regulations-Title 29,
    Part 1926 (OSHA)
Superintendent of Documents
U.S. Government Printing Office
Washington, DC 20402

Employer's Tax Guide, Circular E
Current issue
Contact your local IRS office

Handy Reference Guide to the Fair Labor
    Standards Act, WH Publication 1282
U.S. Department of Labor
Employment Standards Administration,
Wage & Hour Division,
Room S-3516,
200 Constitution Avenue, NW
Washington, DC 20210

Overtime Compensation Under the Fair
    Labor Standards Act
WH Publication
U.S. Department of Labor
Employment Standards Administration
Wage & Hour Division,
Room S-3516
200 Constitution Avenue, NW
Washington, DC 20210

Some questions on law and business management exams are based on field experience and knowledge of trade practices. Therefore, all exam questions will not be limited to printed text books.

The questions in this chapter are designed to give you a "feel" for the types of questions that you can expect on a law and business management examination, including those based on field experience. However, you will still need to study the labor laws of the state in which you plan to take the exam.

3-1   Which of the following business organizations is the easiest to form?

A) Sole proprietorship

B) General partnership

C) Limited partnership

D) Corporation

Answer: A

An individual or sole proprietorship is the easiest business to form because the owner is the business and it involves the least amount of government regulation.

3-2   Which of the following is a true statement concerning a sole proprietorship business organization?

A) The owner must use his or her own name in the business name

B) The owner may do business under a trade or "assumed" name

C) The trade or business name must be followed by either Inc. or Ltd.

D) A name will be given the business by the licensing agency

Answer: B

A person engaged in a sole proprietorship organization may use a trade or assumed name. For example, John Doe trading as Doe's Building Service, or John Doe trading as Fast Building, etc.

3-3   Which of the following is a disadvantage when operating a business as a sole proprietorship?

A) The owner of the business makes all decisions

B) The owner has full control of the business

C) Ownership is freely transferable

D) The owner has unlimited personal liability

Answer: D

The owner of a sole proprietorship business organization is personally responsible for all debts and damages that occur from the business operation. If these liabilities are not satisfied, the owner's personal property and assets may be attached by debtors.

3-4 Which of the following is a true statement concerning a general partnership business?

A) The business terminates upon the death of a partner

B) General partners do not have personal liability for the business

C) The ability to raise outside capital is decreased

D) A partnership interest is transferable without the consent of all the partners

Answer: A

A general partnership business terminates upon the death of a partner, the withdrawal of a partner, or by bankruptcy.

3-5 Which of the following is the chief disadvantage of a general partnership?

A) Pooling of financial resources

B) All partners have unlimited personal liability

C) Pooling of individual capabilities to better the business

D) Each partner shares in the responsibilities of the business

Answer: B

General partners are equally liable to creditors. Each partner shares equally in the profits and losses from the business.

3-6 Which of the following best describes a limited partnership business organization?

A) A business with one general partner and at least two limited partners

B) A business with one limited partner and at least six general partners

C) A business partnership consisting of one or more general partners and one or more limited partners

D) A business consisting of no general partners and two or more limited partners

Answer: C

A business specifically created as limited partnership, and that has filed the appropriate documents as required by state law, must have one or more general partners and one or more limited partners.

3-7   If a corporation is known as a foreign corporation in all states except Connecticut, what type of corporation would the business be known as in Connecticut?

A) Foreign corporation

B) Exotic corporation

C) Limited corporation

D) Domestic corporation

Answer: D

A corporation is known as a domestic corporation in the state in which the corporation was formed, and operates by that state's laws. This same corporation is known as a foreign corporation in all other states.

3-8   Which of the following best describes a corporation?

A) A business organization that is exempt from any possible double taxation

B) A separate legal entity created under the laws of a specific state

C) The easiest possible business organization to form

D) A business organization with low start up costs

Answer: B

A corporation is always subject to possible double taxation — first on the corporation's profits and then on the shareholders dividends. A corporation is also the most costly and complex type of business to organize. Consequently, Answer B best describes a corporation.

3-9   If a contracting business is incorporated in one state and the firm desires to work in another state, which of the following places should be contacted to make certain that the business complies with all requirements for a foreign corporation in the state in which the contractor will be working?

A) The State Corporation Commission in the state where the contractor is incorporated

B) The Department of Labor in Washington, DC

C) The nearest IRS office

D) The State Corporation Commission in the state where the contractor will be working

Answer: D

The State Corporation Commission in the state where the contractor will be working should be contacted first. This commission will provide further details as to who to contact prior to beginning construction.

3-10   What is the first and most important element of a contract between the parties involved?

A) The type of form used to write the contract

B) Mutual agreement

C) The ability to present a good-looking document

D) Proper punctuation

Answer: B

An offer to perform some type of work or services and an acceptance of the offer are considered by law to be the natural expressions of mutual agreement.

3-11   In contractual language, what does "consideration" mean?

A) Kindly

B) Charitable

C) Something of value

D) Compassionate treatment

Answer: C

Consideration means that something of value is given by one party to another party in exchange for work or services.

3-12   Which of the following is necessary for a contract to be enforceable?

A) The performance of the work or services must be legal

B) The contract must be typewritten

C) All parties involved must be present at the time the contract is signed

D) The contract must be typewritten or printed by some other mechanical or electronic means

Answer: A

The courts will not enforce a contract for work or services that are illegal. For example, if a contractor is hired to install a septic system and drain field in an area that was disapproved by the local health department, the contractor may not get paid. Since the work is illegal, the law will not enforce the contract. Furthermore, both parties may be subject to criminal action by the city, county, or state.

3-13   Which of the following elements is not required in a contractor's offer or proposal to do work?

A) The contractor's name, address, and license number

B) A description and address of the work

C) The amount that will be charged for the work

D) The contractor's age and physical condition

Answer: D

The elements in A through C are essential in any offer or proposal to do work. Answer D may be necessary in some cases of individual employment, but not necessary in a proposal from a contractor.

3-14   What are the two basic types of construction contracts?

A) General partnership

B) Hourly and weekly rates

C) Competitive-bid and negotiated

D) Limited partnership

Answer: C

One type of contract is based on selecting a contractor as the result of a competitive bid; the other is the result of direct owner-contractor negotiation.

3-15   Which of the following may be a competitive-bid contract?

A) Lump-sum and unit-price contracts

B) Cost-plus-fee contracts

C) The owner purchases all materials, and the contractor works by the hour at a predetermined rate for each hour worked

D) The contractor buys all materials and charges the owner 20% profit above the contractor's cost

Answer: A

Competitive-bid contracts are usually prepared on a fixed-price basis, and consist of either a lump-sum contract or a unit-price contract.

3-16   Which of the following best describes a lump-sum contract?

A) A contract in which the total construction cost is not known until the project has been completed

B) A contract in which the contractor agrees to perform stipulated work or services in exchange for a fixed amount of money

C) A contract that is based on estimated quantities of well-defined items of work and a cost-per-unit amount for each

D) A contract in which the contractor's profit will be a certain percentage of the total cost of the work

Answer: B

A lump-sum contract is as stated in Answer B. The contractor is obligated to perform the work for the exact dollar amount regardless of the ease or difficulty of the work during the construction activities.

3-17   Construction estimating is the analysis of all the elements involved in the cost of a project. Which of the following costs best describes this analysis?

A) Material, labor, equipment, job and company overhead, and profit

B) Material and labor only

C) Material, labor and overhead

D) Profit, material and labor

Answer: A

Estimating involves a careful study of all the factors in Answer A.

3-18   What is the type of contract called when a contractor agrees to perform work or services for a given labor rate per hour and a 15% profit on the cost of all materials?

A) Cost-plus-fee contract

B) Lump-sum contract

C) Unit-price contract

D) Fixed-price contract

Answer: A

A cost-plus-fee contract is normally negotiated between the owner and the contractor and the details vary considerably. However, in most cases, the owner pays actual costs of construction plus an additional amount based on a fixed percentage of the project's cost.

3-19   Which of the following is *not* a possible arrangement with a cost-plus-fee contract?

A) A fixed fee above the cost of the work

B) The contractor agrees to perform a certain amount of work for a fixed sum of money

C) A sliding-scale percentage of the cost of the work

D) A fixed fee with a bonus

Answer: B

Answer B is considered a lump-sum contract and therefore cannot be termed a cost-plus-fee contract.

3-20   Which of the following is necessary for a contractor to submit a competitive bid on any construction project?

A) A resume from the owner or architect

B) A plot plan showing the project's location

C) A set of construction documents

D) A building permit

Answer: C

Construction documents for a given project basically consist of a complete set of working drawings and written specifications. Sometimes there are several additional separate documents, such as bidding documents, owner-contractor agreement, general conditions, supplementary and/or special conditions, addenda, etc. However, in many cases, all of these documents are combined in a set of written specifications and bound in book or booklet form. See Chapter 1 of this book.

3-21   Which section of written project specifications normally summarizes the work, and the project close-out?

A) General requirements

B) Addenda

C) Modifications

D) Shop drawings

Answer: A

Division 1 — General Requirements of written specifications summarizes the work, alternatives, project meetings, submissions, quality control, temporary facilities and controls, products, and the project close-out. Every responsible person involved with the project should become familiar with this division.

3-22   What is the purpose of an addendum to the construction and bidding documents?

A) To specify the close-out date of the project

B) To stipulate the bidding date

C) To clarify complex design details

D) To make changes to the documents

Answer: D

When changes are required for any given construction project, prior to awarding the contract, an addendum is issued that contains information that may affect bid prices.

3-23   On projects of any consequence, who is normally responsible for ensuring that the project drawings comply with all building codes and local ordinances?

A) Contractor

B) Architect/engineer

C) Owner

D) Material supplier

Answer: B

The person or firm who designs the project drawings is responsible for ensuring that the construction documents conform to all codes and ordinances. However, a clause in most written specifications state that "all work must conform to all codes and ordinances," which generally makes it the contractor's responsibility to point out any discrepancies to the owner or architect, and not to knowingly continue with faulty work.

3-24   If changes are made to the original construction documents after the project has been awarded, and work is in progress, what is the normal procedure that the contractor should take?

A) The contractor should put in a claim for additional costs

B) The contractor must perform the work as though it was stated in the original construction documents

C) All work must be stopped and a new contract must be negotiated

D) The contractor may charge any amount for this work

Answer: A

Most contracts provide for processing contractor's claims for extra work during the construction of any project. These procedures must be followed exactly to avoid waiver or forfeiture of an otherwise valid claim.

3-25 **Most successful contractors have a full-time employee who prepares materials lists, labor units, and all other costs for each construction project that the firm bids. What is the job title of this person?**

A) Architect

B) Estimator

C) Engineer

D) Bondsman

Answer: B

A good estimator knows the building process and all the work items and materials required for each project. A good estimator is an essential part of any successful contractor's business.

3-26 **After the construction documents are prepared, bids are taken, and the contract is awarded, when may the contractor start planning to begin construction?**

A) When the building permit is signed

B) When the owner gives his or her permission

C) When the contract is signed

D) When the building inspector says so

Answer: C

The contract should be signed by all parties involved before the contractor orders any materials, hires subcontractors, etc.

3-27 **Many construction contracts contain a clause stating that "time is of the essence in this agreement." Which of the following best describes this phrase?**

A) Specified completion dates must be met

B) An accurate time sheet must be kept for workers in all trades, including subcontractors

C) Specified completion dates must be met within a reasonable time

D) Specified completion dates must be met except for all subcontractors

Answer: A

All performance and completion dates specified in the contract are intended to be met as stated, and performance or completion beyond those dates will be considered a material breach of the contract.

3-28   In a standard building construction contract, who assumes responsibility for the subcontractor's work?

A) Owner

B) Architect

C) Building inspector

D) General contractor

Answer: D

The general contractor assumes all the risks for work performed by the subcontractors if hired by the general contractor. The owner holds the general contractor responsible to complete the entire project as agreed in the signed contract.

3-29   Do most construction contracts give the owner the right to change work during the course of construction?

A) No

B) Only by a court order

C) Yes, but the contractor must be compensated

D) Yes, and the contractor will not be compensated

Answer: C

Almost all construction contracts recognize the right of the owner to add, delete, or change work during the construction process. The contractor should be compensated for any additional costs, or the owner credited with any savings, that result from the changes.

3-30   To whom is a building construction contract normally awarded?

A) Highest bidder

B) Most popular contractor

C) Lowest bidder

D) Closest contractor to the project's location

Answer: C

Normally, the lowest bidder gets the job. However, in most bidding documents, a clause is inserted which states, "the owner has the right to reject any and all bids." This clause is inserted in case all bids are higher than the allotted budget, or if the architect/owner thinks the low bidder is not qualified to do the work.

3-31   Which of the following best describes "project scheduling" as related to the building construction industry?

A) The process of assigning each construction activity to a time slot so that the requirements of the project may be completed on time

B) Determining the amount of material needed for a project and the amount of labor required to install it

C) Finishing up a project's "punch list" in order to close out the job

D) The process of analyzing each of the tasks required to complete a project and then determining the most efficient way to accomplish each one

Answer: A

Project scheduling is a necessary construction activity to complete a construction project in the most efficient manner. For example, the footings must be dug and the reinforcing steel in place before the concrete is ordered and poured. If project scheduling is neglected, it is conceivable that the concrete would be on the job before it could be used.

3-32   Which of the following best describes "project planning" as related to the building construction industry?

A) The process of assigning each construction activity to a time slot so that the requirements of the project may be completed on time

B) Determining the amount of material needed for a project and the amount of labor required to install it

C) Finishing up a project's "punch list" in order to close out the job

D) The process of analyzing each of the tasks required to complete a project and then determining the most efficient way to accomplish each one

Answer: D

Project planning must take into account the sequence of events necessary to complete a construction project. For example, excavation will normally come first, forms built for the footings, rebars installed in place, footings poured, etc. Project planning differs from project scheduling in that exact time slots are usually not assigned during the planning process. However, during the planning stage, the contractor must approximate the need for equipment, materials, and the time for the various subcontractors to come on the job. For example, the electrical trade may be needed to install a temporary electric service prior to beginning construction, but will not be needed further until the building is under roof.

3-33   Who is normally responsible for material receiving and storage on the job site?

A) The project superintendent

C) The architect

B) The estimator

D) The consulting engineer

Answer: A

Job site supervision on projects of any consequence is normally handled by the site or project superintendent. His or her duties include directing the various trades and subcontractors, receiving and storing materials, etc.

3-34   Which of the following best describes "cost control" as related to the building construction industry?

A) The process of delaying payments to vendors

C) The ongoing process of monitoring job costs while the project is underway

B) The process of seeking quotations on materials to obtain the lowest possible price

D) The process of negotiating wage scales with labor organizations

Answer: C

Job progress must be constantly monitored to keep the project on schedule. Doing so helps to ensure an adequate cash flow and also enables the contractor to derive the most profit from the project.

3-35   Who should be contacted if the working drawings are unclear during the process of construction?

A) The owner

C) The local building inspector

B) The architect

D) The local labor organization

Answer: B

An architect is normally commissioned to plan and design building projects. The architect also prepares complete sets of working drawings and written specifications. If a conflict is encountered, or if a portion of the drawings is not clear, the architect or the architect's consultants should be contacted.

3-36   Who is normally responsible for job-site safety?

A) Owner

B) Building inspector

C) Architect

D) General contractor

Answer: D

Job-site safety is one of the many responsibilities of the building contractor. The contractor is usually represented on the job site by his or her project superintendent, but the responsibility still remains on the shoulders of the contractor.

3-37   Which of the following job-site employees is most likely to approve labor time sheets for the contractor's payroll?

A) Crane operator

B) Job superintendent

C) The local labor organization's representative

D) The trade apprentice with the most time on the job

Answer: B

The approval of labor time sheets is one of the many jobs required of the project superintendent.

3-38   Which of the following is considered one of the best ways that contractors can reduce their losses due to exposure to risks caused by natural disasters, fire, theft, and accidents?

A) Insurance

B) Proper training of employees

C) Being selective in the type of work performed

D) Keeping the work force to a bare minimum

Answer: A

All contractors should carry adequate insurance at all times. Many contractors have lost their business overnight because of a single natural disaster or major accident. A reputable and knowledgeable insurance broker can determine the best coverage for each contractor and project.

3-39   Which of the following best describes an insurance policy?

A) An agreement whereas the insurer guarantees that the contractor will not be sued by any party

B) A policy that is in no way related to a contract

C) A contract under which the contractor agrees to perform a certain amount of work for a specified payment

D) A contract under which the underwriter promises to assume financial responsibility for a specified loss or liability

Answer: D

An insurance policy is basically a form of contract, and the laws pertaining to contracts and insurance policies are quite similar.

3-40   Which of the following insurance policies for contractors is not usually required by law?

A) Workers' Compensation

B) Unemployment insurance

C) Fire insurance

D) Medicare insurance

Answer: C

While all contractors should have fire insurance on their buildings and equipment, fire insurance is not normally required by law, whereas the other policies listed are compulsory.

3-41   Which of the following is normally not covered in an all-risk builder's risk insurance policy?

A) Protection against any physical loss or damage to the project or project materials

B) Coverage for the cost of correcting faulty workmanship

C) Coverage of temporary construction job site structures

D) Protection against fire and theft of construction tools

Answer: B

Unless the policy is specifically modified, all-risk builder's risk insurance does not include the cost of correcting faulty workmanship, materials, specifications or design. Many policies also exclude any losses from natural disasters.

3-42   When a firm or company assumes liability for the performance of a contractor's legal obligations, what is this type of bond called?

A) Performance bond

B) Contract surety bond

C) Bid bond

D) Payment bond

Answer: B

Should a contractor default on his or her obligations, a surety bond guarantees that the work will be completed at no additional cost to the owner.

3-43   What type of bond guarantees that the successful bidder on a project will sign a contract with the owner for the amount of the contractor's bid?

A) Performance bond

B) Contract surety bond

C) Bid bond

D) Payment bond

Answer: C

If the contractor who is the successful bidder on a project defaults, the surety company will either pay the owner the entire bond amount, or else pay the difference in cost between the contractor who defaulted and the next lowest bidder.

3-44   What type of bond guarantees that all materials used on the project will be paid for and that all wages to workers and subcontractors used on the project will also be paid so that liens being filed against the property title can be avoided?

A) Performance bond

B) Contract surety bond

C) Bid bond as specified by the Miller Act of 1935

D) Payment bond

Answer: D

A payment bond protects suppliers, subcontractors, and workers against nonpayment. This type of bond also protects the owner and developer against liens filed by unpaid parties that participate in the project's development. A lien bond is also sometimes required to protect the owner, lender, or title company from a claim or lien filed by a subcontractor that could impair the title to the property. This type of bond, however, varies greatly from state to state and each contractor should determine the filing requirements before submitting a bid if such a bond is required.

3-45   What percentage of the total contract price are performance bonds normally required to cover?

A) 50%

B) 75%

C) 80%

D) 100%

Answer: D

Performance bonds are typically required for 100% of the contract amount.

3-46   Payment bond amounts on smaller projects (under $5 million) are usually what percent of the total contract price?

A) 50%

B) 75%

C) 80%

D) 100%

Answer: A

Payment bonds are typically 50% of the total contract price if the total project cost is less than $5 million. Over $5 million, the payment bond amount is usually a fixed $2.5 million amount.

3-47   Which federal act sets the safety standard for most construction projects in the United States?

A) NFPA

B) NEMA

C) OSHA

D) ASMI

Answer: C

The Federal Occupational Safety and Health Act (OSHA), Volume 29 CFR 1926/1910 contains the minimum safety standards that apply to the construction industry. In general, this act establishes the safety and health obligations of employers toward their employees. Most states have adopted this safety standard, but many states also have provided additional safety requirements not covered in the OSHA standards. Therefore, each contractor should obtain a copy of his or her own state's safety standards.

3-48   Which of the following is an OSHA safety standard for the construction industry?

A) Handrails must be provided in all toilets for handicapped workers

B) A contract surety bond must be obtained before hiring any workers

C) Employers must instruct their employees to recognize and avoid unsafe conditions

D) Employers must be aware of any medication taken by their employees and keep an adequate supply of all medications on the job site during working hours

Answer: C

OSHA safety standard 1926.21 requires all contractors to instruct their employees to recognize and avoid unsafe working conditions.

3-49   At what height must guardrails and toeboards be provided on scaffolds?

A) At any height above the finished floor

B) On platforms that are more than 10 feet above the ground or floor level

C) On platforms that are more than 12 feet above the ground or floor level

D) On platforms that are more than 20 feet above the ground or floor level

Answer: B

OSHA safety standard 1926.451 requires guardrails and toeboards on scaffolding platforms that are higher than 10 feet above the ground, grade, or floor.

3-50   When asbestos can be crumbled in the palm of the hand, it is said to be:

A) Patchable

B) Pliable

C) Friable

D) Crumbly

Answer: C

When asbestos is friable, tiny fibers can readily break away into fine dust which can be easily inhaled or swallowed, causing a severe health hazard.

3-51   What is the best way to prevent asbestos-related diseases among construction workers?

A) Hire a specialist to identify the level of exposure to asbestos

B) Make certain that employees do not exceed the "action level" by more than 35%

C) Use only workers that have already contracted an asbestos-related disease

D) Limit exposure

Answer: D

Limiting exposure to hazardous materials is the best way to prevent diseases.

3-52   Which of the following best describes contractor liability insurance?

A) An insurance policy designed to protect the contractor against claims brought by third parties who are not employees

B) An insurance policy designed to provide coverage for offices, sheds, warehouses, and stored materials

C) An insurance policy that protects the contractor's property while it is being transported

D) An insurance policy that protects the contractor against burglary, theft, or robbery

Answer: A

Third-party law suits are common, and liability and property damage insurance is deemed necessary for all contractors.

3-53   What is the main purpose of the contractor in taking out liability insurance for his or her own employees?

A) To increase the dollar limits of underlying insurance

B) To have a policy that protects the contractor from liabilities arising out of his or her own business

C) To have insurance that protects the contractor from liability arising out of errors or omissions during the construction process

D) To have a policy that provides coverage over and above Workers' Compensation in case of serious injury or death of an employee while working on the contractor's job site

Answer: D

Liability insurance on the contractor's employees is normally written in combination with Workers' Compensation insurance and provides additional coverage for the contractor's employees.

3-54   Which of the following Acts deal with child labor and minimum wage laws?

A) Federal Depository Act

B) Federal Income Tax Act

C) Fair Labor Standards Act

D) National Fire Prevention Act

Answer: C

The Fair Labor Standards Act establishes minimum wage compensation, overtime pay, record keeping, and child labor standards affecting workers in the United States. This Act is enforced by the Wage and Hour Division of the U.S. Department of Labor.

3-55   The federal law that guarantees equal opportunity for persons with disabilities was enacted in 1990. What is this Act called?

A) ABA

B) ACA

C) ADA

D) AEA

Answer: C

The Americans With Disabilities Act (ADA) was enacted in 1990 and became effective July 26, 1992 for all employers with 25 or more employees; employers with 15 to 24 employees are required to conform to the provisions of this Act after July 26, 1994.

3-56   The ADA protects qualified individuals with disabilities from which of the following?

A) Working overtime

B) Employment discrimination

C) Paying excessive amounts of withholding tax

D) Getting less income than would normally be paid to a person without a disability

Answer: B

An employer cannot discriminate against a person because of a physical or mental impairment that substantially limits a major life activity.

3-57   Which of the following is not considered to be a major life activity limitation?

A) Impaired hearing

C) Impaired speech

B) Impaired sight

D) Missing a finger from one's hand

Answer: D

Besides impaired hearing, sight, and speech, other limitations include impaired breathing, and the inability to perform manual tasks, walk, care for oneself, learn, or work.

3-58   The Immigration and Naturalization Service is responsible for implementing the Act that requires employers to hire only American citizens or aliens who:

A) Are over 21

C) Have obtained a driver's license

B) Are authorized to work in the United States

D) Are married with dependents

Answer: B

Employers must verify the employment eligibility of anyone hired after November 6, 1986. The employee completes Section 1 and the employer completes Section 2 of the INS Form I-9.

3-59   The Fair Labor Standards Act (FLSA) requires employers to pay employees overtime pay after employees work how many hours in a workweek?

A) After 60 hours

C) After 45 hours

B) After 50 hours

D) After 40 hours

Answer: D

Overtime pay is required for all nonexempt workers for any time worked after 40 hours per workweek.

3-60   What is the minimum overtime pay allowed by the FLSA?

A) 1¼ times the employees' regular pay

C) 2 times the employees' regular pay

B) 1½ times the employees' regular pay

D) 2¼ times the employees' regular pay

Answer: B

Overtime pay must not be less than 1½ times the employees' regular rate of pay.

3-61 If a contractor hires an employee on the basis of a 30-hour week for $10 per hour, and this employee works 37 hours one week, what should the employee's gross pay be for that week, based on FLSA regulations?

A) $450

B) $405

C) $350

D) $370

Answer: **D**

Since the employee did not work more than 40 hours in the workweek, no overtime pay is due. Therefore, the employee's total hours are multiplied by $10 for a total of $370.

3-62 The same employee in Question 3-61 worked 39 hours one week and 45 hours the next week. What is this employee's gross pay for the 2 weeks?

A) $750

B) $865

C) $975

D) $1005

Answer: **B**

The employee had no overtime pay due the first week so his gross pay would be $390. The second week, his gross pay would be $400 for the 40 regular hours, plus 1½ times his regular pay ($10 × 1½ = $15) for the 5 hours worked over 40 hours during the workweek. Consequently, his gross pay for the 2-week period would be $390 + $400 + $75 = $865.

3-63 If the employee in Question 3-61 received a raise in pay to $12 per hour, what would his gross pay be for the same amount of hours and conditions worked in Question 3-62?

A) $920

B) $950

C) $980

D) $1038

Answer: **D**

The employee had no overtime pay due the first week so his gross pay would be $468. The second week, his gross pay would be $480 for the 40 regular hours, plus 1½ times his regular pay ($12 × 1½ = $18) for the 5 hours over 40 hours he worked during the one workweek. Consequently, his gross pay for the 2-week period would be $468 + $480 + $90 = $1038.

3-64   Which of the following is the most common reason for the failure of a contracting business?

A) Overstocking materials

B) Financial problems

C) The contractor is unable to meet deadlines

D) The contractor hires unqualified employees

Answer: B

Any of the answers can cause the failure of a contracting business, but the main reason for failure will normally be financial problems caused by underbidding projects, lack of sufficient working capital or credit, and slow payments from customers.

3-65   Which of the following is a true statement concerning financial organization and management?

A) The process is largely wasteful and unproductive

B) It is just as important as time spent on the construction site

C) The process should be left entirely to the contractor's accountant

D) The process should never receive top priority in any business

Answer: B

Financial organization and management is a critical part of staying in business and the process is equally important as the time spent on the construction site.

3-66   While a contractor does not need a college business degree to stay in business or a complete knowledge of bookkeeping and accounting, he or she should have the ability to perform which of the following tasks?

A) Interpret credit reports received for potential customers

B) Know how to select a suitable bookkeeping system for the business without consulting an accountant or CPA

C) Understand computer programming so that the contractor can write an accounting program for the business

D) Spot financial problems early

Answer: D

The ability to spot financial problems early gives the contractor a better chance of correcting the problems before the business is seriously jeopardized.

3-67   In Answer B of Question 3-66, what does CPA mean?

A) Corporate paid accountant

B) Correct public accountant

C) Certified public accountant

D) Certified private accountant

Answer: C

There are many licensed people who do bookkeeping, prepare tax returns, and offer financial advice to businesses and individuals. A certified public accountant (CPA) has undergone rigorous training and education before being licensed to advertise as a financial adviser.

3-68   To ensure good records, all payments made by contractors should be made by check. However, if a contractor must pay in cash, what should the contractor do?

A) Request a receipt for the payment

B) Record the name and address of the place where payment was made

C) Record only the phone number of the place where payment was made in case the contractor is questioned by the IRS

D) Make the purchase elsewhere, where they will accept a check

Answer: A

A valid receipt showing amount of payment, date of payment, and to whom payment was made is an acceptable method of ensuring good records.

3-69   If a cash payment is made and the contractor does not get a receipt, what should the contractor do about this payment?

A) Record the name and address of the business where the payment was made

B) Write a statement in the contractor's records to explain the payment

C) Keep the phone number of the business where payment was made in case the contractor is questioned by the IRS

D) Without a receipt, the contractor must not report the payment to the IRS

Answer: B

The IRS will usually accept cash payments as valid tax deductions, even without a receipt, if good records are kept explaining the payment.

3-70   How long does the IRS require a contractor keep his or her bank statements and canceled checks?

A) 1 year

B) 2 years

C) 3 years

D) 4 years

Answer: D

The IRS can audit an account back 4 years; more if fraud is suspected.

3-71   Information obtained from canceled checks, invoices, and receipts is entered into bookkeeping journals, summarized, and then transferred to the firm's general ledger. The information from the general ledger shows the contractor's financial condition. Which of the following is a report showing the company's financial condition?

A) Income statement

B) Balance sheet

C) Financial statement

D) General ledger statement

Answer: C

Financial statements are used by the contractor to evaluate the company's assets. A financial statement is also needed when the contractor deals with bonding companies, banks, and investors.

3-72   What is another name for a firm's income statement?

A) Profit and loss statement

B) Balance sheet

C) Statement of cash flow

D) General ledger

Answer: A

A contractor's income statement shows the income and expenses that occurred over a given period of time and the final profit and loss that resulted. Therefore, this statement is frequently called a "profit and loss statement."

3-73   Contractors must withhold certain amounts from employees' wages for taxes. Which of the following is not a required federal withholding tax?

A) Federal Income Tax

B) Social Security Tax

C) State Income Tax (if applicable)

D) Profit-sharing

Answer: D

Contractors must withhold Federal Income Tax, State Income Tax (if applicable), Social Security Tax, and Medicare Tax. While some contractors may deduct other amounts such as for employees' saving bonds, IRAs, or for a profit-sharing program, these are not required by the Federal Government.

3-74   Which of the following is not deducted from an employee's pay?

A) Medicare Tax

B) Federal Unemployment Tax

C) Federal Income Tax

D) Social Security Tax

Answer: B

Only the employer pays Federal Unemployment Tax (FUTA). It is not deducted from an employee's wages.

3-75   Contractors are required to pay a certain portion of employees' Social Security Taxes. How much?

A) An amount that equals the employee's share

B) 10% of the employee's gross pay

C) 3% of the employee's net pay

D) An amount that equals half the employee's share

Answer: A

The contractor must pay Social Security Taxes matching the employee's share. The contractor is also required to match the employee's share of Medicare Taxes.

3-76   If a contractor is operating as the sole proprietor of his business, how must he file his income tax return?

A) Submit Form 1120 on the 15th day of the third month after the end of the contractor's fiscal year

B) Submit Form 1120-S on the 15th day of the third month after the end of the contractor's fiscal year

C) Submit Form 1065 on the 15th day of the fourth month after the end of the contractor's fiscal year

D) Submit Schedule C with his individual income tax return

Answer: D

A sole proprietor should submit Schedule C with his or her individual income tax on or before April 15 of each year.

3-77   If a contracting business is operating as a partnership, how should the income tax return be filed?

A) Submit Form 1120 on the 15th day of the third month after the end of the contractor's fiscal year

B) Submit Form 1120-S on the 15th day of the third month after the end of the contractor's fiscal year

C) Submit Form 1065 on the 15th day of the fourth month after the end of the contractor's fiscal year

D) Submit Schedule C with his individual income tax return

Answer: C

A partnership must submit Form 1065 on the 15th day of the fourth month after the end of the contractor's fiscal year.

3-78   If a contracting business is incorporated, how should the income tax return be filed?

A) Submit Form 1120 on the 15th day of the third month after the end of the contractor's fiscal year

B) Submit Form 1120 S on the 15th day of the third month after the end of the contractor's fiscal year

C) Submit Form 1065 on the 15th day of the fourth month after the end of the contractor's fiscal year

D) Submit Schedule C with his individual income tax return

Answer: A

A corporation must submit Form 1120 on the 15th day of the third month after the end of the contractor's fiscal year.

3-79 **What document can be issued by a property owner or his architect to direct a contractor to install some portion of the building or system in a manner other than described in the original construction documents?**

A) Bond

B) Certificate of substantial completion

C) Change order

D) Progress report

Answer: C

A change order usually has an effect on the price and completion date. A change order may be requested by the owner, architect, engineer, or contractor.

3-80 **When is the deadline for employees' W-2 forms to be mailed?**

A) December 31

B) January 31

C) Last day in February

D) April 15

Answer: B

W-2 forms must be sent to each employee from whom taxes were withheld by January 31 of each year.

3-81 **When is the deadline for sending W-3 forms to the IRS, summarizing the W-2 forms mailed to employees?**

A) December 31

B) January 31

C) Last day in February

D) April 15

Answer: C

W-3 forms must be sent to the IRS by the last day in February of each year.

3-82 **Form 1099 must be sent to each employee or consultant for any compensation that was not subject to withholding taxes. What is the due date of this form?**

A) December 31

B) January 31

C) Last day in February

D) April 15

Answer: B

1099 forms are due by January 31 for the preceding year.

3-83   When must a 1096 form be sent to the IRS summarizing the 1099s sent to employees or consultants for any compensation not subject to withholding taxes?

A) December 31

B) February 31

C) Last day in February

D) April 15

Answer: C

1096 forms must be sent to IRS by the last day of February for the previous year.

3-84   How does a contractor know how many deductions an employee is claiming?

A) From the employees' W-4 form

B) From the employees' W-2 form

C) From the employees' 1099 form

D) From the employees' 1096 form

Answer: A

Each employee is required to fill out Form W-4 for his or her employer. This form shows how many deductions the employee is claiming.

3-85   How does a contractor calculate the amount of Federal Income Tax to withhold?

A) Using information from the employees' W-4 form and IRS Circular B

B) Using information from the employees' W-4 form and IRS Circular C

C) Using information from the employees' W-4, W-2, 1066, and 1097 forms and also IRS Circular D

D) Using information from the employees' W-4 form and IRS Circular E

Answer: D

IRS Circular E contains information describing the regulations for deducting income tax. A chart is also included that shows the exact amount of Federal Income Tax to withhold from each employee, depending upon the employee's gross pay and number of deductions. See Figure 3-1.

SINGLE Persons- Weekly Payroll Period

If the wages are-		And the number of withholding allowances claimed is-										
At least	But less than	0	1	2	3	4	5	6	7	8	9	10
		The amount of income tax to be withheld is-										
$0	$55	0	0	0	0	0	0	0	0	0	0	0
55	60	1	0	0	0	0	0	0	0	0	0	0
60	65	2	0	0	0	0	0	0	0	0	0	0
65	70	2	0	0	0	0	0	0	0	0	0	0
70	75	3	0	0	0	0	0	0	0	0	0	0
75	80	4	0	0	0	0	0	0	0	0	0	0
80	85	5	0	0	0	0	0	0	0	0	0	0
85	90	5	0	0	0	0	0	0	0	0	0	0
90	95	6	0	0	0	0	0	0	0	0	0	0
95	100	7	0	0	0	0	0	0	0	0	0	0
100	105	8	0	0	0	0	0	0	0	0	0	0
105	110	8	0	0	0	0	0	0	0	0	0	0
110	115	9	1	0	0	0	0	0	0	0	0	0
115	120	10	2	0	0	0	0	0	0	0	0	0
120	125	11	3	0	0	0	0	0	0	0	0	0
125	130	11	3	0	0	0	0	0	0	0	0	0
130	135	12	4	0	0	0	0	0	0	0	0	0
135	140	13	5	0	0	0	0	0	0	0	0	0
140	145	14	6	0	0	0	0	0	0	0	0	0
145	150	14	6	0	0	0	0	0	0	0	0	0
150	155	15	7	0	0	0	0	0	0	0	0	0
155	160	16	8	0	0	0	0	0	0	0	0	0
160	165	17	9	1	0	0	0	0	0	0	0	0
165	170	17	9	1	0	0	0	0	0	0	0	0
170	175	18	10	2	0	0	0	0	0	0	0	0
175	180	19	11	3	0	0	0	0	0	0	0	0
180	185	20	12	4	0	0	0	0	0	0	0	0
185	190	20	12	4	0	0	0	0	0	0	0	0
190	195	21	13	5	0	0	0	0	0	0	0	0
195	200	22	14	6	0	0	0	0	0	0	0	0
200	210	23	15	7	0	0	0	0	0	0	0	0
210	220	25	17	8	0	0	0	0	0	0	0	0
220	230	26	18	10	2	0	0	0	0	0	0	0
230	240	28	20	11	3	0	0	0	0	0	0	0
240	250	29	21	13	5	0	0	0	0	0	0	0
250	260	31	23	14	6	0	0	0	0	0	0	0
260	270	32	24	16	8	0	0	0	0	0	0	0
270	280	34	26	17	9	1	0	0	0	0	0	0
280	290	35	27	19	11	3	0	0	0	0	0	0
290	300	37	29	20	12	4	0	0	0	0	0	0
300	310	38	30	22	14	6	0	0	0	0	0	0
310	320	40	32	23	15	7	0	0	0	0	0	0
320	330	41	33	25	17	9	1	0	0	0	0	0
330	340	43	35	26	18	10	2	0	0	0	0	0
340	350	44	36	28	20	12	4	0	0	0	0	0
350	360	46	38	29	21	13	5	0	0	0	0	0
360	370	47	39	31	23	15	7	0	0	0	0	0
370	380	49	41	32	24	16	8	0	0	0	0	0
380	390	50	42	34	26	18	10	2	0	0	0	0
390	400	52	44	35	27	19	11	3	0	0	0	0
400	410	53	45	37	29	21	13	5	0	0	0	0
410	420	55	47	38	30	22	14	6	0	0	0	0
420	430	56	48	40	32	24	16	8	0	0	0	0
430	440	58	50	41	33	25	17	9	1	0	0	0
440	450	59	51	43	35	27	19	11	3	0	0	0
450	460	61	53	44	36	28	20	12	4	0	0	0
460	470	62	54	46	38	30	22	14	6	0	0	0
470	480	64	56	47	39	31	23	15	7	0	0	0
480	490	65	57	49	41	33	25	17	9	0	0	0
490	500	67	59	50	42	34	26	18	10	2	0	0
500	510	68	60	52	44	36	28	20	12	3	0	0
510	520	70	62	53	45	37	29	21	13	5	0	0
520	530	71	63	55	47	39	31	23	15	6	0	0
530	540	73	65	56	48	40	32	24	16	8	0	0
540	550	75	66	58	50	42	34	26	18	9	1	0
550	560	78	68	59	51	43	35	27	19	11	3	0
560	570	81	69	61	53	45	37	29	21	12	4	0
570	580	84	71	62	54	46	38	30	22	14	6	0
580	590	87	72	64	56	48	40	32	24	15	7	0
590	600	89	74	65	57	49	41	33	25	17	9	1

Figure 3-1: Chart from IRS Circular E for determining amount of federal tax to withhold from employees' wages.

3-86   What is the amount of Federal Income Tax that should be withheld from a single employee, with 1 dependent, if his gross weekly pay is $575? See Figure 3-1.

A) $69

B) $71

C) $92

D) $97

Answer: B

IRS Circular E contains a chart showing the exact amount of Federal Income Tax to withhold from each employee, depending upon the employee's gross pay and number of deductions. In this case, the amount is $71.

3-87   What is the amount of Federal Income Tax that should be withheld from a single employee, with 7 dependents, if his gross weekly pay is $491?

A) $10

B) $20

C) $30

D) $40

Answer: A

IRS Circular E in Figure 3-1 shows this amount to be $10.

3-88   Which of the following best describes a "lien?"

A) A note given as security against the payment of a just debt

B) To reinforce a structure or object with bracing or forms

C) A claim on the property of another as security against the payment of a just debt

D) Not perpendicular

Answer: C

A lien is a specific type of legal document that can be used by contractors and others to secure payment for labor or materials which have been used to improve another person's property. Lien laws are based on the theory that if an owner's property has been improved, the owner should not benefit from the improvements unless he pays for it.

3-89   Who is entitled to file a lien?

A) Only subcontractors or specialty contractors who work on a building construction project

B) Any person who furnishes labor or materials used in a construction project

C) Any person to whom the property owner owes money

D) Only workers who are paid a salary, not hourly wages

Answer: B

Any person who furnishes labor or materials used in the construction, alteration, or repair of any building, land, or other structure, is entitled to file a lien.

3-90   What is usually the maximum amount of a lien filed against a building or property?

A) $10,000

B) $100,000

C) $1,000,000

D) An amount equal to the contract price or agreed-upon charge

Answer: D

A lien will usually equal the amount of the contract or the agreed-upon price. For example, if the contractor was hired on a cost-plus-profit basis, the contractor may obtain a lien to cover the cost of all labor, materials, overhead, and the agreed-upon profit, provided the contractor can show proof of these charges.

3-91   If a contractor has not been paid for work on a construction project, how long does the contractor have to file a lien?

A) Within 10 days

B) Within 20 days

C) Within 30 days

D) Varies from state to state

Answer: D

The lien laws vary from state to state, but in many states, the law gives all parties 90 days to file a claim for a lien. The lien claim must be filed with the county court in which the property is located. The claim must state the name of the owner or reputed owner of the property, the address of the property, and the amount due. The claim must also include a statement of the terms, time, and conditions of the contract, and a description of the property to be charged with the lien, sufficient for identification. The claim must usually be verified by oath. Each contractor should review the lien laws of his/her state.

Chapter 4

Site Work, Demolition and Construction

Selecting a building site for any new structure requires an investigation not only of the legal history and future plans for the land and surrounding areas, but also of the physical characteristics of the soils and underlying geology. In some cases, the investigation is best performed by a qualified land planner or engineer. In other cases, local municipalities can be of assistance.

Investigation of the legal history of the property, commonly called a title search, is usually performed by an attorney or title search agency. A title search involves checking to see that no outstanding liens are held against the property and that all previous title transfers were correctly recorded.

Other important information necessary to verify prior to construction is the current zoning status of the property and surrounding areas; and of the status of the area in the master plan for the local municipality. This investigation includes an examination of plans for the expansion of the transportation network to see how these plans may affect the location of the building or buildings on the building site.

The physical characteristics of the lot include a boundary description or survey. The land recording procedures often require an official survey, which must be performed by a licensed surveyor.

Local offices of the U.S. Department of Agriculture Soil Conservation Service are an excellent source of data describing soil conditions and the geology of the area. This information is important in choosing the foundation system, particularly in areas with unstable soils.

Soil Conditions

Excavation of earth and rock involves four basic operations:

- Loosening
- Loading
- Hauling
- Dumping

Rock, hardpan, and frozen ground may be loosened more economically with explosives, although many types of pneumatic tools are available where explosives are not permitted.

In soft ground, with a minimum of large rocks, loosening and loading becomes one operation. Backhoes and front-end loaders are frequently used on small work, while huge excavation equipment is used on larger jobs.

4-1   Most building codes and building inspection departments in the United States will accept compaction test results for fill material if the tests are performed in accordance with which of the following standards?

A) ASTM D 698   C) NFPA

B) NEC   D) ASHRAE

Answer: A

Most building codes, building inspectors, and building inspection departments accept testing procedures as provided by the American Society for Testing and Materials (ASTM). ASTM Document 698 gives the standards for performing compaction tests.

4-2   AASHTO sets construction standards for which of the following?

A) Plywood siding   C) Highway bridges

B) Steel structures   D) Refrigeration piping

Answer: C

The American Association of State Highway and Transportation Officials sets standards for highways and related construction, such as highway bridges.

4-3   Which of the following best describes an analysis of foundation soils?

A) Corrosion resistance   C) Iron content

B) Organic content   D) The ability to resist heat and fire if used around building foundation walls

Answer: B

Most building codes limit the amount of organic material allowed in acceptable foundation soils. Organic material consists of compounds that formerly comprised, or where derived from, plants and animals.

4-4   Which of the following best describes the purpose of local building site-work requirements?

A) Such requirements are intended to override federal regulations

B) Such requirements are intended to override other local state regulations

C) Such requirements are intended to give minimum standards for the local soil conditions

D) Site-work requirements are always left to local officials

Answer: C

Most building codes give standards of minimum quality that are allowed in a given locale and are not intended to nullify other state or federal laws.

4-5   Which of the following federal departments has developed regulations and guidelines on the use of explosives for demolition projects and for other building construction practices?

A) HUD

B) DOTn

C) Department of Agriculture

D) Department of Labor

Answer: B

The Department of Transportation (DOTn) has developed many regulations and safeguards which apply to explosives due to the use of explosives in massive highway construction activities.

4-6   Which of the following best describes the requirements for portable fire extinguishers that are required on most job sites?

A) They must be A:B:C rated

B) They must be A rated

C) If B rated, the extinguishers must be inspected twice weekly

D) If C rated, the extinguishers must be inspected daily

Answer: A

Job-site fire extinguishers must be capable of extinguishing all types of fires; the A:B:C rated extinguishers meet this requirement.

4-7   Temporary job-site facilities such as sidewalk sheds and guard fences are required by all building codes. When must these safety barriers be installed?

A) Before applying for a building permit

B) Before beginning any type of construction, including the delivery of materials

C) Immediately (within 24 hours) after the building contract is signed

D) After the foundation has been excavated

Answer: B

Safety barriers, sidewalk sheds, and other required safeguards must be in place early, before any construction begins, to properly safeguard the public from normal job-site hazards.

4-8   When it becomes necessary to temporarily store materials on public property or to temporarily block existing roadways, which best describes the requirements of most localities?

A) Permission is automatically granted when the building permit is obtained

B) Special permission is required

C) If police protection is available, no other permits are required

D) It is acceptable to all building codes if the pavements are marked

Answer: B

Special permission is required to store building materials on public property or to temporarily block existing roads or highways in most situations. This permission is in addition to the normal building permit.

4-9   Which of the following is an acceptable safeguard around the perimeter of a construction site?

A) Armed guards

B) The installation of two-way radios on all sides of the job site

C) Approved fences or barricades

D) Around-the-clock lighting

Answer: C

Approved fences are an acceptable and necessary safeguard.

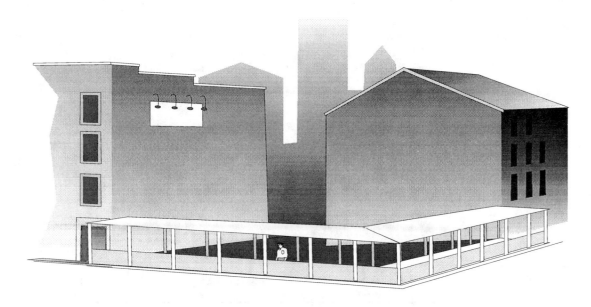

Figure 4-1: Typical sidewalk shed that offers protection to the public from falling objects on a building construction project.

4-10   What protection is required for public sidewalks that are in use by the public during building construction?

A) Steel barriers

B) Persons hired as lookouts

C) Concrete ramps

D) Sidewalk sheds

Answer: D

Sidewalk sheds (Figure 4-1) are required in most towns and cities where sidewalks pass near the construction site.

4-11   Public walks or walkways under sidewalk sheds must comply with which of the following?

A) All such walkways must be constructed of concrete

B) Walkways under sidewalk sheds must be absolutely level

C) Such walkways must comply with the requirements for interior egress corridors and ramps

D) All such walkways must never exceed 20 feet in length

Answer: C

The same rules apply to outside enclosed corridors as to those inside of a building.

Figure 4-2: Four methods that may be used for fighting fires. Which is the most common for job-site protection?

4-12   Which representation in Figure 4-2 do most codes require as protection against small construction fires?

A) Firefighters

B) Fire hydrant

C) Fire alarms

D) Fire extinguishers

Answer: D

Portable fire extinguishers are an economical and effective method of controlling small construction-site fires.

4-13   Most building codes require that the construction materials and methods used for sidewalk sheds be based on which of the following?

A) Time of day that blasting (demolition) will take place

B) Height of the building and the distance to the public street

C) Amount of rush-hour traffic

D) The distance to the covered shelter

Answer: B

Construction activities at great heights and the proximity of construction activities to the street increase the chances for hazardous flying debris, and dictates the construction materials and methods for sidewalk sheds.

4-14   Most building codes require that fire hazards caused by demolition activities and building construction work comply with which of the following?

A) Rules of common sense

B) Local ordinances

C) ANSI standards

D) NFPA standards

Answer: D

The accepted standards for fire prevention in all types of construction work are those compiled by the National Fire Protection Association (NFPA) of Quincy, MA.

4-15   Which of the following best describes the requirements for a building standpipe water system which is used to fight fires?

A) It may be temporarily blocked for deliveries only

B) The system may be blocked if space is needed to store construction materials or equipment

C) The system may be blocked for any construction activity that is monitored

D) The system should never be blocked

Answer: D

A functioning building standpipe system cannot be made inaccessible at any time.

4-16   Which of the following is a requirement for retaining walls that are built adjacent to an adjoining property or building?

A) Night lighting must be provided

B) Such walls are limited in height

C) Such walls may not be constructed of concrete

D) Retaining walls must be provided with a guardrail or fence

Answer: D

General public safety is always a concern and requirement of all building codes.

4-17   Before demolition activities on any building can begin, which of the following best describes the requirements for existing utilities?

A) All utility bills must be paid in full

B) All utilities must be disconnected and capped off at a safe distance from the demolition activities

C) Existing electrical wires must be protected by steel shields

D) Existing utilities must be constantly monitored during the demolition activities

Answer: B

Public utilities entering the demolition site must be properly disconnected and capped in a manner prescribed by the utility authorities and the local building inspection department.

4-18   If a building has been demolished and the site properly cleared, what further requirements are considered necessary by most building codes and local ordinances?

A) Safeguards must be taken to prevent water damage to foundations of adjoining structures

B) A means to prevent vandalism must be taken

C) A means to prevent fires on the vacant lot must be provided before the contractor leaves the site

D) Barriers must be installed to prevent damage to existing utilities

Answer: A

The owner of a demolished construction site, which then becomes a vacant lot, must leave the lot so as not to cause harm or damage to adjoining buildings.

4-19   What is another requirement for the vacant lot after a building is demolished?

A) Grass must be planted on the vacant lot if it remains vacant for a period of 6 months

B) Shrubs and trees must be planted if the lot remains vacant, without any construction activity, for 1 year

C) The site must be graded so that it conforms to existing adjoining grades

D) Trails across the lot must be lighted

Answer: C

The site must be properly graded to protect the general public and also adjacent buildings or lots.

4-20 **If a contractor is denied access to a structure adjoining a construction site on which the contractor is working, and as a result, will be unable to protect the adjoining building from possible damage caused by the contractor's construction activities, which of the following is a building code requirement?**

A) Notify the appropriate law-enforcement authority

B) Forcibly enter the property

C) Notify the adjoining property owner and the local building inspection office in writing and have the notification delivered by certified mail

D) Notify the adjoining property owner's insurance carrier

Answer: C

Such notification is required by most building codes; it should be in writing with proof of delivery.

4-21 **The owner of a structure adjoining a new building construction site may have to pay for damage to his or her own property even if the damage was caused by the new construction. Under which of the following conditions could this happen?**

A) The owner refuses to communicate with the building contractor in person

B) The owner of the adjoining property refuses to allow the building contractor access to the existing structure

C) The owner refuses to monitor the new construction

D) The owner refuses to attend construction meetings held by the general contractor

Answer: B

Most building codes require the owner of a building adjoining a construction site to allow those in charge of the new construction to effect measures that will insure proper construction safeguards.

4-22 **To protect the public against intermittent hazards across a walkway, which of the following is usually a code requirement?**

A) Traffic light

B) Barricades

C) Alarms

D) A watchman

Answer: D

If there are hazards at a walkway at various times during the day, the best way of protecting the public, short of closing the walk, is to provide a watchman as shown in Figure 4-3 on the next page.

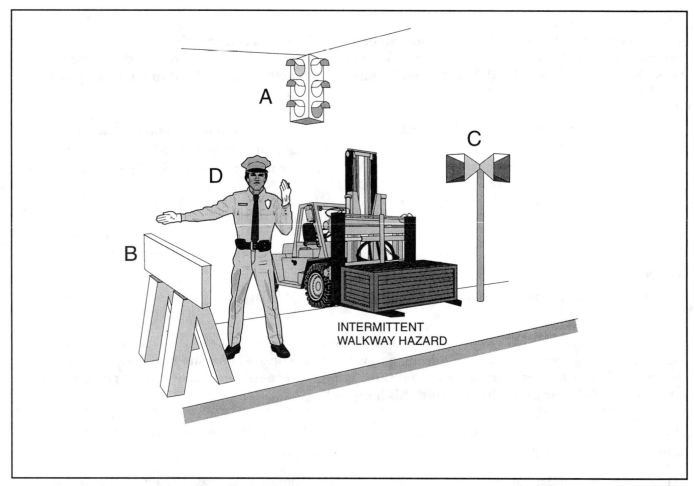

Figure 4-3: Placing a watchman at the site is the usual method of protecting pedestrians from intermittent hazards when construction activities must cross a passageway.

4-23 **The demolition of a building may involve structural collapse, yet structural collapse violates the requirements of most building codes. How is this dilemma normally addressed by building codes?**

A) Structural collapse is acceptable for building demolition

B) Structural collapse is never acceptable

C) An architect or professional engineer must monitor any building collapse

D) All building code requirements are suspended during a collapse

Answer: A

Most codes require safeguards to prevent the structural collapse of a building except when the process of the work itself is to effect the collapse. For example, during the construction of a new building, forms, braces, and other safeguards are required to prevent structural collapse. However, during the demolition of an existing structure, the main purpose of the work is to collapse the building structure.

4-24 Which of the following is a common building code requirement for standpipe systems during the construction of each floor level?

A) It must be complete and ready for use only if there is water in the system

B) There are no building code requirements during the construction process; only after the building is complete and ready for occupants

C) All standpipes must be brightly painted during the construction of the building

D) The standpipe system must be ready for use on each level as that level is completed

Answer: D

The standpipe system must be completed with all fittings, valves, etc. and ready for use at each level, even if there is no water supply system in place.

4-25 Which of the following best describes the requirements for neighboring walls adjoining or shared by a new building under construction?

A) New construction work must stop at the first sign of any cracks in the existing structure

B) New construction must not cause damage to any existing structure

C) The existing wall must be temporarily relocated during the new construction

D) Any new construction must be no less than 6 inches from the existing wall

Answer: B

The contractor of the new building must protect the structural integrity of any existing structures.

4-26 Which of the following fire-protection systems is required in all high-rise buildings?

A) A sign on each floor giving the phone number of the nearest fire department

B) Portable fire extinguishers

C) Computer-monitored closed-circuit TV cameras in each office space

D) A standpipe water-supply system

Answer: D

A standpipe system is required in all high-rise buildings. (See Figure 4-4 on the next page.) Exit signs are also required, but these are only a part of a fire-protection system and are also required in buildings other than the high-rise type. They are provided to direct personnel out of buildings in case of fire.

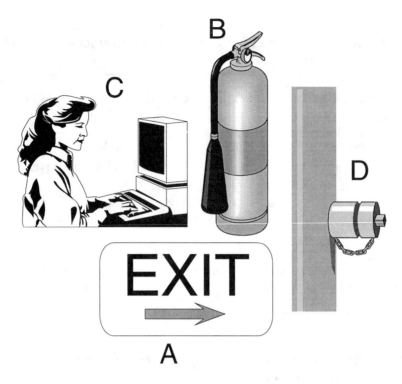

Figure 4-4: A standpipe system is required in all high-rise buildings.

4-27   Hose connections to standpipes are required to comply with which representation in Figure 4-5?

A) The hose connection must have a removable cap

B) The connection outlet must be installed at 36 inches above floor level

C) The connection must be concealed in a wall cabinet

D) The connection must be locked and made tamperproof

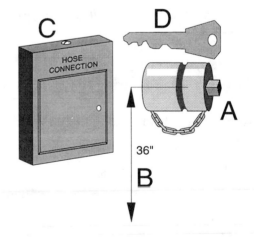

Answer: A

Hose connections for standpipe systems must be provided with a removable cap which is attached to the hose connection with a chain.

Figure 4-5: Which of these is a code requirement for hose connections to a standpipe system?

4-28   Which of the following is *not* a Code requirement for demolition activities?

A) Material dropped by gravity or thrown outside exterior walls shall be wetted down first to contain dust

B) Adequate ventilation must be provided in all work areas

C) Demolition activities shall not endanger people, adjacent property or public right-of-way

D) If material removal causes excess dust, it shall be wetted down to prevent a nuisance

Answer: A

Demolition material may not be dropped by gravity, or thrown. Metal or wooden chutes must be used.

4-29   Which of the following is a common code requirement for standpipe systems when a building is being demolished?

A) The standpipe system must be kept in operable condition up to one floor below the one being demolished

B) The complete standpipe system must remain in place until after the building has been completely demolished

C) A temporary standpipe system must be built before the old system is removed

D) The entire standpipe system must be removed from the building before demolition takes place

Answer: A

When a building is demolished floor by floor, the standpipe system must be maintained up to the floor below the one being demolished.

4-30   Permanent or temporary stairs are required when a building has been constructed to a height of more than:

A) 25 feet

B) 50 feet

C) 100 feet

D) 200 feet

Answer: B

The required threshold beyond which a temporary stair must be in place is 50 feet, unless the permanent stairs are constructed and ready for use.

4-31   Which of the following meets building code requirements in regard to party walls when a building is demolished?

A) The owner of the building adjoining the one being demolished is responsible for maintaining his or her own wall

B) City or county officials are responsible for arbitrating exactly who is responsible for maintaining party walls

C) The owner of the demolished building is responsible for maintaining the usefulness of the party wall

D) Local utilities are always responsible for maintaining party walls

Answer: C

The owner of the demolished building is responsible for plugging up beam holes in the party wall, keeping the wall safe at all times during demolition, and maintaining the wall's usefulness.

Chapter 5

Foundations, Formwork, and Retaining Walls

In general, the type of foundation selected for a structure depends on the weight of the structure and the allowable bearing capacity of the soil.

Foundations that must carry heavy loads require careful attention to the bearing capacity of the soil. The following table gives the generally accepted bearing capacities of various soil types in tons per square foot:

SOIL-BEARING CAPACITIES	
Material	**Allowable Bearing Tons per Square Foot**
Quicksand and alluvial soil	½
Soft clay	1
Moderately dry clay, fine sand	2
Firm and dry loam or clay	3
Compact coarse sand or stiff gravel	4
Coarse gravel	6
Gravel and sand, well-cemented	8

SOIL-BEARING CAPACITIES *(Cont.)*	
Material	**Allowable Bearing Tons per Square Foot**
Good hardpan or hard shale	10
Very hard native bedrock	20
Rock under caissons	25

The unit soil pressure exerted by a foundation is computed by dividing the total weight by the bearing area.

Footings

Footings act as the base for the foundation walls and transmit the superimposed load to the soil. The type and size of footings should be suitable for the soil condition, and in cold climates, the footings should be far enough below the finished grade level to be protected from frost. State, county and city building codes usually establish this depth, which can be 4 feet or more in the northern sections of the United States and Canada.

Poured concrete is generally used for footings, although gravel is recommended as footing for foundations of pressure-treated wood. Developments in treated wood foundation systems permit all-weather construction and provide reliable foundations as well.

Where fill has been used to raise the level of the building, the footings must extend below the fill to undisturbed earth. In areas having fine clay soil, which expands when it becomes wet and shrinks when it dries, irregular settlement of the foundation system and building may occur. A professional engineer should be consulted when building a structure on this type of expansive clay soil.

Foundations

Foundation walls form an enclosure for basements or crawl spaces and also carry the building loads. The types of foundations most commonly used includes poured concrete, reinforced poured concrete, and concrete block. Pressure-treated wood foundation walls are being more often used and are accepted by most codes for specific types of structures. Preservative-treated posts and poles offer many possibilities for low-cost foundation systems and can also serve as a structural framework for the walls and roof.

Forms for Concrete

Forms are a major part of concrete construction work. They must support the plastic concrete until it hardens. Forms protect the concrete, assist in curing it, and support any reinforcing rods (rebars) or conduit embedded in it.

Forms for concrete must be tight, rigid, and strong. If not tight, loss of mortar may cause a honeycomb effect or loss of water may cause sand streaking. The forms must be braced enough to stay in alignment. Special care is needed in bracing and tying down forms, such as for retainer walls, where the mass of concrete is larger at the bottom and tapers toward the top. In this type of construction and in the first pour for walls and columns, the concrete tends to lift the form above the proper elevation.

Concrete forms are generally constructed from one of these materials:

- Earth
- Metal
- Wood
- Fiberglass

5-1   For larger buildings, a number of soil load-bearing tests are required. These tests are usually based on which of the following?

A) 25% of the building floor area

B) 50% of the building floor area

C) The ground area to be covered by the building

D) The number of rock outcroppings on the site

Answer: C

The tests required are based on a percentage of the ground coverage of the building. Such percentages vary depending on the size of the building.

5-2   Which of the following is a required soil test for deep foundations?

A) A perk test

B) An exploratory boring to solid rock

C) A test to determine soft clay content

D) An exploratory boring 6 feet into solid rock

Answer: B

Most building codes will require that a boring be made all the way down to solid bedrock for deep foundations.

5-3   When the test in Question 5-2 is performed, what will most code officials require in addition to the actual test?

A) Samples of actual rock strata

B) Samples of actual soil strata

C) Documentation describing the type of drill used to make the test

D) A chemical analysis of the soil strata

Answer: B

Most code officials will want to look at actual soil samples in order to visually confirm soil type and verify the contractor's written report. With such soil samples in hand, the code officials can readily have them tested if there are any signs of doubtful characteristics.

5-4   The data recorded as a result of a soil-test boring are required to be interpreted by which of the following?

A) Local health department

C) County administrator

B) Registered professional engineer

D) Soil Conservation Service

Answer: B

The structural analysis of the load-bearing characteristics of soil is a highly specialized area of study. A registered engineer experienced in this field of study is generally the only person qualified to analyze soil samples.

5-5   Settlement of soil under a foundation is deemed within acceptable limits to most building code officials if which of the following specifications are met?

A) The soil settles less than $\frac{1}{4}$ inch per ton of loading

C) The soil settles less than $\frac{1}{8}$ inch per ton of loading

B) The soil settles less than $\frac{1}{10}$ inch per foot of loading

D) The soil settles less than $\frac{1}{10}$ inch per ton of loading

Answer: D

Most all buildings can be expected to settle. The goal is to design foundations that will result in as little settlement as possible; $\frac{1}{10}$ inch per ton is generally accepted as a maximum.

5-6   Which of the following is the most suitable foundation soil for high-rise buildings?

A) Packed gravel

C) Organic salt

B) Bedrock

D) Packed sand

Answer: B

In most cases, solid bedrock is the best foundation for a building ("skyscrapers" in New York City, for example, are conveniently located in an area that has an abundance of underlying bedrock).

5-7   Which of the following best describes building code requirements for the load-bearing capacity of soil?

A) The load-bearing capacity may be temporarily exceeded for snow loads

B) The load-bearing capacity may be exceeded only by the amount of the specified live loading

C) The load-bearing capacity must never be exceeded

D) The load-bearing capacity may be exceeded after the building has undergone initial settlement

Answer: C

Good engineering practice always employs safety factors that allow overstress. However, if the actual load-bearing capacity is exceeded, the soil will fail.

5-8   When a structure is to be built on a foundation material of doubtful characteristics, which of the following is required by most code officials before the construction work may proceed?

A) The exact nature of the soil must be determined with test borings

B) Aerial photographs of the building site must be taken with infared film

C) A perk test must be made to determine the ability of the soil to absorb water

D) Pilings must always be used when such conditions are encountered

Answer: A

A soil test performed by a qualified individual is nearly always required, along with a written report and actual soil samples.

5-9   Which of the following is a "deciding factor" when determining footing depth?

A) The weight of the foundation

B) The depth of the frost line

C) The ambient temperature of the footings at the time of installation

D) The distance from ground surface to organic soil strata

Answer: B

In most circumstances, good engineering practice dictates that a footing must be taken down below the frost line due to the expansion and contraction of the underlying bearing soil strata.

5-10   Which of the following best describes typical building code restrictions on footings bearing on bedrock that is above the frost line?

A) This condition is never acceptable

B) Boring or blasting is required to place the footing below the frost line

C) Another building site must be selected

D) This condition is acceptable by most building codes

Answer: D

Generally, bedrock that will not shift or heave due to frost action is suitable as a bearing strata regardless of the frost depth.

5-11   Which of the following is the best criteria for restrictions on footing depth in areas of temperate climate?

A) Excessive moisture

B) Unstable soil conditions always prevail in such areas

C) Frost action

D) Organic soils prevail in such areas

Answer: C

Temperate regions are the areas most commonly affected by freezing and thawing.

5-12   When a foundation footing is widened, which of the following occurs?

A) The unit pressure on the soil becomes less

B) The unit pressure on the footing increases

C) The unit pressure will always remain the same

D) The unit pressure on the footing will double for every 6 inches that it is widened

Answer: A

The more square area of footing there is in contact with the soil, the more area of soil there is to absorb the loads placed on it. Therefore, the wider the footing the less pounds per square foot unit stress there is on the soil.

5-13   In considering the problem of foundation settlement, most building codes require a structural design that:

A) Ensures even building settlement

B) Depends on 28-day concrete strength

C) Ensures differing rates of settlement for columns and walls

D) Guarantees no settlement

Answer: A

If a building settles at all, it should settle within acceptable limits and it should settle evenly throughout its parts.

5-14   Which of the following is most likely to affect the structural integrity of a foundation?

A) Moderate to high winds up to 50 mph

B) The slope of the land on which the foundation is constructed

C) The type of soil above the foundation

D) Vibrations from nearby railways or other heavy equipment

Answer: D

Most building codes address the problems of vibration adjacent to foundations. Heavy equipment vibrations can cause soil settlement and a whole host of other structual-related problems that must be considered in initial foundation design.

5-15   What type of building superstructure is allowed when a wood foundation system is utilized?

A) Concrete block

B) Wood frame and concrete block

C) Solid brick

D) Wood frame only

Answer: D

Most building codes allow wood foundation systems for wood frame buildings provided the footing loads are within acceptable limits. This foundation method is allowed because of the relative light weight of the framing materials.

5-16   When wood is subjected to constant change from wet to dry, which of the following will occur?

A) The wood will decay faster than if it were constantly wet or constantly dry

C) There will be no difference in the length of time it takes for the wood to decay

B) The wood will decay less than if it were constantly wet or constantly dry

D) Joints tend to become rigid

Answer: A

Decay is set into motion when wood constantly changes moisture content. This is why most codes require residential wood foundations and wood wall studs and sheathing above grade to be protected and kept dry at all times.

5-17   At what distance must reinforcing steel (rebars) used in reinforced concrete footings be kept from the footing edges?

A) 4 inches

C) $1\frac{1}{2}$ to 2 inches

B) 6 inches

D) 3 inches

Answer: D

The clear distance between the face of the steel, embedded in concrete, and the earth must be at least 3 inches.

5-18   The minimum concrete compression strength required for residential footings is:

A) 2,000 pounds per sq. in.

C) 4,000 pounds per sq. in.

B) 2,500 pounds per sq. in.

D) 4,500 – 6,000 pounds per sq. in.

Answer: B

A minimum of 2,500 pounds per sq. in. in a 28-day concrete strength is required in most areas for residential footings.

5-19   If the top of the foundation wall in Figure 5-1 on the next page is exposed 4 inches above grade, which of the following is a correct statement?

A) This exposure does not meet building code requirements

B) This exposure meets code requirements only if masonry veneer is used on the outside wall of the foundation

C) This exposure meets code requirements only if the waterproofing extends to the top of the wall

D) To meet code requirements, the top of the foundation must be extended another 4 inches

Answer: B

Most building codes require foundation walls to extend at least 6 inches above the finished grade except when masonry veneer is installed on the exposed wall. Then the exposed height can be reduced to 4 inches.

5-20   What is the main reason that the porous fill in Figure 5-1 will not meet code requirements?

A) The fill does not extend far enough beyond the edge of the footing

B) The fill extends too far from the edge of the footing

C) The height of the fill above the footing is insufficient

D) There is no footing drain tile

Answer: A

The fill does not extend at least 1 foot beyond the footing edge; a requirement of most building codes.

5-21   What is the required thickness of the moisture barrier that must be used under the basement floor (slab) in Figure 5-1?

A) 2 mils

B) 4 mils

C) 6 mils

D) 8 mils

Answer: C

A 6-mil polyethylene moisture barrier must be placed under the basement floor.

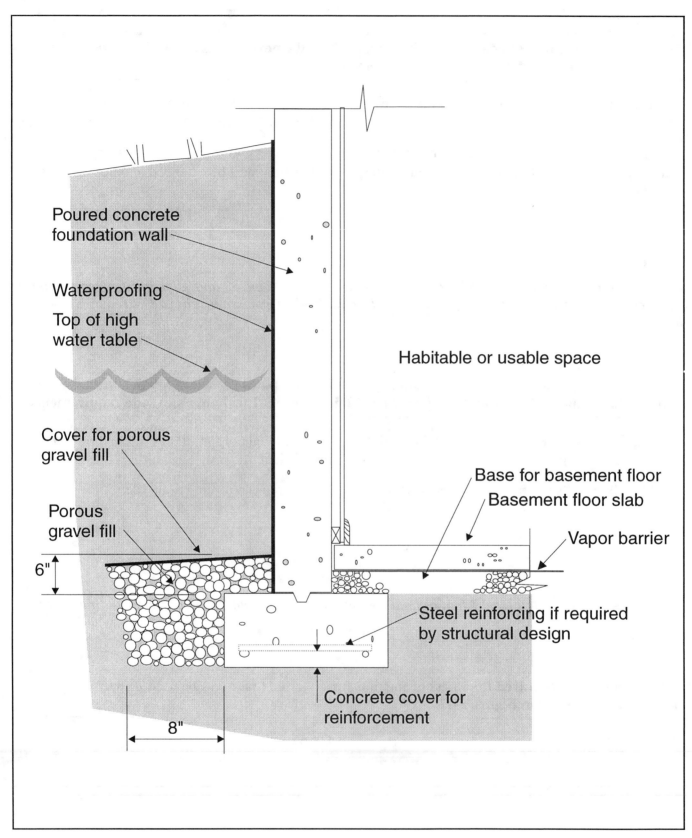

Figure 5-1: Cross-sectional view of a residential building foundation for use with Questions 19 through 24.

5-22   What is the minimum allowable thickness of the floor base in Figure 5-1?

A) 2 inches

B) 4 inches

C) 6 inches

D) 8 inches

Answer: B

The floor base that is covered by the moisture barrier in Figure 5-1 must be at least 4 inches thick to comply with most building codes.

5-23   Due to the high water table in the foundation view shown in Figure 5-1, which of the following must be done to comply with most building codes?

A) The outside of the entire foundation wall must be cement parged and then a dampproof covering applied over the parging

B) The outside of the entire foundation wall must be cement parged and then a waterproof cover added over the parging

C) A waterproofing membrane must be applied over the entire exterior face of the foundation wall

D) A waterproofing membrane must be applied over the exterior face of the foundation wall up to grade level

Answer: D

Most building codes differentiate between dampproofing and waterproofing. If a high-water table is present, a waterproofing membrane is required to cover the foundation wall up to finish-grade height.

5-24   If approved drain tiles are to be used along the footing of the foundation wall in Figure 5-1 rather than just the porous gravel fill, what are the coverage requirements of the fill?

A) 1 inch of porous gravel base, and 4 inches of porous gravel cover for the tile

B) 2 inches of porous gravel base, and 4 inches of porous gravel cover for the tile

C) 4 inches of porous gravel base and 6 inches of porous gravel cover for the tile

D) 2 inches of porous gravel base and 6 inches of porous gravel cover for the tile

Answer: D

Changing the drainage system in this situation would then permit using only 2 inches of gravel base with 6 inches of gravel cover over the tiles.

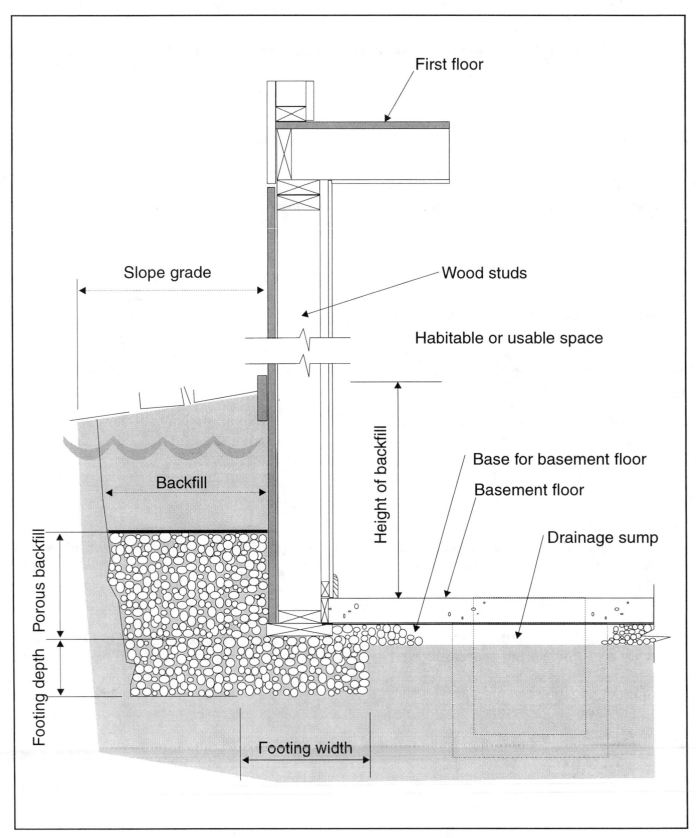

Figure 5-2: Cross-sectional view of a residential building foundation for use with Question 5-25.

5-25   The standard maximum height of backfill for the wood foundation system in Figure 5-2 is which of the following?

A) 4 feet

B) 5 feet

C) 6 feet

D) 7 feet

Answer: A

Due to the lightweight nature of this foundation system and the lack of inherent resistance to overturning, backfill must be limited to a height of no more than 4 feet above the top of the basement floor.

5-26   If the residential foundation wall in Figure 5-3 on the next page is 6-inch solid concrete block, the vertical distance between finish grade and the top of the floor slab is limited to:

A) 4 feet

B) 1 foot

C) 2 feet

D) 3 feet

Answer: D

Most building codes will allow a foundation wall to be nominal 6-inch solid masonry provided that the height of unbalanced fill does not exceed 3 feet, the soil is of a stable nature, and there is limited seismic risk.

5-27   If the residential foundation wall (Figure 5-3) is standard concrete block construction and consists of 13 block courses, what is the wall height?

A) 8 feet

B) 8 feet 8 inches

C) 7 feet 4 inches

D) 7 feet

Answer: B

The standard height for one course of concrete block is 8 inches. 13 courses = 13 × 8 inches or 8 feet 8 inches.

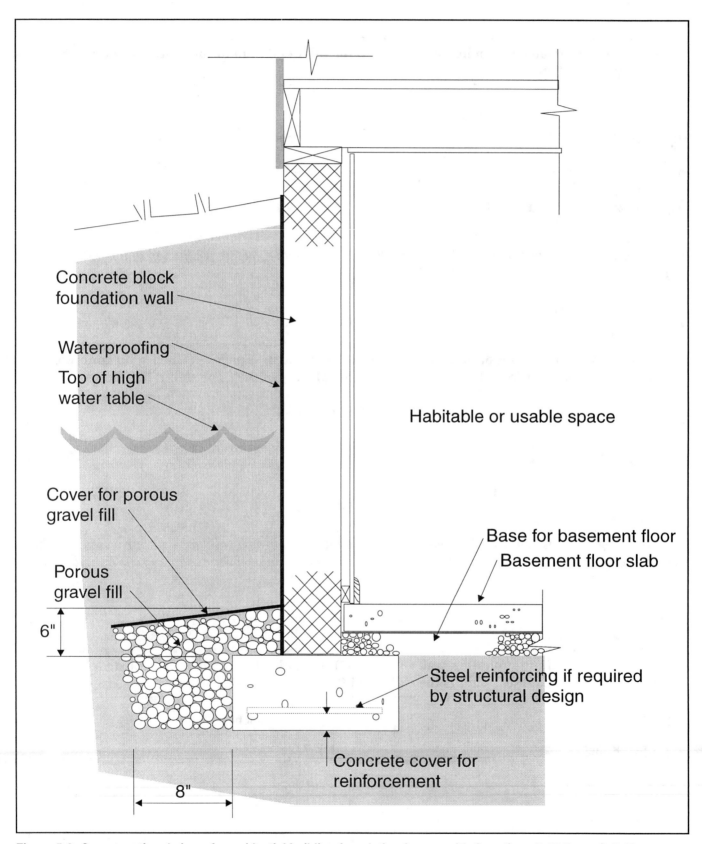

Figure 5-3: Cross-sectional view of a residential building foundation for use with Questions 5-26 through 5-29.

5-28   A drainage sump, as shown in Figure 5-3, will probably be required when:

A) The soil has good drainage characteristics

B) The soil is a silty gravel mixture

C) The soil is primarily clay

D) The soil is a silty sand mixture

Answer: C

According to the Unified Soil Classification System, clay soil has only medium drainage characteristics. Most codes will require a sump when the soil has been classified as anything other than Group I — having good drainage characteristics.

5-29   When required due to poor soil drainage, the drainage sump shown in Figure 5-3 must be at least:

A) 3 feet square

B) 6 feet deep

C) Capable of retaining 50 gallons of water

D) 24 inches in diameter

Answer: D

Most residential code requirements specify a sump that is at least 24 inches in diameter or 20 inches square. The depth must be at least 24 inches below the bottom of the floor slab.

5-30   Which of the following best describes a retaining wall?

A) A supplemental wall used in conjunction with a standard wall to retain sound in one area

B) A wall designed and constructed to hold drain tile in place for carrying off excess water

C) A wall designed and constructed to hold a mass of earth in place

D) A wall that is held in place by bracing on one side

Answer: C

The main use of a retaining wall is to hold a mass of earth in place such as the edge of a terrace or excavation. See Figure 5-4 on the next page.

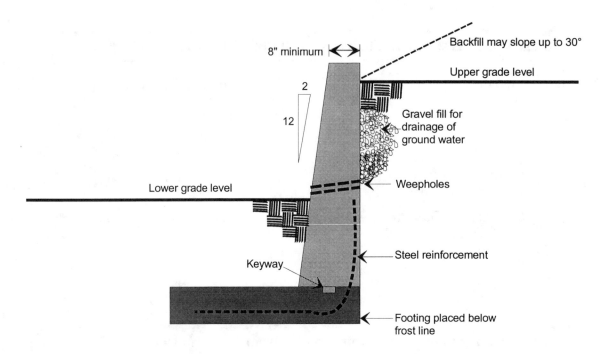

Figure 5-4: Cross-sectional view of a typical L-type retaining wall.

5-31 **Which of the following represents the vertical pitch of the retaining wall in Figure 5-4? I. Starting from the top of the wall, the wall thickness increases at the rate of 2 inches in every 12 inches. II. Starting from the top of the wall, the wall thickness decreases at the rate of 2 inches in every 12 inches.**

A) I

B) II

C) Neither I or II

D) Both I and II

Answer: A

The pitch is shown as 2/12 which means the thickness of the wall increases at the rate of 2 inches for every 12 inches of vertical distance. For example, if the top of the wall is 8 inches thick, the wall would taper to 10 inches thick 1 foot below the top; 12 inches thick 2 feet below the top, etc. If the total height of the wall is 5 feet, then the thickness at the base would be 2 × 5 = 10 inches, plus the thickness of the top (8 inches), for a total thickness of 18 inches.

Chapter 6

Interior Finishes

The most widely used wall and ceiling finish is gypsum board, commonly known as "drywall." It has the advantages of being economical, noncombustible, and easy to install and repair. Another popular wall covering is paneling, such as tongue-and-groove or shiplap boards, or panels of 4- by 8-foot sheets of plywood, hardboards, or particleboard.

Gypsum Board

Several types of gypsum board are available for building construction:

- Fire-rated
- Water-resistant
- Sound-deadening
- Regular

Regular gypsum board is faced with a strong paper that accommodates almost any type of decorative treatment. The edges may be tapered, square, beveled, or tapered with a round edge. The tapered edges are designed to be finished with joint compound and tape. Square edges are used where another finish surface, such as wallpaper, paneling, or tile is to be applied. Beveled edges give the effect of paneling. Gypsum board is commonly available in 4-foot widths and in lengths up to 16 feet.

Although all gypsum board is noncombustible — providing some degree of fire protection — fire-rated board gives added protection. The core is reinforced so that it remains intact even after the chemically combined water has been released from the gypsum. This type of board is primarily used where a rated firewall is required or where major structural members need fire protection. They are usually required in multifamily or special types of buildings, but not normally needed in single-family dwellings, except that some codes may require fire-rated board on a wall between the garage and the living area of the house. Fire-rated board may provide a finished surface or be used as a backer board for some other type of finish.

Water-resistant board is most often used as a backer for tile, but can be used with other finishes in high-moisture areas such as bathrooms or kitchens. It is particularly important that it be used around bathtubs and showers where leaks could develop and cause deterioration of regular gypsum board. The water resistance is provided by an asphalt-wax emulsion combined with the gypsum.

Sound-deadening board is normally used between living units in multifamily dwellings, but can also improve privacy in single-family houses. This board is also primarily a backer with regular gypsum board applied over it.

Regular and fire-rated boards are available with a variety of finishes laminated to the face. The most widely used finish is vinyl with colors, textures, or patterns imprinted. The patterns may be wood grain applied with a photographic process that gives the appearance of wood paneling. These usually have a finished beveled edge, so that no further finish is required. The following table lists maximum spacing for studs and ceiling joists for the various thicknesses of gypsum board.

Orientation of Length of Sheet to Framing Members	Maximum Thickness	Maximum Spacing of Supports (on center) in Inches	
		Walls	Ceilings
Parallel	3/8	16	—
	1/2	24	16
	5/8	24	16
Perpendicular	3/8	16	16
	1/2	24	24
	5/8	24	24

GYPSUM BOARD THICKNESS AND SPACING

When single-layer sheets of gypsum board are used, the 4-foot-wide sheets are applied vertically or horizontally on the walls after the ceiling has been covered. Vertical application covers 3 stud spaces when studs are spaced 16 inches on center, and 2 when spacing is 24 inches. The sheet edges should be centered on studs, and other moderate contact should be made between edges of adjacent sheets.

The horizontal method of application is best adapted to rooms in which full-length sheets can be used, because then it minimizes the number of vertical joints. Where joints are necessary, they should be made at windows or doors. Nail spacing for both horizontal and vertical applications is the same. Normally, horizontal nailing blocks between studs are not required, if stud spacing is not greater than 16 inches on center and gypsum board is 3/4 inch or thicker. However, nailing blocks may be used when spacing is greater, or when an impact-resistant joint is required.

Nails and screws in the regular gypsum wallboard should be driven slightly below the surface. The crowned head of the hammer forms a small dimple in the wallboard. A nail set should not be used, and care should be taken to avoid breaking the paper face.

Joint compound, or spackle, is used to apply the tape over the tapered edge joints and to smooth and level the surface. Although joint cement is available in powder form, most builders use the pre-mixed type.

Interior corners may be cornered with tape. Fold the tape down the center to make a right angle and apply compound at the corner, press the tape in place, and finish the corner with joint compound. Sand smooth when dry and then apply a second coat.

The interior corners between the walls and ceiling may also be concealed with some type of molding. When moldings are used, the joint usually does not require taping.

Drywall corner beads (metal) used at exterior corners prevent damage to the gypsum board. They are fastened in place and covered with joint cement.

6-1   Which of the following best describes the type of flooring shown in A of Figure 6-1?

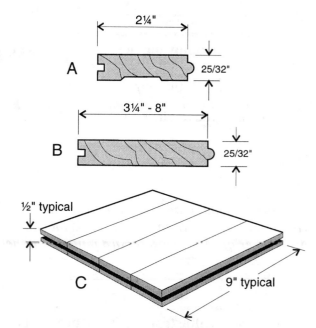

A) Square-edge plank flooring

B) Tongue-and-groove plank flooring

C) Strip flooring

D) Block flooring

Answer: C

The flooring shown in A of Figure 6-1 is a widely used tongue-and-groove strip flooring.

Figure 6-1: Three types of wood flooring.

6-2   What is the purpose of the hollow back of the strip flooring in A of Figure 6-1?

A) To allow glue or other mastic to adhere better

B) Permits the strips to bear firmly on both edges to allow for slight irregularities in the subfloor surface

C) To lighten the weight of the overall flooring which, in turn, reduces the dead load of the building

D) The hollow back provides a channel for any moisture that may be trapped between the subflooring and finished floor

Answer: B

The hollow back of the strip flooring shown in A of Figure 6-1 allows both bottom edges to bear firmly on the subfloor. Some patterns have more than one hollow channel, but they serve the same purpose.

6-3   Which of the following best describes the type of flooring shown in B of Figure 6-1?

A) Square edge plank flooring

B) Tongue-and-groove plank flooring

C) Strip flooring

D) Block flooring

Answer: B

Plank flooring is a term used to describe flooring boards that are wider than 3¼ inches.

6-4   Which of the following best describes the type of flooring shown in C in Figure 6-1?

A) Square edge plank flooring

B) Tongue-and-groove plank flooring

C) Strip flooring

D) Block flooring

Answer: D

Block flooring is manufactured in 3 basic types: unit block flooring, laminated block, and slat block flooring. The type shown in Figure 6-1 is the unit block type which consists of strip flooring laid parallel to one another or in a checkerboard pattern and held together with metal or wood splines.

6-5   Which of the illustrations in Figure 6-2 is an acceptable method of laying wood flooring over a concrete slab that is on or below grade?

A) I

B) II

C) Both I and II

D) Neither I or II

Answer: B

Method II prevents the wood flooring from directly contacting the below-grade cement slab which has a tendency to attract and hold moisture.

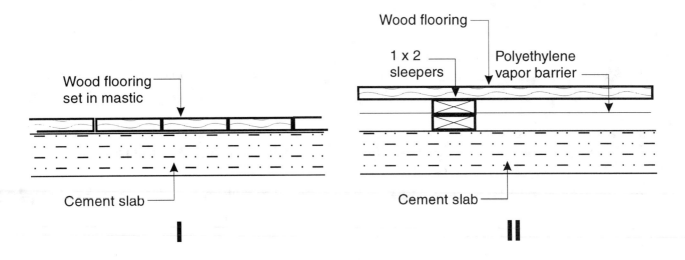

Figure 6-2: Cross-sectional views of two methods used to install wood flooring over concrete slabs.

6-6   Which of the following methods is the best way to install the sleepers in Figure 6-2, II?

A) A threaded stud anchor should be "shot" into the cement floor, and then both sleepers secured with a recessed washer and nut before the wood flooring is nailed to the top sleeper

B) The concrete floor should be drilled for lead anchors at distances not to exceed 3 feet on center and then both sleepers are secured with machine screws before the wood flooring is nailed to the top sleeper

C) The bottom sleeper should be secured to the cement floor with waterproof mastic with the top sleeper secured to the bottom sleeper with glue and wood screws before the wood flooring is nailed to the top sleeper

D) All wooden members should be glued to each other and also to the cement floor without using any other fasteners

Answer: C

Answers A and B would both harm the integrity of the cement floor and require more labor units (worker hours) to install. Answer D is better, but C gives the most secure installation.

6-7   A prefabricated residential shower with moisture-resistant fiberglass walls 66 inches high has been installed in a residential bathroom. The installation was rejected by the local building inspector. Why?

A) The shower walls are too high

B) The shower walls are too short

C) The drain is not big enough

D) Fiberglass is not an approved shower wall

Answer: B

Residential shower and tub walls of an approriate material, such as fiberglass, must be extended to a height of 72 inches.

6-8   The spacing of fasteners is different when applying wall finishes to wood studs rather than light gage metal studs because:

A) Metal studs are not as stable as wood studs

B) Nails don't hold as well in metal studs

C) Fastener spacing is the same for wood or metal studs

D) Finishes are screwed to metal studs

Answer: C

Nail or screw spacing for fasteners is the same regardless of the type of stud support.

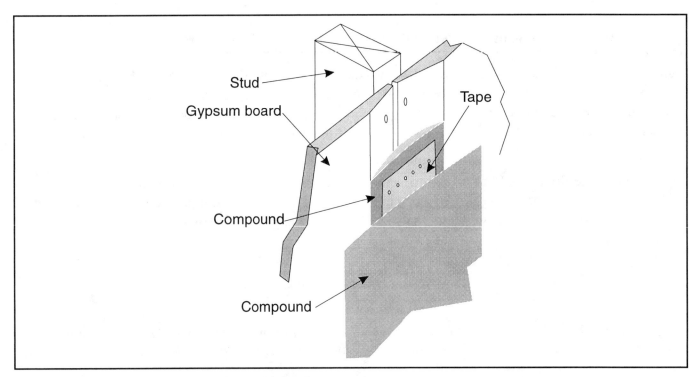

Figure 6-3: Joint detail for gypsum board (drywall).

6-9   Which of the following best describes the application of joint tape in Figure 6-3?

A) Apply over wet joint compound

B) Apply over dried joint compound

C) Apply directly to the base gypsum board

D) The tape must be folded before application

Answer: A

Joint tape is placed onto wet joint compound just after the compound has been applied to the face of the gypsum board surface.

6-10   How many steps (risers) are required for a set of stairs that has a floor-to-floor height of 9 feet 6 inches, if the height of the risers are to be approximately 7 inches each?

A) 12

B) 14

C) 16

D) 18

Answer: C

The floor-to-floor height is divided by 7 inches to obtain the number of risers. 9 feet 6 inches = 114 inches. 114 inches ÷ 7 inches = 16.29. Consequently, 16 risers will be required.

6-11   Since there will be 16 risers used for the staircase in Question 6-10, what will be the exact height of each riser?

A) 7 inches

B) $7\frac{1}{8}$ inches

C) $7\frac{1}{4}$ inches

D) $7\frac{1}{2}$ inches

Answer: B

The total floor-to-floor height is 9 feet 6 inches or 114 inches. Since there are 16 risers, $114 \div 16 = 7.125$. Therefore, the exact height of each riser will be 7.125 or $7\frac{1}{8}$ inches.

6-12   The run (tread) of each step in Questions 6-10 and 6-11 is 10 inches. What is the total run (length) of the stair?

A) 9 feet 8 inches

B) 13 feet 4 inches

C) 11 feet 8 inches

D) 12 feet 6 inches

Answer: D

Since the stair in question has 16 risers, there will be 15 treads at 10 inches each. 15×10 inches = 150 inches or 12 feet 6 inches.

6-13   What is the minimum allowable headroom for the stairway in Figure 6-4 on the next page if the first floor ceiling height is 7 feet 11 inches?

A) 6 feet

B) 6 feet 8 inches

C) 7 feet

D) 7 feet 10 inches

Answer: B

The minimum headroom for all parts of any stairway must not be less than 6 feet 8 inches, measured vertically from the sloped plane adjoining the tread nosing or from the floor surface of the landing or platform. When nosing is not present, as allowed in stair treads of 11 inches or more, the measurement is taken from the outer edge of the tread.

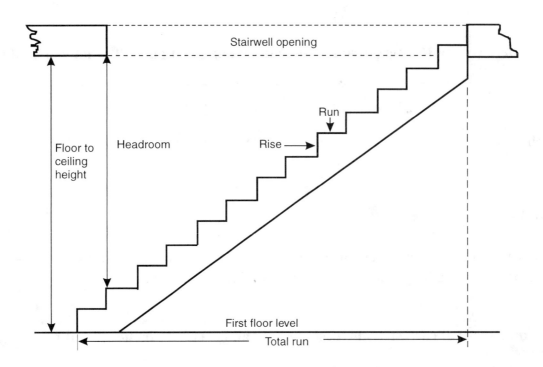

Figure 6-4: Cross-sectional view of a flight of stairs.

6-14   What is the maximum allowable riser height for the stairs in Figure 6-4?

A) 7 inches

B) $7\frac{1}{4}$ inches

C) $7\frac{1}{2}$ inches

D) $7\frac{3}{4}$ inches

Answer: A

The International Building Code holds the maximum height of stair risers in non-private buildings to 7 inches. Since there is no indication if this is a private or public building, you must go with the more-demanding requirement.

6-15   If a handrail is installed on each side of the stairs in Figure 6-4, what is the minimum allowable clear width of the stairway at and below the handrails?

A) 24 inches

B) 28 inches

C) 32 inches

D) 36 inches

Answer: B

Building codes require a minimum stair width of 28 inches when 2 handrails are used; 32 inches when only 1 handrail is used.

6-16 What is the minimum allowable thickness of gypsum board installed on a wall with vertical studs placed every 24 inches on center?

A) $\frac{3}{8}$ inch

C) $\frac{5}{8}$ inch

B) $\frac{1}{2}$ inch

D) $\frac{7}{8}$ inch

Answer: B

Gypsum board installed in a perpendicular position with supports every 24 inches must be at least $\frac{1}{2}$ inch thick. Any thickness less than $\frac{1}{2}$ inch must be supported 16 inches on center.

6-17 Gypsum board used for plaster lath must be installed at right angles to support framing. Which of the following is another requirement for the installation of gypsum board?

A) End joints of gypsum board must be in alignment with each other

C) End joints of gypsum board must be staggered

B) Fasteners must not be installed within 3 inches of the edges

D) No fastener shall be less than 48 inches on center

Answer: C

Gypsum lath must be installed at right angles to support framing with the end joints staggered if it is used as plaster lathing.

6-18 When screws are used for attaching gypsum wallboard to wood studs, they must be Type W, in accordance with ASTM C 1002, and must penetrate the wood to what depth?

A) $\frac{1}{4}$ inch

C) $\frac{5}{8}$ inch

B) $\frac{1}{2}$ inch

D) $\frac{3}{4}$ inch

Answer: C

Section 702.3.5 of the Council of American Building Officials (CABO) states the required penetration depth of $\frac{5}{8}$ inch.

6-19 **Screws for attaching gypsum wallboard to light-gage steel must be Type S, in accordance with ASTM C 1002, and penetrate the steel no less than which of the following depths?**

A) $\frac{1}{4}$ inch

C) $\frac{5}{8}$ inch

B) $\frac{1}{2}$ inch

D) $\frac{3}{4}$ inch

Answer: **A**

Section 702.3.5 of CABO specifies the minimum depth to be $\frac{1}{4}$ inch.

6-20 **The horizontal application of drywall, shown in Figure 6-5, indicates nailing blocks at mid-height in the wall. At what stud spacing should such nailing blocks be used?**

A) 16 inches on center

C) 30 inches on center

B) 24 inches on center

D) 32 inches on center

Answer: **B**

When wall studs are placed 16 inches on center, horizontal nailing blocks are usually not required in most areas. However, when the wall studs are spaced 24 inches on center, horizontal nailing blocks must be used.

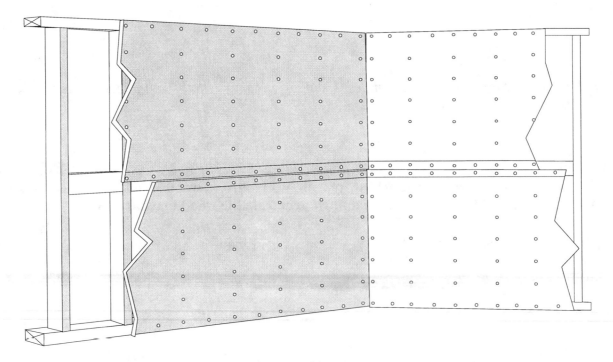

Figure 6-5: Horizontal application of drywall, using horizontal nailing blocks for added support.

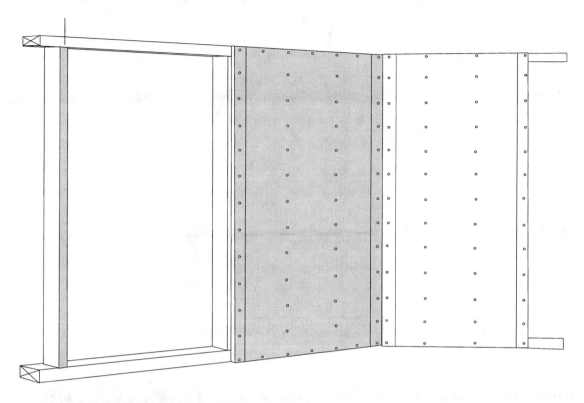

Figure 6-6: Vertical application of gypsum board (drywall).

6-21   How far apart should fasteners be spaced for the gypsum board installation in Figure 6-6?

A) 2 to 4 inches

B) 4 to 6 inches

C) 6 to 8 inches

D) 8 to 10 inches

Answer: C

Fivepenny drywall nails (about $1\frac{5}{8}$ inches long) should be used on $\frac{1}{2}$-inch gypsum board. They should be driven in every 6 to 8 inches vertically, and also 6 to 8 inches horizontally along the sill and plate.

6-22   When installing regular gypsum wallboard, the nails should be driven in so that the heads are slightly below the surface and surrounded by a round dimple. What tool is used to make this dimple?

A) The ball of a ball peen hammer

B) A drywall dimpling tool

C) The handle of a wedge-blade screwdriver

D) The crowned head of a claw hammer

Answer: D

The dimple is readily made with the crown of a claw hammer, as shown in Figure 6-7 on the next page.

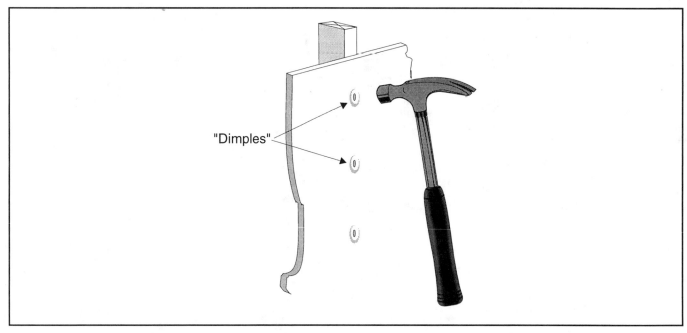

Figure 6-7: Dimples over drywall fasteners made with the crowned head of a claw hammer.

6-23   Figure 6-8 on the opposite page shows an inside corner of adjoining walls and the application of wood trim at the base of each. How should Joint A be cut?

A) Butt joint

B) Coped joint

C) Mitered joint

D) Milled joint

Answer: B

The cut for Joint A should be made with a coping saw, with the cut following the contour of the molding to which it abutts.

6-24   Figure 6-8 on the opposite page shows an inside corner of adjoining walls and the application of wood trim at the base of each. What type of joint is shown at Joint B?

A) Butt joint

B) Coped joint

C) Mitered joint

D) Milled joint

Answer: A

A butt joint is sufficient for Joint B, although some carpenters may prefer to use a mitered joint. Either type is okay, but the mitered joint takes more labor.

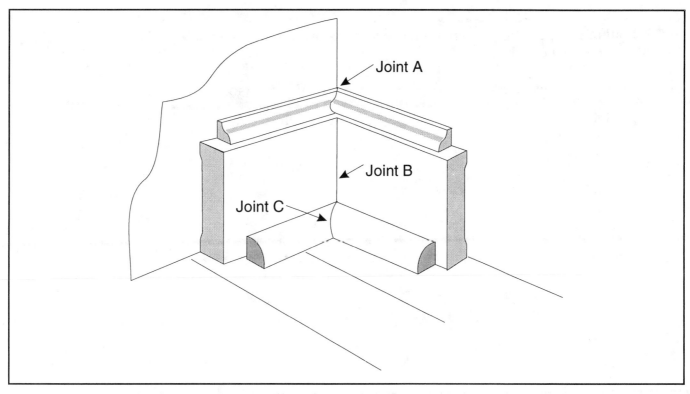

Figure 6-8: Types of conventional base molding.

6-25   Referring again to Figure 6-8, how should Joint C be cut?

A) Butt joint

B) Coped joint

C) Mitered joint

D) Milled joint

Answer: B

The cut for Joint A should also be made with a coping saw, with the cut following the contour of the molding to which it abutts.

6-26   What is the best description of the molding shown as Joint A in Figure 6-8?

A) Crown molding

B) Base shoe

C) Baseboard

D) Base cap

Answer: D

The base cap is applied directly to the top of the base molding to make a neat transistion from the flat top of the molding to the adjacent wall.

6-27 If all of the moldings shown in Figure 6-8 are installed at an outside corner of the wall, how should the molding cuts be made?

A) Same as for the inside corner

B) Coped joint

C) Mitered joint

D) Milled joint

Answer: C

All cuts should be mitered for an outside corner.

Chapter 7

Exterior Finishes

All exterior walls of buildings must be covered with approved materials , designed and installed to provide a barrier against weather and insects. This barrier also enables environmental control of the interior spaces.

Exterior Wall Sheathing

Exterior wall sheathing is the covering applied over the outside wall framework of studs, plates, and window and door headers. It forms a base upon which the exterior finish can be applied. Certain types of sheathing and methods of application can provide great rigidity to the building, eliminating the need for special corner bracing. Sheathing also serves to reduce air infiltration and, in certain forms, provides significant insulation.

Types of sheathing include the following:

- Plywood
- Reconstituted wood panels
- Wood boards
- Insulating Fiberboards
- Foil-faced laminated paperboards
- Gypsum boards
- Rigid formed-plastic boards (with or without facings)

Plywood: This sheathing is available in thicknesses ranging from $5/16$ inch to $3/4$ inch in various grades and construction for stud spacings of 16 and 24 inches on center. When plywood sheathing is adequately nailed (and sometimes glued), additional corner bracing is not required. Entire walls can be sheathed with 4- × 8-foot sheets applied vertically or horizontally. Plywood sheathing can also be used at corners only, with the remainder of the wall being covered with other sheathing materials — eliminating the need for corner bracing.

Reconstituted Wood Panels: Several types of reconstituted wood panels are used for wall sheathing; structural flakeboard (including waferboard and oriented strandboard), particleboard, and composite panels.

Waferboard is commonly available in thicknesses ranging from $7/16$ inch to $3/4$ inch. The most common panel size is 4 × 8 feet, but it can be obtained in sizes up to 4 × 16 feet or larger.

Waferboard sheathing is installed in much the same manner as plywood sheathing, although many local codes require that the waferboard be $1/8$ inch thicker than plywood for the same applications.

Oriented strandboard, often called OSB, is a composite panel of compressed strand-like wood particles arranged in layers, usually 3 to 5, oriented at right angles to each other in the same fashion as plywood. Bonding is accomplished with a phenolic resin as with waferboard. Production thicknesses and panel sizes are similar to waferboard.

Particleboard is composed of small wood particles, usually arranged in layers by particle size, but not usually with a particular strand orientation. As with other reconstituted wood panel sheathing materials, the particles are bonded together with a phenolic resin. Available thicknesses and panel sizes are similar to waferboard.

Composite panels consist of a reconstituted wood core bonded between a wood veneer face and back plies. This material has a surface appearance similar to plywood and, like plywood, is available in various thickness and panel sizes.

Wood Boards: These are the oldest form of sheathing, but are now infrequently used and may be unavailable in some areas. When available, wood sheathing is usually of nominal 1-inch thickness or resawn $\frac{5}{8}$-inch boards in a square-edge pattern. Widths used are 6, 8, and 10 inches. The boards may be applied horizontally or diagonally. When they are applied diagonally, corner bracing can be eliminated.

Insulating Fiberboard: These sheathings consist of an organic fiber that is coated or impregnated with asphalt or other treatment for water resistance. Occasional wetting and drying that might occur during construction does not damage the sheathing significantly. Galvanized or other corrosion-resistant fasteners are recommended for installation.

Three types of insulating fiberboards are: regular density, intermediate density, and nail base. Regular density is used for cover only, where no racking resistance or structural support is needed. Where structural support is required, intermediate density is used. Nail-base fiberboard will hold nails; it is well suited as a sheathing beneath sidings that require nailing at other than stud locations. Addi-

tional corner bracing is usually not required for intermediate and nail-base sheathing when they are properly applied with the long edges aligned vertically. Shingles used for siding can be applied directly to nail-base sheathing if they are fastened with special annular-grooved nails.

Insulating fiberboards are manufactured in $\frac{1}{2}$-inch thickness and in 4- × 8-foot and 4- × 9-foot sizes. Some are produced in $48\frac{3}{4}$-inch widths for overlapping. Their thickness is commonly slightly less than $\frac{1}{8}$ inch. When panels are nailed in accordance with the manufacturers' recommendations, corner bracing may be eliminated.

Gypsum Wallboard: This sheathing is composed of treated gypsum filler faced on two sides with water-resistant paper. Panels are $\frac{1}{2}$ inch thick, and are either 2 × 8 feet in size for horizontal application, or 4 × 8 feet or 4 × 9 feet for vertical application. The 2- × 8-foot size either has one edge grooved and the other with a matched V-edge, or has square-edged sides. The 4- × 8-foot and 4- × 9-foot sizes have square edges only. If panels are properly nailed, corner bracing is not required.

Rigid Foam Plastic: This sheathing consists of polystyrene, urethane, isocyanurate, or phenolic foam panels, in some instances faced with aluminum foil, aluminum foil laminated Kraft paper, or polyethylene sheet on one or both sides. These materials, with thermal resistance (R) values ranging from less than R-4 to over R-8 per inch of material thickness, are used primarily to enhance the total thermal resistance values of wall construction. All are nonstructural; that is, some form of wall corner bracing is required. Panels for wall sheathing are usually produced in thicknesses for $\frac{3}{8}$ inch to 1 inch and in panel sizes of 2 × 8 feet, 4 × 8 feet, or 4 × 9 feet, or longer.

7-1   What does A in Figure 7-1 indicate?

A) Wall sheathing

B) Insulation

C) A moisture barrier

D) A 1 inch air space

Answer: D

A 1-inch wide air space is required between the masonry veneer and the sheathing.

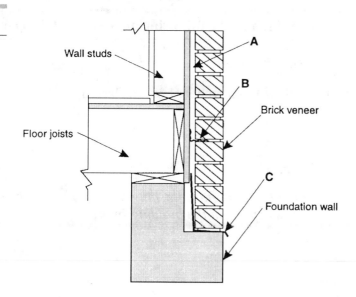

Figure 7-1: Cross-sectional view of frame construction with brick veneer.

7-2   Which of the following answers best describes B in Figure 7-1?

A) Metal ties

B) Wall flashing

C) Toggle bolts

D) Brick spacers

Answer: A

Building codes require masonry veneer to be attached to the backing or supporting wall by metal ties.

7-3   What is the minimum allowable spacing for metal ties used to attach masonry to supporting walls?

A) 12 inches on center, horizontally

B) 16 inches on center, horizontally

C) 24 inches on center, horizontally

D) 36 inches on center, horizontally

Answer: C

The ties must be spaced a minimum of 24 inches on center, horizontally, and support a maximum brick area of 3¼ square feet.

7-4   Which of the following answers best describes item C in Figure 7-1 on the preceding page?

A) Termite shield

B) Below-grade veneer bottom flashing

C) Above-grade veneer bottom flashing

D) Building paper

Answer: C

Building codes require flashing at the bottom of brick veneer so that water penetration behind the veneer is kept from the building interior.

7-5   When installing metal veneer as an exterior finish on building, which of the following is a requirement of the National Fire Protection Association?

A) The siding should be installed horizontally

B) The siding should be installed vertically

C) The siding should be installed diagonally

D) The siding must be electrically and mechanically grounded

Answer: D

The National Fire Protection Association (NFPA) issues guidelines for grounding metal veneers on buildings.

7-6   Which of the following is required at all roof intersections?

A) Caulking

B) Flashing

C) Gutters and downspouts

D) A double layer of shingles

Answer: B

Flashing is required at all roof intersections to prevent water penetration under the shingles and onto the roof sheathing.

7-7   When applying asphalt-saturated felt over studs or sheathing on exterior walls, what is the minimum overlap that must be provided at each joint?

A) 2 inches

B) 4 inches

C) 6 inches

D) 7 inches

Answer: C

Where joints occur in weather-resistant sheathing paper, they should be lapped no less than 6 inches.

7-8   In which of the following positions or patterns should weather-resistant asphalt-saturated felt sheathing paper be applied to the sheathing or studs of exterior walls in frame-constructed buildings?

A) Horizontally

B) Vertically

C) Diagonally

D) In a checkerboard pattern

Answer: A

Section 703.2 of the CABO building code requires sheathing paper to be installed horizontally in all situations.

7-9   When weather-resistant asphalt-saturated felt sheathing paper is installed horizontally over exterior-wall sheathing, what is the minimum amount that the upper layer must overlap the bottom layer?

A) 2 inches

B) 4 inches

C) 6 inches

D) 8 inches

Answer: A

Section 703.2 of the CABO building code requires the upper layer of sheathing paper to be lapped over the lower layer no less than 2 inches.

7-10   When installing steel siding, which of the following is a building code requirement to help prevent corrosion?

A) All joints must be caulked

B) All joints must be riveted

C) The starting strip must be above grade

D) The siding must not be installed when the ambient temperature is less than 40°F

Answer: C

Building codes require the bottom starting strip or edge to be elevated high enough above grade to prevent corrosion of the siding.

7-11   What is the minimum allowable thickness for wood siding used for exterior finishes on buildings if it is not installed over any type of sheathing?

A) $\frac{1}{4}$ inch

B) $\frac{1}{2}$ inch

C) $\frac{3}{4}$ inch

D) 1 inch

Answer: B

When wood siding has no backing, such as sheathing, building codes in most areas require a minimum thickness of ½ inch.

7-12   A brick-veneer finish for wood-frame construction is a common exterior finish. Which of the following is the best definition of veneer?

A) A nonstructural cover

B) A building frame support

C) A support backing

D) A sheathing

Answer: A

Building codes require a veneer wall be attached to some type of backing, such as plywood sheathing, but it must not support any building loads, other than providing for its own stability.

7-13   Which of the following is a building code requirement for exterior window glaze?

A) All exposed glazing must be protected by window shutters

B) It must be structurally resistant to wind

C) It must be painted with an exterior paint within 24 hours after installation

D) It must be non-reflective

Answer: B

Building codes require all exterior window glazing to be structurally resistant to wind loading.

7-14   Which of the following is a building code requirement for load-bearing walls that provide an attachment backing for brick, stone, or other masonry veneer?

A) A separate footing and foundation is required

B) Wall studs must not be less than 48 inches on center

C) The walls must be designed to support the veneer as well as other building loads

D) The walls are required to support the veneer, but not any other dead loads

Answer: C

Since veneer is nonstructural, it depends on the footing and/or foundation as well as its backing for support. Most exterior walls are load-bearing walls. Therefore, such walls must be able to support the veneer as well as other building loads.

7-15   What is the minimum allowable thickness of wood shingles when they are used as an exterior finish?

A) $\frac{1}{16}$ inch

B) $\frac{1}{4}$ inch

C) $\frac{3}{8}$ inch

D) 1 inch

Answer: C

Building codes list the allowable thickness for most common building finishes. Building codes require wood shingles to be at least $\frac{3}{8}$ inch thick when used as an exterior finish.

7-16   What is the minimum allowable thickness for hardboard when used as an exterior finish on buildings?

A) $\frac{1}{4}$ inch

C) $\frac{5}{8}$ inch

B) $\frac{1}{2}$ inch

D) $\frac{3}{4}$ inch

Answer: B

Building codes require hardboard to have a thickness of at least ½ inch when used as an exterior finish on buildings.

7-17   Which of the following nail types are allowed for the installation of exterior wall sheathing or weather boards?

A) Zinc-coated steel

C) Neither A or B

B) Aluminum

D) Both A and B

Answer: D

Building codes allow any nails that are made from corrosion-resistant material to be used for installing exterior sheathing. Materials include zinc, zinc-coated iron or steel, copper, aluminum, etc.

7-18   What is the minimum allowable thickness of adhered masonry veneer when applied to an exterior wall?

A) $\frac{3}{4}$ inch

C) $1\frac{1}{4}$ inch

B) $1\frac{3}{8}$ inch

D) $1\frac{5}{8}$ inch

Answer: D

Adhered masonry veneer units must not be less than $1\frac{5}{8}$ inches thick and they must not support any superimposed loads. Furthermore, the veneer must be designed to provide a bond to the supporting element sufficient to withstand a shearing stress of 50 psi after curing 28 days.

7-19   What is the minimum allowable thickness of anchored terra cotta or ceramic veneer when applied to an exterior wall?

A) $\frac{3}{4}$ inch

B) $1\frac{3}{8}$ inch

C) $1\frac{1}{4}$ inch

D) $1\frac{5}{8}$ inch

Answer: D

Anchored terra cotta or ceramic veneer units must not be less than $1\frac{5}{8}$ inches thick. They are allowed to be anchored directly to masonry, concrete or stud construction.

7-20   What is the maximum size of adhered veneer weighing more than 3 pounds per sq. ft. when used as an exterior finish on concrete block walls?

A) 18 inches in the greatest dimension

B) 24 inches in the greatest dimension

C) 36 inches in the greatest dimension

D) 48 inches in the greatest dimension

Answer: C

Adhered veneer units must not exceed 36 inches (914 mm) in the greatest dimension, nor more than 720 sq. in. in total area.

7-21   What is the maximum height that adhered veneer may be installed to a wood-frame constructed building wall?

A) 10 feet

B) 20 feet

C) 30 feet

D) 40 feet

Answer: C

Exterior adhered veneer must not be attached to wood-frame construction at a point more than 30 feet in height above the noncombustible foundation unless an engineering analysis is prepared by a registered design professional and approved by the local building authority.

7-22   Building codes require building paper to be attached to the sheathing when veneers of brick, clay tile, concrete or natural or artificial stone are used. What is the required grade weight of this building paper?

A) 10-pound

B) 14-pound

C) 28-pound

D) 36-pound

Answer: B

BOCA Section 1405.3.6 requires 14-pound paper or felt to be attached to the sheathing when the above veneers are used. Flashing is also required where necessary to prevent moisture penetration behind the veneer.

7-23   Which of the following must be installed at the top and sides of all exterior window and door openings if an approved water-resistant sheathing and caulking are not used?

A) Flashing

B) A vapor-barrier film

C) Built-in gutters

D) I beams at least 4 inches thick

Answer: A

Approved corrosion-resistant flashings must be provided at the top and sides of all exterior window and door openings and must be installed in such a manner as to be leakproof. However, such flashing is not required where an approved water-resistant sheathing is installed, and an approved water-resistant caulking is applied at the top and sides of window and door opening, and it is done in such a manner as to be leakproof.

7-24   What is the minimum allowable thickness of aluminum siding when used as an exterior finish on plywood sheathing?

A) 0.019 inch

B) 0.024 inch

C) 0.035 inch

D) 0.025 inch

Answer: A

BOCA Table 1405.3 specifies the minimum thickness of weather coverings for buildings. The minimum thickness for aluminum siding is 0.019 inch.

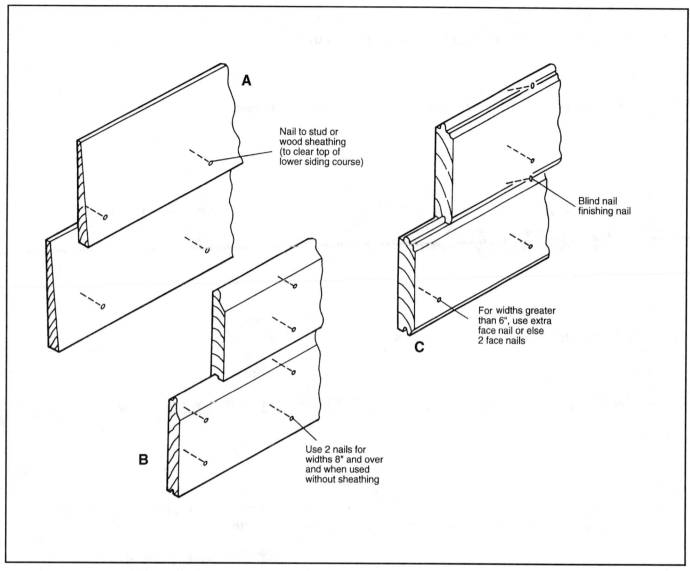

Figure 7-2: Types of wood siding in common use.

7-25   Which of the following best describes siding A in Figure 7-2?

A) Board and batten

B) Paneling pattern

C) Drop pattern

D) Bevel pattern

Answer: D

The bevel siding shown in A of Figure 7-2 should have a lap of not less than 1 inch. For weather resistance and appearance, the butt edge of the first course of siding above windows should coincide with the top of the window drip cap. It is also desirable that the bottom of a siding course be flush with the underside of window sills.

7-26 Which of the following best describes siding B in Figure 7-2?

A) Board and batten

B) Paneling pattern

C) Drop pattern

D) Bevel pattern

Answer: C

Drop siding with shiplap edges, shown in B of Figure 7-2, is installed in much the same way as lap siding except for spacing and nailing. One or two 8d nails should be used at each stud crossing when installing drop siding. Two nails are used for widths greater than 8 inches.

7-27 Which of the following best describes siding C in Figure 7-2?

A) Board and batten

B) Paneling pattern

C) Drop pattern

D) Bevel pattern

Answer: B

The paneling pattern siding in C of Figure 7-2 is very similar to drop siding except the boards used in the paneling pattern are the true tongue-and-groove type, usually with a V-notch at the joint.

7-28 When installing drop siding, which of the following is the most appropriate nail size to use at each stud crossing?

A) 8d

B) 12d

C) 16d

D) 20d

Answer: A

8d corrosion-resistant nails made of galvanized steel, stainless steel, or aluminum, should be used to install drop siding. Ordinary steel-wire nails tend to rust a short time after being installed and can cause disfiguring stains on the face of the siding. In most cases, the nail heads will show rust spots through putty and paint.

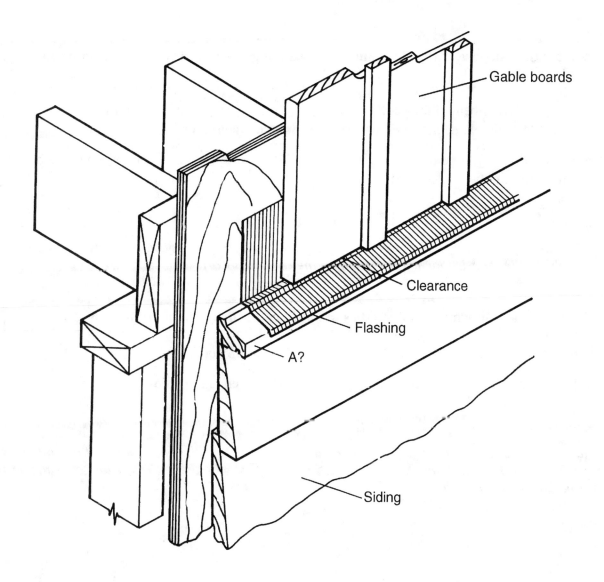

Figure 7-3: Transition of siding types at gable end.

7-29 **When making a transistion from bevel horizontal siding to vertical siding at the gable, as shown in Figure 7-3, what is the name of the molding that is used at A?**

A) Drip loop

B) Flashing

C) Gable board

D) Drip cap

Answer: *D*

The drip cap in Figure 7-3 caps the top bevel board, offers a support for the flashing, and ensures good drainage at the junction of the two materials.

7-30   What is the purpose of the clearance between the gable boards and the flashing in Figure 7-3?

A) To allow ventilation behind the gable boards which also helps to prevent decay

B) To allow the flashing to be replaced at a later date without removing the gable boards

C) To ensure that dropping moisture clears the gable material

D) To allow for swelling of the gable boards

Answer: C

Flashing should be used over and above the drip cap so that dropping moisture clears the gable material. If the gable boards touched the flashing, they would absorb some moisture.

7-31   Which of the following best describes the pattern of the gable boards in Figure 7-3?

A) Batten and board

B) Board and batten

C) Board and board

D) Batten and batten

Answer: B

When wider boards are installed first and then battens used to cover the board joints, this pattern is known as board and batten. When the battens are installed first with the boards nailed over them, the pattern is called batten and board.

Chapter 8

Roofs and Roof Structures

Roofs function as the primary sheltering element of buildings, protecting interior spaces from the natural elements. The roof should also control the flow of water (from rain and snow), water vapor, heat, and air. In addition, it must be structured to carry its own weight as well as live loads such as snow, ice, and wind. The roof system should be fire-resistant, and in many cases, it may be required to accommodate mechanical and electrical equipment.

Roof frames provide structural members to which roofing, vents, and materials to finish the ceiling may be attached, and within which insulation materials may be placed. Pitching of roof surfaces creates storage space and living space that costs less than the main floor space because no additional foundation is required, and because roof costs do not increase proportionately with the increase in living space.

Roof Designs

Roofs sometimes use one structural member as both ceiling and roofing support as in flat or shed roofs. However, the most common roof configuration is an isosceles triangle; that is, rafters or top chords of trusses that form equal-length sloping sides to which roofing materials are attached. Ceiling joists or bottom truss chords form the horizontal base to which ceiling materials are fastened.

In a single-member roof, support must be provided at both ends by walls or beams. In the triangular roof, the ceiling joists require intermediate bearing support within the building, but the roof rafters usually do not. Since their weight and the weight they support is all transferred to the bottom, the rafters tend to push out at the bottom and fall in the center where they meet. They are restrained from doing so by the ceiling joists, which are placed in tension, and consequently, must be securely fastened to the rafters and to each other where spliced.

Roofs are frequently built with triangular trusses in which the three sides of the triangle are fastened together with steel plates or plywood gussets, and reinforced with interior web members. Wood trusses can span up to 50 feet, and they are designed to require support only at the two ends of the base or bottom chord.

Roof Pitch

The slope of a roof is generally expressed as the number of inches of vertical rise in 12 inches of horizontal run. The rise is given first; so a 4-inch rise in 12 inches gives a 4/12 pitch.

The architectural style of a building often determines the type of roof and the roof slope. In deciding roof slope, another consideration is the type of roofing desired. For example, a built-up roof is permitted on flat roofs or slopes up to a 2/12 pitch, depending on the type of asphalt or coal-tar pitch and aggregate surfacing materials used. Rolled roofing can be used on roofs with a pitch of 1/12 or steeper, while wood shingles are permitted on roofs with a pitch of 3/12 or steeper. Asphalt shingles are permitted on roofs with a pitch of 2/12 or steeper.

The most popular roof style for residential construction is the gable roof — a triangular roof system in which the triangles are terminated at the ends of the house by triangular end walls called *gables*. The gables close in the building's attic space, and some means of ventilating the attic is usually provided. However, many other designs are common, including the hip, mansard, gambrel, shed, and flat roofs.

The questions in this chapter are typical of those found on contractor's exams throughout the United States.

8-1   What water depth is required for roof-ponding design when the south parapet of Figure 8-1 is 6 inches high, and all other parapets are 12 inches high?

A) 12 inches

B) 3 inches

C) 9 inches

D) 6 inches

Answer: D

Ponding is an accumlation of water on a roof deck that is relatively flat. The parapets in this example would hold water to a maximum depth of 6 inches. Most building codes require that the full depth of potentially blocked-up water must be used for ponding design, assuming that all normal water outlets, such as scuppers and drains, are blocked.

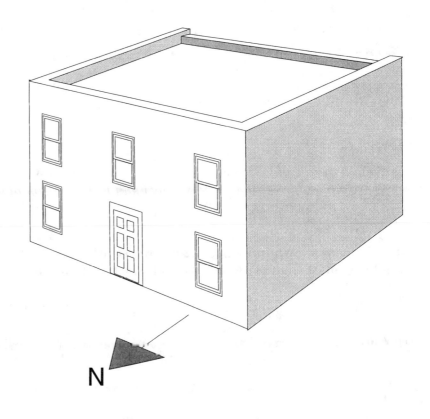

Figure 8-1: Flat-roof building with parapet walls surrounding the roof structure.

8-2   If the roof in Figure 8-1 is perfectly flat, which of the following best gives the building code requirements for the roof?

A) It is acceptable if provisions are made to prevent water ponding

B) It is acceptable if the surface covering meets with code regulations

C) The roof must have at least one drain at mid-span

D) The roof is not acceptable under the specified circumstances

Answer: D

Most building codes do not allow perfectly flat roof structures. The roof must be sloped to some degree as explained in the next question and answer.

8-3   The minimum slope for a built-up, coal-tar type roof is:

A) $\frac{1}{2}$:12

B) $\frac{3}{4}$:12

C) $\frac{1}{8}$:12

D) No minimum pitch is required

Answer: C

The minimum allowable roof slope for all roofs is $\frac{1}{4}$:12, except for coal-tar type roofs, which can be sloped as little as $\frac{1}{8}$:12; that is, $\frac{1}{8}$ vertical unit to 12 horizontal units.

8-4   The roof shown in Figure 8-2 is covered with a non-ballasted thermoset roofing system and has a horizontal span of 16 feet. What is the minimum fall or pitch from ridge to eave?

A) $2\frac{1}{4}$ inches

B) 2 inches

C) 3 inches

D) 4 inches

Answer: D

The minimum allowed roof slope is $\frac{1}{4}$:12. Since the roof has a horizontal projection of 16 feet, the vertical rise allowed is $16 \times \frac{1}{4} = 4$ inches.

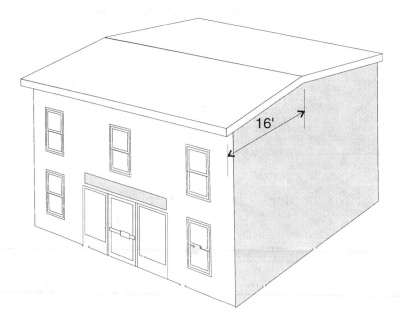

Figure 8-2: Perspective view of a commercial building with a sloped roof.

8-5 **If the roof covering in Figure 8-2 is changed to a ballasted thermoset system, what would be the minimum vertical fall allowed from ridge to eave?**

A) 4 inches

B) 8 inches

C) 16 inches

D) 24 inches

Answer: A

The minimum slope required is the same for both ballasted and non-ballasted roof systems.

8-6 **If the roof in Figure 8-2 is covered with a ballasted roof system, what is the maximum vertical fall allowed from the ridge to the eave?**

A) 8 inches

B) 16 inches

C) 32 inches

D) 12 inches

Answer: C

Most building codes limit the slope of ballasted roof coverings to 2:12; that is, for every 12 inches of horizontal run, there can be no more than 2 inches of vertical rise in the pitch. Therefore, a ballasted roof with a horizontal run of 16 feet may not rise more than (2 × 16 =) 32 inches.

8-7 **Which of the following statements is true concerning the classification of roof coverings?**

A) Class A coverings offer the highest degree of fire resistance

B) Class B coverings offer the highest degree of fire resistance

C) Class C coverings offer the highest degree of fire resistance

D) Class D coverings offer the highest degree of fire resistance

Answer: A

The Class System indicates the relative fire resistance of the roof covering. The American Society for Testing and Materials (ASTM) is the accepted authority for assigning classifications of A, B, or C to roofing materials. Class A is the most fire resistant, while Class C is the least fire resistant.

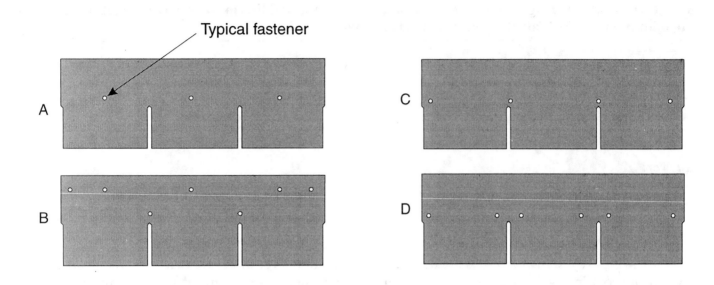

Figure 8-3: Nailing configurations for asphalt shingles.

8-8   Asphalt shingles, such as depicted in Figure 8-3, are required to be secured with a number of fasteners. Which one of the diagrams in Figure 8-3 meets minimum building code requirements?

A) Diagram A   C) Diagram C

B) Diagram B   D) Diagram D

Answer: C

Diagram C of Figure 8-3 shows four fasteners, the minimum number required for each shingle strip.

8-9   When strip asphalt shingles are installed in coastal hurricane-prone areas, which of the diagrams in Figure 8-3 shows the minimum number of fasteners allowed?

A) Diagram A   C) Diagram C

B) Diagram B   D) Diagram D

Answer: D

Six fasteners are required in coastal areas, and to within 100 miles inland, of the Atlantic Ocean and Gulf of Mexico where wind velocities frequently reach 80 miles per hours (mph).

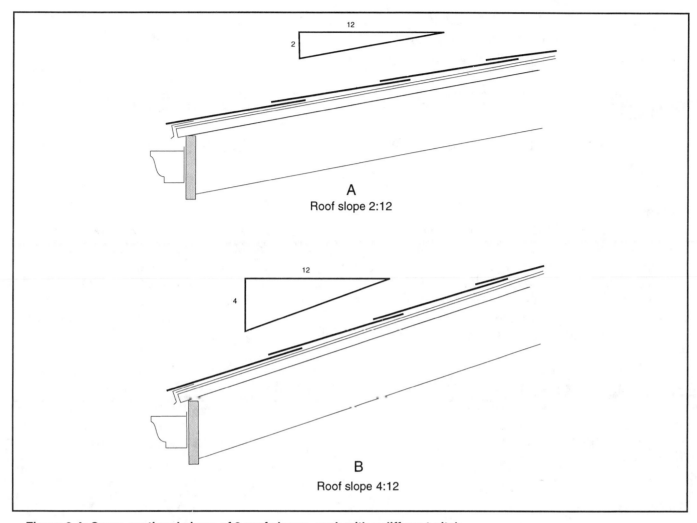

Figure 8-4: Cross-sectional views of 2 roof slopes, each with a different pitch.

8-10   Roof profiles or cross-sectional views are shown in Figure 8-4. If the roof coverings are asphalt shingles, which of the following does not comply with most building codes?

A) Single-layer underlayment (roofing felt) is acceptable for both situations

B) Double-layer underlayment is acceptable for both situations

C) Asphalt shingles are acceptable for the roof slopes shown

D) An underlayment is required in both situations

Answer: A

While a single layer of underlayment is acceptable for diagram B, which has a slope of 4:12, diagram A has a slope of less than 4:12 and therefore requires a double layer of roofing felt. Most building codes accept a single layer of underlayment for roof pitches of 4:12 or steeper, but a double layer is required for pitches less than 4:12.

8-11 If the roof slope shown in Diagram A of Figure 8-4 is changed to an angle of 8 degrees with the horizon, which of the following statements would be true?

A) Asphalt shingles are an acceptable roof covering

B) Asphalt shingles are not an acceptable roof covering

C) The roof slope becomes 3:12

D) The roof slope becomes 4:12

Answer: B

Since a roof pitch of 2:12 is the minimum acceptable roof slope for asphalt shingles, compare a pitch of 2:12 with 8 degrees. The angle (between the roof surface and the horizon) can be found using the equation, tan A = a/b, where A is the angle in degrees, a is the unit rise, and b is the unit run. Since the minimum roof slope for asphalt shingles is 2:12, tan A = 2/12 or .167. Using an electronic calculator, slide rule, or a chart giving the tangents of angles, the angle of tangent .167 is 9.425 degrees — the minimum allowable slope. Since the sample roof in the question slopes only 8 degrees from the horizon, this is less than 9.425 degrees and is therefore not acceptable for asphalt shingles.

8-12 What is the minimum allowable roof pitch when wood shingles are used?

A) 2:12

B) 2½:12

C) 3:12

D) 4:12

Answer: C

A minimum roof pitch of 3:12 is required when wood shingles are used.

8-13 Which of the following best describes the type of roof shown in Figure 8-5?

A) Shed

B) Gable

C) Hip

D) Mansard

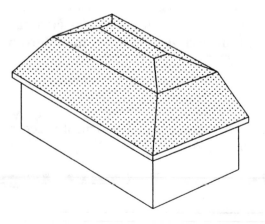

Answer: D

The mansard roof is used for some residential construction, and the design is also popular with commercial buildings, especially those that do not exceed 2 stories. This roof design is seldom used on buildings with more than 2 stories.

Figure 8-5: One type of popular roof for residences and some commercial buildings.

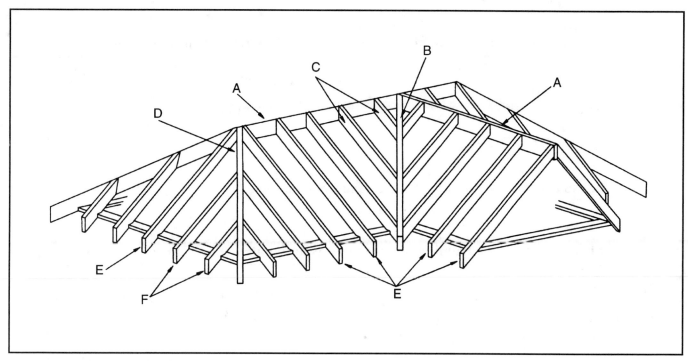

Figure 8-6: Typical roof framing.

8-14   What are the roof-framing members called that are designated A in Figure 8-6?

A) Hip rafter

B) Ridge board

C) Valley jack rafter

D) Hip jack rafter

Answer: B

Two ridge boards are shown in the drawing, one along the ridge of the hip roof, and one along the ridge of the gable roof or dormer.

8-15   What is the roof-framing member called that is designated B in Figure 8-6?

A) Hip rafter

B) Ridge board

C) Valley jack rafter

D) Valley rafter

Answer: D

The valley rafter is the single rafter to which the valley jack rafters abutt.

8-16   What are the roof-framing members called that are designated C in Figure 8-6?

A) Hip rafter

B) Ridge board

C) Valley jack rafter

D) Hip jack rafter

Answer: C

Valley jack rafters are the wood members that extend from the ridge board to the valley rafter.

8-17   What is the name of the framing member that is designated D in Figure 8-6?

A) Hip rafter

B) Ridge board

C) Valley jack rafter

D) Common rafter

Answer: A

Hip rafters form the main sloping end ridges of a hip roof and the hip jack rafters run from the top plate to abutt against the hip rafters.

8-18   What is the name of the framing members that are designated E in Figure 8-6 ?

A) Hip rafter

B) Ridge board

C) Valley jack rafter

D) Common rafter

Answer: D

Common rafters run from the top ridge board to the top plate of the building. A "birdsmouth" notch is made in each rafter where it meets the top plate.

8-19   What is the name of the framing members that are designated F in Figure 8-6?

A) Hip rafter

B) Hip jack rafter

C) Valley jack rafter

D) Common rafter

Answer: B

Hip jack rafters run from the top plate to abutt against the hip rafter. They differ from common rafters since they do not run all the way to the top ridge board.

8-20   When slate shingles are used as a roof covering, how many layers of slate must always overlap?

A) 1

C) 3

B) 2

D) 4

Answer: C

Slate shingles must be arranged and overlapped so there are always 3 layers of slate shingles at each joint.

8-21   When installing California Mission tile, as shown in Figure 8-7, what must be used to support the cap tile?

A) 30-pound felt underlayment

B) A gable fascia

C) A 2- × 3-inch furring strip

D) Guide strings

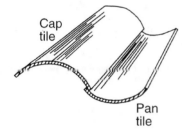

Figure 8-7: California Mission tile.

Answer: C

A 2- × 3-inch furring strip is normally installed between the roof sheathing and the cap tile. The pan tile rests directly on the felt underlayment. See Figure 8-8 on the next page.

8-22   Which of the following best describes the material used around roof protrusions, chimneys, and roof valleys to prevent water from seeping under the roof covering?

A) Louvers

C) Asphalt roll roofing

B) Flashing

D) Teflon-coated fiberglass

Answer: B

A metallic exposed sheeting is required between the felt underlayment and roofing material at roof valleys and around any roof protrusions, such as plumbing vents. Roofing cement, or flashing compound, further guards against leakage. See Figure 8-9 on the next page.

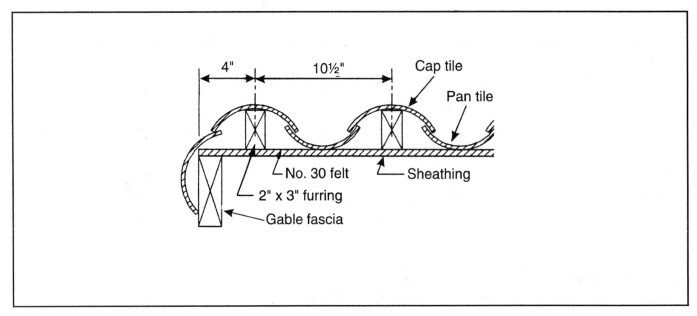

Figure 8-8: Cross-sectional view of California Mission tile.

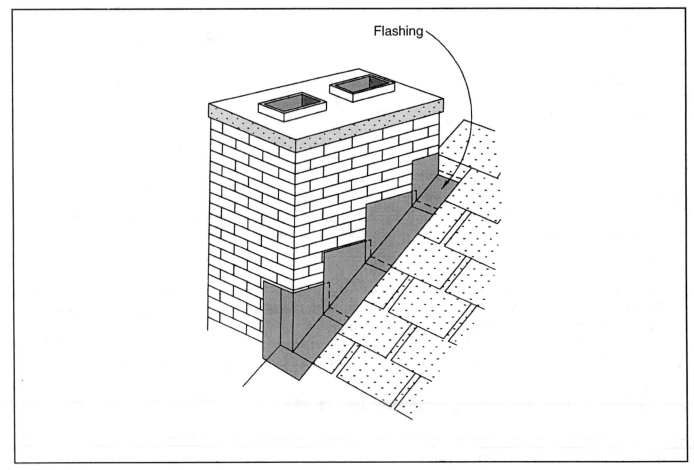

Figure 8-9: Flashing is used along the roof line where the roof meets a chimney. Flashing prevents water from seeping under the roof covering.

Chapter 9

Structural Loads

All of the following forces must be considered in the design of a building structure:

- Dead loads
- Live loads
- Wind loads
- Impact loads
- Shock waves
- Vibrations
- Seismic loading

Dead Loads: Dead loads are the weight of the walls, partitions, framing, floors, ceilings, roofs and all other permanent stationary construction entering into and becoming a part of the building.

Live Loads: Live loads are transient and moving loads such as occupants, furnishings, snow, rain, etc.

Wind Loads: Wind pressure may result in lateral loading on walls and in downward pressure or uplift forces on roof planes. Wind loads are critical in coastal areas of the Southeast because of the frequent hurricanes.

Impact Loads: These loads include shock waves and vibrations from explosions, earthquakes, nearby railroads, or heavy machinery operating within or near a structure. Snow and mud slides may also cause impact loads. Although tornadoes normally fall under wind loads, some impact and

vibration will also be prevalent. Obviously, impact loads are the most difficult to calculate.

Seismic Loading: Seismic loads are critical on the West Coast, where earthquakes are a constant threat.

Except for a building's dead load, which is fixed, all the other forces listed can vary in duration, magnitude, and point of application. A building structure must therefore be designed and constructed for these possibilities. Some geographic locations have loading requirements beyond those expected in the usual conventional construction. These loads are considered in local building codes and the appropriate structural design is required.

Wind Load

The primary consideration for good performance under extreme wind load is ensuring that all members of the structure are tied together. The roof is most vulnerable and should be well secured to the walls. The walls must also be adequately secured to the floor and foundation system. A good connection to the foundation is necessary; do not depend on the weight of the building to hold it in place on the foundation. Wide roof overhangs, carports, and porches need to be well anchored because of the large area for uplift. Connectors should load nails and other fasteners laterally rather than in a withdrawal position. To accomplish this, sheet metal connectors or straps are often required.

For wood-frame construction, instead of depending on toenailing to the top plate, use commercially available connectors for connecting roof trusses or rafters to the wall. Where a rafter and joist system is used, collar beams or gussets are important to hold the roof together at the ridge. Metal straps or plates can be used to tie walls to the floor and sill plate. This tie can also be accomplished with structural wall sheathing that extends down over the floor framing and is well nailed. Finally, the sill plate must be anchored to the foundation.

The principle of tying all components of the structure together is often best accomplished with engineered components such as roof trusses. Connectors are specifically engineered to hold all the parts together.

Observation of wind damage has shown that building shape has some influence on overall damage. Hip roofs sustain less shingle damage than gable roofs because turbulence around the gable end starts the removal of shingles at the edge.

Snow Load

The major preparation for snow load is simply the use of larger structural members. The size of structural members is usually specified by the local building code.

Rafters and beams in particular are designed for maximal snow-load conditions. Observations have shown little evidence of failures in light-frame buildings. Failures generally occur in commercial buildings with long spans over large open spaces.

There are some general shape considerations that may influence snow loads. Snow usually slides off steep sloping roofs, and often blows from flat roofs where the roof is all at one elevation. The problem of snow build-up on sloped roofs develops when the wind is perpendicular to the ridge. Turbulence at the ridge causes drifting on the downwind side, resulting in an unbalanced load on the roof structure. Another drift problem occurs where two building sections of different heights join. Snow blows off the higher section onto the lower section, resulting in a deep drift. This is particularly critical when the lower section is a flat roof.

Seismic Load

The major items needed to provide earthquake resistance are adequate lateral bracing, shear resistance in walls, and good connections between all major components. Buildings that have performed best have had simple rectangular configurations, continuous floors, and small window and door openings. They may be described as having a symmetric box-like lateral resistive system. In addition to the building acting as a unit, anchorage to the foundation is particularly important to avoid having the foundation move out from under the building.

Large openings in walls have been a major cause of building failure during earthquakes. The openings appear to be more critical when they are near a corner. Particular danger exists where large openings have a second story over them. The weight of the second story added to the lack of racking resistance increases the risk of failure.

The joining of two elements of a building of different heights can also cause problems. The two sections will have different frequencies of vibration, and so may not move together.

9-1   In addition to plans and sections, dimensions and sizes, what other information should be provided on construction drawings?

A) All point loads

B) An isometric layout

C) Design loads

D) Impact loading criteria

Answer: C

Information that shows design load criteria must be submitted in the construction documents and must include all factors affecting structural calculations, including point loads and/or impact loads.

9-2   Which of the following types of design-load information must be selected from information specifically provided in building codes?

A) Both dead and live loads

B) Dead loads

C) Live loads

D) Impact loads

Answer: C

Live loads that must be used in structural calculations for a given area are provided in most of the major building codes used in the United States.

9-3   Which of the following best defines wind loads?

A) A design load calculated as a live load

B) A load that is never used when calculating column loads, since it is a horizontal, not a vertical, force

C) A design load calculated as a dead load

D) An independent load that is neither live or dead

Answer: A

Wind loads are live loads that must be calculated using appropriate criteria listed in the building code. Wind loads depend on several factors, including the geographical location of the structure.

9-4   Wind moving at 1 mph is the same as which of the following?

A) A motor car moving at 60 mph

B) 2.0 feet per second (fps)

C) 1.47 fps

D) 88 fps

Answer: C

One mile per hour (1 mph) = 1 mile per 60 minutes or 5280 feet ÷ 60 = 88 feet per minute or 1.47 feet per second.

9-5   Which of the following is the best definition of dead load?

A) The weight of the roof, floors, and walls

B) The weight of all permanent parts of a building

C) The weight of people and furniture inside of a building

D) The weight of all stationary parts of a building

Answer: B

All permanent building components such as structural members, built-in equipment and similar items, are dead loads.

9-6   Which of the following best describes seismic loads?

A) Vertical loads

B) Moving loads

C) Horizontal loads acting parallel to the building axis

D) Horizontal loads acting in any horizontal direction

Answer: D

Seismic or earthquake loads are considered to be horizontal (lateral) loads that can impact a building from any horizontal direction.

9-7   Which of the following is a lateral building load?

A) The weight of the soil that abuts against a basement wall

B) Falling snow

C) Heavy roof loading

D) Excessive basement floor loading

Answer: A

Any soil adjacent to a building's foundation exerts pressure (loading) on the foundation walls. Such pressure acts in a lateral fashion.

9-8   Which of the following are good examples of live loads?

A) A train and a child

B) Built-in book shelves

C) Steel basement columns

D) Rooftop HVAC equipment

Answer: A

Live loads are not permanent parts of a building. A moving train, for example, may not pass into the building, but if it is nearby, it will cause vibrations that will affect the building structure. A child and all other people are always considered to be live loads.

9-9   Which of the following best describes the design criteria for elevator loads and the surrounding building structure?

A) Allow 200 pounds per person

B) Limit the elevator load to three persons

C) Impact loading

D) Nonuniform live loads

Answer: C

If an elevator falls only a short distance, there will be resulting impact loads. Consequently, building codes require that impact loading be considered when designing elevator structures. There are many other types of moving machinery that can cause building impact or kinetic loads as well.

9-10   What is a factor that may affect the structural performance of a roof that is subjected to snow loading?

A) The roof insulation

B) The surrounding terrain

C) The design of the penthouse

D) The shingle texture; that is, either smooth or rough

Answer: B

Most building codes consider the nature of the surrounding terrain when specifying installation requirements. For example, if a low-sloping roof is located in an open, unobstructed area, the snow-loading requirements can be reduced.

9-11   When a building contains rooftop landscaping materials, such as shrubbery, how should the materials be handled according to the building code?

A) The weight of the materials must be handled as a dead load

B) The weight of the materials must be handled as a live load

C) The weight of the materials must be handled as an impact load

D) The weight of the materials must be handled as a lateral load

Answer: A

Landscaping materials are considered a permanent part of the roof. Therefore, their weight must be treated as a design dead load.

9-12   When planning for snow loads on roof structures, which of the following must be considered during the design stage?

A) There may be more snow on the ground than on the roof

B) There may be more snow on one part of a roof than on another part

C) There may be snow on the roof, but none on the ground

D) The unit weight of snow may vary considerably in only a few sq. ft. of roof structure

Answer: B

Blowing snow has a tendency to drift, or accumulate, depending on the terrain. The same is true for certain rooftop situations. For example, a gable roof may accumulate more snow on one side of the roof than on the other. Therefore, the structure design must consider the possibility of unbalanced loads.

9-13   What is the main reason that greenhouse roofs usually have few snow-loading problems?

A) Building codes require high-strength plexiglass roofs

B) The low pitch of greenhouse roofs gives more structural strength

C) The steep pitch of greenhouse roofs allows snow to fall off before it can accumulate

D) Greenhouse roofs are continuously heated

Answer: D

Greenhouse roofs are continuously heated, which prevents the build-up of snow loads. However, when a greenhouse is inactive (no heat), additional structural protection is usually required in areas with heavy snow fall.

9-14   Building codes show maps of ground snow loads for various areas of the United States. On what unit snow weight are these maps based?

A) 10 pounds per cu. ft.

B) 12 pounds per cu. ft.

C) 15 pounds per cu. ft.

D) None of the above

Answer: D

Building codes give snow loading criteria that is based on the weight of accumulated snow on a square foot of ground. It is impractical to give the weight of snow per cu. ft. because wet compacted snow differs greatly in weight from the same amount of fresh-fallen snow.

9-15   Handrails in a commercial stairway must resist which of the following forces?

A) A 200-pound concentrated force

B) A 200-pound uniform force

C) A 50-pound concentrated force

D) A concentrated force exerted by a 200-pound person

Answer: A

A handrail must be able to withstand a concentrated 200-pound force applied from any direction.

9-16   When is a building usually subjected to its most strenuous loading?

A) When it is first occupied

B) When occupants are gathered mostly to one side

C) When the building's normal life expectancy has been exceeded

D) When the building is under construction

Answer: D

Heavy construction equipment, materials, and workers can overstress a building's structural design. Therefore, building codes give specific requirements for buildings under construction. In general, the codes require construction loads not to exceed those for which the finished occupied building is designed.

9-17   Buildings located in flood zones must be designed to resist structural damage to building components that are located in which of the following areas?

A) Within 3 feet of the base flood elevation

B) Below the base flood elevation

C) Below the 50-year flood elevation

D) Below the high-water mark

Answer: B

Most building codes accept the base flood elevation as the benchmark for determining flood hazards. The base flood elevation must be determined by persons qualifed to provide the appropriate survey data.

9-18   Some buildings located in earthquake-prone areas are required to have an in-depth engineered seismic design prepared by a qualified registered professional. Which of the following building types are usually exempt from this requirement?

A) Wood frame buildings

B) A combination of wood and steel frame buildings

C) Welded steel frame buildings

D) Reinforced concrete structures

Answer: A

Wood frame buildings are usually exempt from an earthquake design analysis. However, there are other code-required elements that are still applicable, but such requirements seldom require a mathematical analysis.

9-19   Residential building codes limit the amount of deflection for floor joists. What deflection is allowed under maximum live loading?

A) The span in inches divided by 240

B) The span in inches divided by 120

C) The span in inches divided by 360

D) The span in inches divided by 208

Answer: C

The amount of deflection allowed for floors in both residential and commercial buildings is total span (in inches) divided by 360. This is considered to be the maximum amount of deflection before a floor is visibly sagging.

9-20   Reinforced concrete beams are manufactured with a slight rise from the ends to the beam midpoint. What is the purpose of this rise?

A) To allow for sagging

B) To provide a pitch in the floor above

C) To increase the strength of the beam

D) To keep moisture and water from settling in any one spot

Answer: A

Most beams sag or deflect after a period of time. Therefore, some types of beams are manufactured to allow for this sag.

9-21   Which of the following wood types produce the strongest framing lumber for all types of building construction?

A) Eastern white pine

B) Douglas fir

C) Maple

D) Cedar

Answer: B

Douglas fir is one of the more common types of framing lumber and is also one of the strongest.

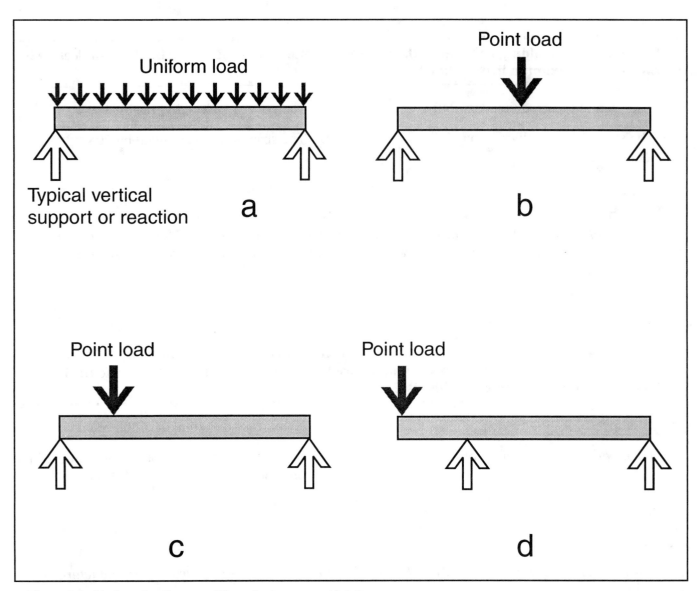

Figure 9-1: Various loading conditions for beams and joists.

9-22   Which diagram in Figure 9-1 best exemplifies live load conditions specified by building code span charts?

A) **a**   C) **c**

B) **b**   D) **d**

Answer: A

*Diagram **a** illustrates uniform loading on a joist or beam. Most codes specify floor live load requirements that are based on loads that are uniformly distributed over the length of a beam.*

9-23   **Which diagram in Figure 9-1 illustrates the loading conditions of a cantilever?**

A) **a**

C) **c**

B) **b**

D) **d**

Answer: D

A cantilever is a loading condition in which a beam or joist extends past its support, and is loaded in part beyond any support.

9-24   **Which diagrams in Figure 9-1 illustrate bearing or joist loading in which the loads are calculated as point loads?**

A) **h**

C) **b** and **c**

B) **b**, **c**, and **d**

D) **d**

Answer: B

*The loadings shown in **b**, **c**, and **d** of this drawing are depicted at a single point over the span of the beam or joist. Consequently, they are referred to as point or concentrated loads.*

9-25   **If a beam is subjected to a concentrated load at mid span as shown in diagram b of Figure 9-1, and a similar beam is subjected to a load between the mid span and a support (diagram c of Figure 9-1), which beam is subjected to the most bending stress?**

A) Both are equally stressed

C) **c**

B) **b**

D) The stress is similar to diagram **a**

Answer: B

A concentrated load (P) placed on a beam will give maximum beam stress at mid span.

9-26   Using diagrams a, b, and c of Figure 9-1, which will cause the most deflection if all dimensions are equal?

A) a

C) c

B) b

D) d

Answer: B

*The loading condition of diagram **b** will cause the most bending stress and the most deflection. Under the conditions given, a general understanding of the dynamics of simple beams can be used to predict certain aspects of their behavior.*

Chapter 10

Concrete and Masonry

Concrete is composed of sand, gravel, crushed rock, or other aggregates held together by a hardened paste of hydraulic cement and water. The thoroughly mixed ingredients, when properly proportioned, make a plastic mass that can be cast or molded into a predetermined size and shape. Upon hydration of the cement by the water, concrete becomes stonelike in strength and hardness and has utility for many purposes.

Improved practices and techniques have added greatly to the ability to produce good concrete, and engineers are in close agreement on the practical needs for producing it. Authorities recognize that, in addition to proper ingredients, a modern formula for successful concrete production includes the following:

- Common sense
- Good judgment
- Vigilance

There is still some concrete which, through carelessness or ignorance in its manufacture and placement, fails to give the service that would otherwise be expected. It is the responsibility of those in charge of construction to make sure that concrete is of uniformly good quality. The extra effort and care required to achieve this objective are small in relation to the benefits. Good construction practice dictates acceptance of only the best. This axiom is especially true of concrete, for the best usually costs no more than the mediocre. In fact, good concrete practices result in better quality concrete and often lower costs by reducing placing difficulties. All that is required to achieve the best is an understanding of the basic principles of making good concrete and paying close attention to proven practices during construction.

Temperatures for Concrete

Most concrete specifications require that concrete, as deposited, must have a temperature no higher than a stipulated value — usually 80°F for concrete to be placed in hot arid climates and 90°F for most other concretes. For mass concrete dams, temperature studies have shown the need for considerably lower maximum placing temperatures. Such placing temperatures, as low as 50°F, are established to control cracking in the structure. On some jobs in the desert regions of the Southwest, concrete placing has been prohibited during the extremely hot weather between June 1 and October 1.

Limitations on maximum temperature and the placing of concrete during hot weather have been imposed because the quality and durability of the resulting concrete is impaired when it is mixed, placed, and cured at high temperatures. The impairment affects several different properties of the concrete: First, the ultimate strength of concrete mixed and cured at high temperatures is never as great as that of concrete mixed and cured at temperatures below 70°F; second, cracking tendencies are increased because of the great range between the high temperature at the time of hardening and the low temperature to which the concrete will later drop; third, the unit water requirement for mixing is increased by higher concrete temperatures, contributing to greater shrinkage on drying; and fourth, concrete that is mixed, placed, and cured at high temperatures has been found to fail sooner, as a result of repeated cycles of moisture and temperature changes above the freezing point, than concrete that is mixed, placed, and cured at lower temperatures.

On the other hand, when there is danger of freezing, certain minimum temperatures of concrete, as placed, are specified because much of the heat generated during hydration of the cement is not immediately available. Specifications require that the temperature of the concrete be not less than 40°F in moderate weather of 50°F when the mean daily temperature drops below 40°F. As an additional precaution, when the mean daily air temperature is lower than 40°F, 1% calcium chloride by weight of cement may be used to bring the concrete

to a stage of greater maturity at the end of the specified period of protection. However, the use of calcium chloride is never justification for reducing the amount of protective cover, heat, or other winter protection which would normally be used. Also, calcium chloride should not be used in concrete that will be subjected to sulfate attack or which contains embedded galvanized metal parts. Where sulfate conditions exist, the water-cement ratio should be reduced to a maximum of 0.47 and Type II or V cement should be used.

To obtain the required temperatures for freshly mixed concrete in cold weather, it is often necessary to heat mixing water or aggregates, or both, depending on the severity of the weather.

Preparations for Placing Concrete

The procedures necessary for satisfactory preparation of foundation surfaces upon or against which concrete is to be placed are governed by design requirements and by the type and condition of the foundation material. Every building contractor should be familiar with these procedures.

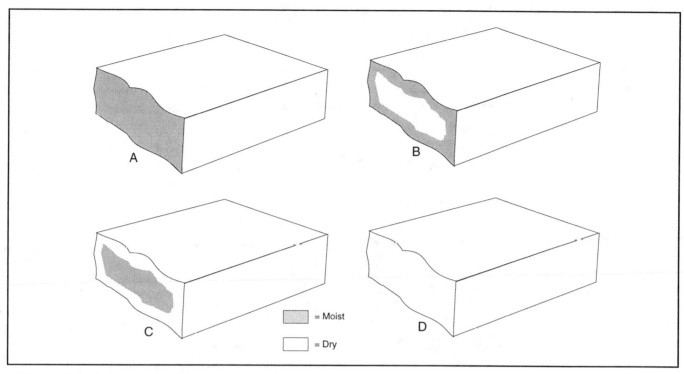

Figure 10-1: Various moisture-content conditions of brick.

10-1   Which diagram in Figure 10-1 shows the best condition for brick at the time of installation?

A) A

B) B

C) C

D) D

Answer: C

The best condition for brick during installation is a dry surface, with a saturated interior. This condition will prevent excessive water absorption from the mortar, and thereby produce a good bond between the mortar and the bricks.

10-2   The application of mortar to brick head joints is shown in Figure 10-2. Which diagram shows the best construction practice?

A) A

B) B

C) C

D) D

Answer: D

The best practice for all brick joints, including head joints, is to completely fill them with mortar. Doing so will result in a wall that is watertight and strong.

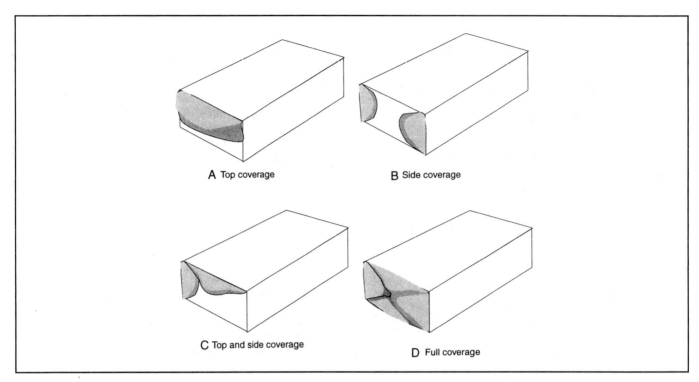

A Top coverage   B Side coverage

C Top and side coverage   D Full coverage

Figure 10-2: Various applications of mortar to brick head joints.

10-3 Mortar for laying brick is acceptable for use in which of the following conditions?

A) Before the mortar has started to set

B) When the mortar has just started to set

C) After the mortar has been remixed with sand

D) When the mortar has set long enough to allow evaporation to take place

Answer: A

Use mortar that has not started to set. Mortar that has begun to set should be discarded; it will not form a proper bond with the masonry.

10-4 Which of the joints in Figure 10-3 is the most weather-resistant?

A) A

B) B

C) C

D) D

Answer: B

The joint in diagram B is known as a concave joint and is the only joint shown in the illustration that is recommended for durability and is weather-resistant for exterior use.

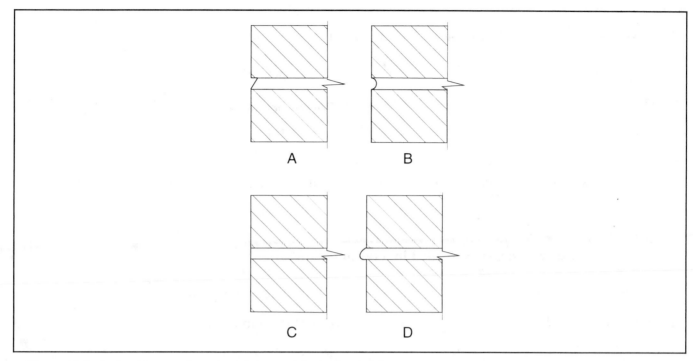

Figure 10-3: Several types of mortar joints used for laying brick.

10-5   What is the minimum allowable thickness and maximum allowable height of an unreinforced masonry parapet wall?

A) 6-inch thickness and 24-inch height

B) 6-inch thickness and 48-inch height

C) 8-inch thickness and 32-inch height

D) 8-inch thickness and 24-inch height

Answer: D

Unreinforced masonry parapet walls are required to be at least 8 inches thick and a height not to exceed 3 times the thickness.

10-6   Which of the following is the best mortar mix for laying brick?

A) One part masonry cement, two parts sand

B) One part masonry cement, three parts sand

C) One part masonry cement, four parts sand

D) One part masonry cement, five parts sand

Answer: B

The standard mix for mortar for laying brick is one part masonry cement to three parts sand.

10-7   What is the required thickness of brick and/or cement block head joints?

A) $\frac{1}{4}$-inch thick

C) $\frac{1}{2}$-inch thick

B) $\frac{3}{8}$-inch thick

D) $\frac{3}{4}$-inch thick

Answer: B

Unless otherwise required or indicated on the project drawings, head and bed joints must be $\frac{3}{8}$-inch thick.

10-8   Where must weepholes be located in a masonry wall?

A) At all corners

C) In the outside wythe

B) In the inside wythe

D) At the unprotected top layer of brick

Answer: C

Weepholes must be provided in the outside wythe of masonry walls at a maximum spacing of 33 inches on center.

10-9   What is the minimum allowable diameter of weepholes?

A) $\frac{3}{16}$ inch

C) $\frac{1}{2}$ inch

B) $\frac{3}{8}$ inch

D) $\frac{5}{8}$ inch

Answer: A

A change in the 1996 BOCA, Section 2111.1.8, requires weepholes in masonry walls to be at least $\frac{3}{16}$ inch in diameter.

10-10   What must be provided when masonry is installed directly above chases or recesses wider than 12 inches?

A) Solid bricks

C) Supporting lintels

B) Hollow masonry units

D) Corbeled masonry

Answer: C

The design of lintels must be in accordance with the engineered masonry design, and the minimum end support of the lintels must not be less than 4 inches.

10-11   What is the minimum allowable distance that the liner of a fireplace wall must extend into the throat of the fireplace?

A) 2 inches

B) 4 inches

C) 6 inches

D) 8 inches

Answer: B

Fireplace liners must extend into the throat of the fireplace a minimum of 4 inches (102 mm).

10-12   What is the minimum allowable thickness of the throat and smoke chamber walls of a fireplace?

A) 2 inches

B) 4 inches

C) 6 inches

D) 8 inches

Answer: D

The walls of the throat and smoke chamber must be constructed of concrete or solid masonry having a minimum total thickness of 8 inches.

10-13   When a concrete block wall is faced with brick, the brick and block must be "tied" together by some means. One method is shown in Figure 10-4. Which of the following best describes this bonding method?

A) 5th course bonding

B) 6th course bonding

C) Cavity bonding

D) Metal-tied wall

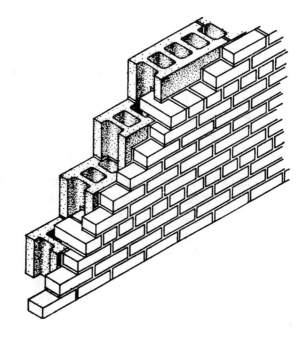

Answer: B

Note that every 6th course of brick is turned at a 90° angle to the remaining courses. Doing so "ties" the brick wall to the block wall and is known as 6th course bonding.

Figure 10-4: One way to bond brick facing to a concrete block wall.

10-14   What test is used to measure the workability of concrete when wet, and also to check the concrete's consistency from batch to batch?

A) Resistance test

B) Slump test

C) Continuity test

D) Plasticizer test

Answer: B

Slump is a measure of the consistency or stiffness of fresh concrete expressed in inches. It is influenced by the amount of water used (more water means more slump), but water is not the only factor. The type of aggregate, the air content, and the proportions of the ingredients all affect slump.

10-15   Which of the following best describes the type of cement that should be used when the concrete will be exposed to freezing, thawing, and the action of salts used for removing ice?

A) Cement with retarders added

B) Cement with plasticizers added

C) Cement with accelerators added

D) Air-entraining cement

Answer: D

Air entrainment is essential for protecting concrete that is exposed to the elements described in the question.

10-16   Which of the following is one characteristic of air-entraining cement?

A) It acts as an antifreeze

B) It forms air bubbles throughout the cement

C) It slows down the setting of concrete

D) It speeds up the setting of concrete

Answer: B

An air-entraining admixture or air-entraining cement causes microscopic air bubbles to form throughout the concrete which act as "relief valves" when the concrete freezes, helping to prevent scaling or spalling of the surfaces.

10-17   Accelerators added to concrete mixtures speed up the setting time and strength development of concrete. Which of the following is the most commonly used concrete accelerator?

A) Calcium nitrate

B) Sodium nitrite

C) Sodium nitrate

D) Calcium chloride

Answer: D

Calcium chloride is the most commonly used accelerator. When added to cement, it speeds up the set and makes freezing damage less likely, especially if the concrete is protected from low temperatures while it is curing.

10-18   What is the purpose of adding retarders to a concrete mixture?

A) To cause the concrete to set faster

B) To increase the amount of water needed to mix concrete

C) To slow down the setting time of concrete

D) To increase shrinkage as the concrete drys

Answer: C

In hot weather, concrete may set so quickly that it cannot be finished properly. Retarders are added to slow the setting time. Retarders are also useful when difficult placements require more time.

10-19   Which admixture is used to make concrete more workable with less water?

A) Air entrainment

B) Accelerators

C) Retarders

D) Plasticizers

Answer: D

Plasticizers make the concrete more workable with less water. Strength is increased by the low water/cement ratio, and the labor costs are usually reduced because the concrete is more workable which, in turn, means faster installations..

10-20   What is the minimum allowable distance that a fireplace hearth must extend beyond the face of a fireplace opening that is less than 6 sq. ft.?

A) 8 inches

B) 16 inches

C) 18 inches

D) 24 inches

Answer: B

Most building codes require the hearth to extend a minimum of 16 inches (406 mm) beyond the face of the fireplace opening and a minimum of 8 inches on each side of the fireplace opening for fireplaces having an opening of less than 6 sq. ft. Fireplaces having larger openings must extend a minimum of 20 inches beyond the face of the fireplace opening and a minimum of 12 inches on each side of the fireplace opening.

10-21   Building codes require a means to shut off the opening to the chimney when a fireplace is not in operation. Which of the following is one approved device for complying with this code requirement?

A) Metal hood

B) Fireblocking

C) Damper

D) Offset

Answer: C

A damper is usually a cast-iron apparatus with a hinged door that may be closed by means of a lever when the fireplace is not in operation.

Chapter 11

Steel Construction

Steel is used for heavy and light structural framing as well as a wide range of building products such as windows, doors, hardware, and fasteners. When used as a structural material, steel combines high strength and stiffness with elasticity. Measured in terms of weight to volume, it is probably the strongest low-cost material available.

Although classified as an incombustible material, steel becomes ductile and loses its strength under high heat conditions (over 1000°F). When used in buildings requiring fireresistance-rated construction, structural steel must be coated, covered, or otherwise protected with fireresistant materials.

Unless specially treated at the time of manufacture, structural steel is normally subject to corrosion, and must therefore be painted, galvanized, or chemically treated for protection against oxidation.

Most structural steel is medium carbon grade steel which is available in plate and bar forms, and in several structural shapes as shown in Figure 11-1. The steel members may be fastened in place by welding or using some mechanical means such as high-tensile strength bolts and nuts or similar fasteners.

Steel may be heat-treated or altered with additives (to form alloys) during its manufacture to develop special properties of strength, hardness or ductility, expansion, corrosion-resistance, or workability.

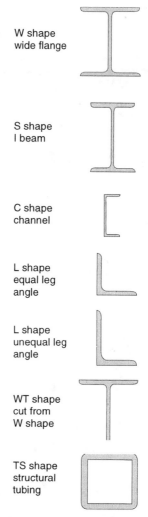

W shape
wide flange

S shape
I beam

C shape
channel

L shape
equal leg
angle

L shape
unequal leg
angle

WT shape
cut from
W shape

TS shape
structural
tubing

Figure 11-1: Various shapes of structural steel.

Types of Steel

Stainless steel is an alloy of steel, nickel, and chromium and has the following features:

- Highly resistant to corrosion, heat, and oxidation
- Has low heat conductivity, but high thermal expansion

Other types of special steels include:

- nickel steel
- chromium steel
- copper-bearing steel

Nickel steel is stronger than regular carbon steel, chromium steel is very hard and corrosion resistant, while copper-bearing steel is corrosion-resistant.

Other ferrous metals used in building construction include:

- Cast iron — which has high carbon content and is brittle, but strong in compression. Cast iron is used for piping and ornamental work.
- Wrought iron — which has extremely low carbon content and is resistant to progressive corrosion. This type of iron is soft, malleable, and tough. It is used for piping, hardware, and ornamental work.

11-1   What is the best description of part A of the steel beam in Figure 11-2?

A) Top web

B) Top flange

C) Web

D) Plate

Answer: B

The I-beam in Figure 11-2 has a top and a bottom flange. The arrow from A is pointing to the top flange.

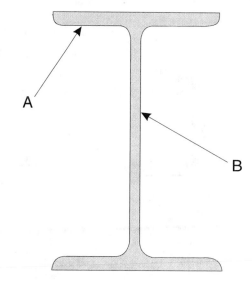

Figure 11-2: Cross-sectional view of a steel wide-flanged beam.

11-2   What is the best description of part B of the steel beam in Figure 11-2?

A) Bottom web

B) Top web

C) Web

D) Plate

Answer: C

The I-beam in Figure 11-2 has top and bottom horizontal flanges and a vertical web between the two. The arrow from B is pointing to the web.

11-3   The American Institute of Seel Construction (AISC) provides specifications for all steel shapes. What is the AISC specification name of the steel shape in Figure 11-2?

A) Standard steel column

B) Structural tubing

C) Wide flange

D) Channel

Answer: C

The shape of the steel beam depicted in Figure 11-2 is a wide flange beam or column, and is specified by the letter W in the AISC specifications. For dimensions, the letter W is followed by its nominal flange width and then by an ×, followed by its weight in pounds per linear foot.

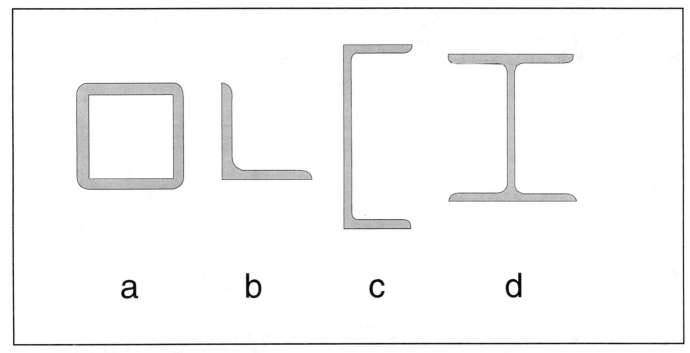

Figure 11-3: Cross-sectional views of structural steel.

11-4   Which illustration in Figure 11-3 best depicts the AISC designation W8×10?

A) **a**   C) **c**

B) **b**   D) **d**

Answer: D

*The AISC publishes The Manual of Steel Construction which is used in the construction industry as **the** guide for heavy structural steel design and installation. W8×10 is a standard designation for a specific piece of structural steel with the shape shown in **d** of Figure 11-3. Most structural details and architectural drawings prepared in the United States use AISC designations for structural steel cross-sectional shapes.*

11-5   What does the steel designation W8×10 indicate in addition to its cross-sectional shape?

A) Nominal depth   C) Nominal depth and unit weight

B) Nominal depth and weight   D) Nominal weight

Answer: C

A W8×10 designation shows the nominal depth of the steel (8 inches) and its weight per linear foot (10 pounds) in addition to its shape (W).

11-6   What is the weight of a structural steel beam designated W14×22 if the beam's length is 24 feet?

A) 528 pounds

B) 336 pounds

C) 308 pounds

D) 22 pounds

Answer: A

A W14×22 steel beam weighs 22 pounds per linear foot. 22 pounds × 24 feet = 528 pounds.

11-7   Which diagram in Figure 11-3 is the most appropriate for a cross-sectional view of a C12×20.7 piece of structural steel?

A) **a**

B) **b**

C) **c**

D) **d**

Answer: C

An AISC designation of C12×20.7 is the designation for a C channel. The remaining numbers designate the depth and its weight per linear foot.

11-8   What is the weight of an AISC structural steel channel that is designated C12×20.7 if it is 13 feet in length?

A) 269.1 pounds

B) 284.4 pounds

C) 156 pounds

D) 341.5 pounds

Answer: A

A channel designated C12×20.7 is 12 inches deep and weighs 20.7 pounds per linear foot. Consequently, 20.7 pounds × 13 feet = 269.1 pounds. Note: It is important that contractors and their estimators and supervisors know the weight of structural steel members. Such information will help determine how a piece of steel is lifted and fitted.

11-9   Which of the diagrams in Figure 11-4 best illustrates a web stiffener?

A) **a**

B) **b**

C) **c**

D) None of the diagrams are web stiffeners

Answer: A

*Structural steel beams and columns are frequently specified with steel web stiffeners. Such stiffeners are normally plates welded between the flanges to brace the web member. The position of plates **b** and **c** in Figure 11-4 would add little, if any, stiffening effect to the web.*

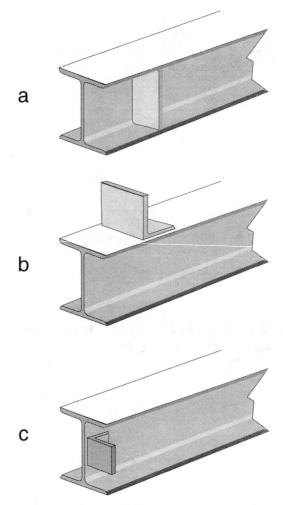

Figure 11-4: I-beams with metal plates welded in 3 different positions.

11-10   Which of the following answers is the most accurate in regard to the design of a steel-column base plate that bears on a concrete pier?

A) Cured concrete eliminates the need for a steel base plate

B) A leveling plate bolted to the concrete will help with column erection and also help to transfer column stresses to the concrete pier

C) A steel base plate should never be used on cured concrete

D) The column should be embedded in the concrete to eliminate the need for a base plate

Answer: B

The base of a steel column is very small in comparison to the high loading stresses that may be transmitted from the bottom of the column to the concrete base. A base plate should always be used to help transfer column stresses to the concrete area.

11-11 Cantilevered floor systems, using light-gage metal floor joists, need reinforcement directly above the load-bearing wall (A in Figure 11-5). What is this reinforcement called?

A) Bending reinforcement

B) Shear support

C) Web stiffening

D) Bracing

Answer: C

Web stiffening is needed to prevent distortion or crippling of the relatively thin beam web.

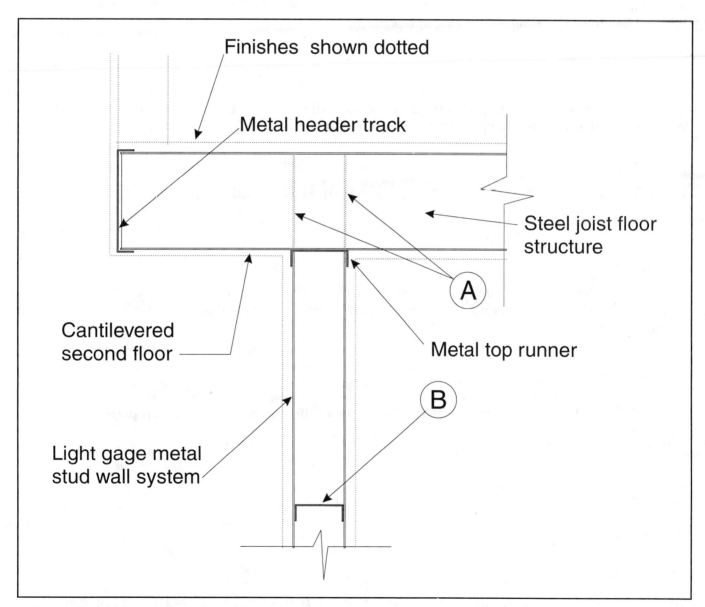

Figure 11-5: Light-gage metal floor and wall system.

11-12 Item B in Figure 11-5 is often used as wall bracing in light-gage metal stud systems. Which of the following is the name given to item B?

A) Diagonal bracing

B) Bridging

C) Shear support

D) Flange bracing

Answer: B

Horizontal wall bracing placed between individual studs is called "bridging." This term is also used to describe horizontal or diagonal bracing of floor joists.

11-13 Shop drawings are required for every project that utilizes structural steel. Which of the following always appears on shop drawings of structural steel?

A) Dimensions

B) Paint primer specs

C) Foundation dimensions

D) Steel deflection tolerances

Answer: A

Shop drawings are details of each piece of steel used on a project. Information includes dimensions, centerlines for drilled bolt holes, bolt dimensions, and other pertinent data. See Figure 11-6 on the opposite page.

11-14 What is the distance above the finished floor to the top of the column cap plate in Figure 11-6?

A) 8' 0"

B) 10' 0"

C) 9' 10"

D) 9' 9½"

Answer: D

The length of the column, including top and bottom plates, is 10' + ³⁄₄" + ³⁄₄" = 10' 1½". Subtract 4" (distance from bottom of column base plate to top of finished floor) from 10' 1½" to get the answer of 9' 9 ½".

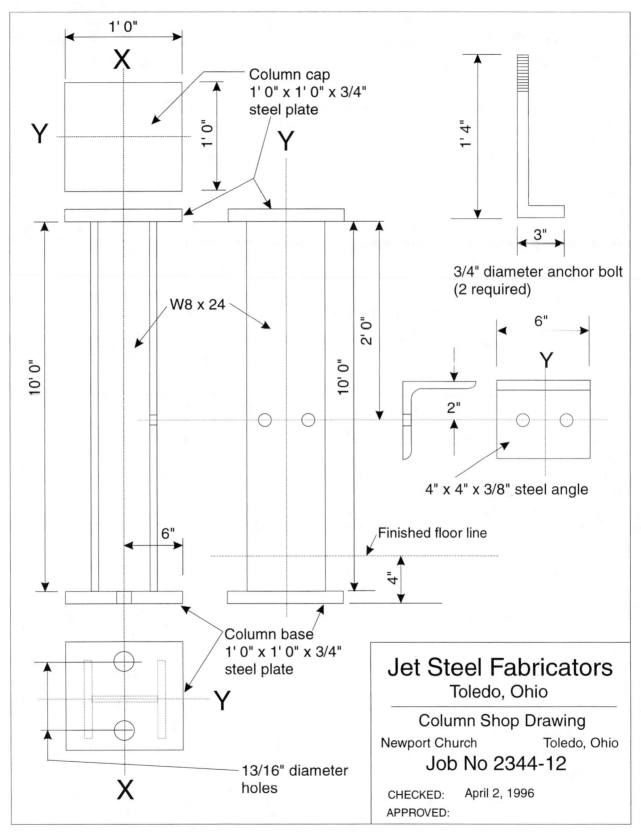

1' 0"

X

Y

Column cap
1' 0" x 1' 0" x 3/4"
steel plate

1' 0"

Y

Y

1' 4"

3"

3/4" diameter anchor bolt
(2 required)

W8 x 24

6"

Y

2"

10' 0"

2' 0"

10' 0"

4" x 4" x 3/8" steel angle

6"

Finished floor line

4"

Column base
1' 0" x 1' 0" x 3/4"
steel plate

Y

13/16" diameter
holes

X

Jet Steel Fabricators
Toledo, Ohio

Column Shop Drawing

Newport Church   Toledo, Ohio

Job No 2344-12

CHECKED: April 2, 1996

APPROVED:

Figure 11-6: Typical shop drawing for structural steel.

11-15   What is the distance from the finished floor to the top bearing surface of the 6-inch long steel angle in Figure 11-6?

A) 8' 0"

C) 8' 2"

B) 2' 0"

D) 7' 10¾"

Answer: D

The distance from the finished floor to the top of the W8×24 column is 10' 0" – 3¼" (the distance from the top of the column base plate to the top of the finished floor) = 9' 8¾". Subtract 2' 0" from the previous figure to determine the distance from the finished floor to the centerline of the angle bolt holes. 9' 8¾" – 2' 0" = 7' 8¾". Adding 2" for the distance from the finished floor to the top of angle gives 7' 10¾".

11-16   What is the appropriate diameter for the 2 bolt holes in the column base plate in Figure 11-6?

A) ¾"

C) ¹¹⁄₁₆"

B) ¹³⁄₁₆"

D) ⅝"

Answer: B

Bolt holes must be consistent with the bolt diameters. Bolt holes must be sized slightly larger than the bolt diameters to facilitate slipping the base plate onto the bolts. A bolt-hole diameter of ¹³⁄₁₆" will give just enough play so that the base plate can be fitted snugly over the bolts. Charts are listed in the AISC manual that give exact dimensions for bolt holes in relation to bolts.

Chapter 12

Fire Protection Systems

Some type of fire protection system is required in practically all types of buildings — from smoke detectors in residential occupancies to extensive fire-alarm, sprinkler, and standpipe systems in larger structures. The extent of fire protection systems depends on the use of the building.

All structures are classified with respect to occupancy in several different use groups stated in the building code. Where a structure is proposed for a purpose which is not specifically provided for in the building code, such structures must be classified in the use group which the occupancy most nearly resembles. The following table lists general classifications.

Occupancy	Use Groups
Assembly	A-1, A-2, A-3, A-4 and A-5
Business	B
Education	E
Factory and industrial	F-1 and F-2
High hazard	H-3 and H-4
Institutional	I-1, I-2, and I-3
Mercantile	M
Residential	R-1, R-2, R-3 and R-4
Storage	S-1 and S-2
Utility and Misc.	U

Assembly Use Groups

All structures which are designed or occupied for the gathering together of persons such as civic, social or religious functions, recreation, food or drink consumption or awaiting transportation, are classified as Use Group A-1, A-2, A-3, A-4 or A-5.

Use Group A-1, Theaters: This use group includes all theaters, and all other buildings and structures intended for the production and viewing of performing arts or motion pictures, and which are usually provided with fixed seats — including theaters, motion picture theaters and television and radio studios that admit an audience.

Use Group A-2 Structures: This use group includes all buildings and places of public assembly, without theatrical stage accessories, designed for occupancy as dance halls, nightclubs and for similar purposes, including all rooms, lobbies and other spaces connected thereto with a common means of egress and entrance.

Use Group A-3 Structures: This use group includes all buildings with or without an auditorium in which persons assemble for amusement, entertainment or recreation purposes, as well as incidental motion picture, dramatic or theatrical presentations, lectures or other similar purposes without theatrical stage other than a raised platform; and which are principally occupied without permanent seating facilities, including art galleries, exhibition halls, museums, lecture halls, libraries, restaurants other than nightclubs, and recreation centers; and buildings designed for similar assembly purposes, including passenger terminals.

Group A-4 Structures: This use group includes all buildings and structures that are occupied exclusively for the purpose of worship or other religious services.

Use Group A-5, Outdoor Assembly: This use group includes structures utilized for outdoor assembly intended for participation in or reviewing activities, including grandstands, bleachers, coliseums, stadiums, amusement park structures and fair or carnival structures.

Business Use Group

The occupancies listed in the following table are indicative of, and must be classified as, Use Group B:

Business Occupancies	
Airport traffic control towers	Fire stations
Animal hospitals, kennels, pounds	Florists and nurseries
Automobile and other motor vehicle showrooms	Laboratories; testing and research
Banks	Laundries; pickup and delivery stations and self-service
Barber shops	Police stations
Beauty shops	Post offices
Car washes	Print shops
Civic administration	Professional services; attorney, dentist, physician, engineer, etc.
Dry cleaning; pickup and delivery stations and self-service	Radio and television studios
Electronic data processing	Telecommunication equipment buildings

Education Use Group

All structures other than those occupied for business training or vocational training, which accommodate more than 5 persons for educational purposes though the 12th grade, are classified as Group E.

Factory and Industrial Use Groups

All structures in which occupants are engaged in work or labor in the fabricating, assembling or processing of products or materials are classified as Group F-1 or F-2.

Use Group F-1 Structures: Factory and industrial occupancies which are not otherwise classified as low-hazard. Use Group F-1 is classified as a moderate-hazard factory and industrial occupancy. The manufacturing processes listed in the following table are indicative of those classified as Use Group F-1.

Moderate-Hazard Factory and Industrial Occupancies	
Aircraft	Disinfectants
Appliances	Dry cleaning using other than flammable liquids in cleaning or dyeing operations
Athletic equipment	Electric light plants and power houses
Automobiles and other motor vehicles	Electrolytic-reducing works and electronics
Bakeries	Engines, including rebuilding
Beverages, alcoholic	Film, photographic
Bicycles	Food processing
Boat building	Furniture
Boiler works	Hemp and jute products
Business machines	Laundries
Cameras and photo equipment	Leather and tanneries, excluding enameling or japanning
Canneries, including food products	Machinery
Clothing	Millwork, woodworking and wood distillation
Condensed and powdered product manufacture	Motion picture and television filming
Construction and agricultural machinery	Musical instruments

Moderate-Hazard Factory and Industrial Occupancies *(Cont.)*	
Optical goods	Soaps and detergents
Paper mills or products	Sugar refineries
Plastic products	Textile mills, including canvas, cotton cloth, bagging, burlap, carpets and rags
Printing or publishing	Tobacco
Recreational vehicles	Trailers
Refuse incinerators	Upholstery and manufacturing shops
Shoes	—

Use Group F-2 Structures: Factory and industrial occupancies which involve the fabrication or manufacturing of noncombustible materials, that, during finishing, packing or processing, do not contribute to a significant fire hazard, are classified as Use Group F-2. The manufacturing processes listed in the following table are indicative of those classified as Use Group F-2.

Low-Hazard Factory and Industrial Occupancies	
Beverages, nonalcoholic	Gypsum
Brick and masonry	Ice
Ceramic products	Metal fabrication and assembly
Foundries	Water-pumping plants
Glass products	

High-Hazard Use Groups

All structures which are occupied for the manufacturing, processing, generation, storage or other use of hazardous materials in excess of the exempt quantities specified in Section 307.8 of the BOCA building code are classified as Use Group H-1, H-2, H-3 or H-4.

Institutional Use Groups

All structures in which people suffering from physical limitations because of health or age are harbored for medical or other care or treatment, or in which people are detained for penal or correction purposes, or in which the liberty of the inmates is restricted, are classified as Use group I-1, I-2 or I-3.

Use Group I-1: This use group includes buildings and structures which house six or more individuals who, because of age, mental disability or other reasons, must live in a supervised environment but who are physically capable of responding to an emergency situation without personal assistance. Where accommodating persons of this description, the following types of facilities are classified as I-1 facilities: board and care facilities, alcohol and drug centers and convalescent facilities. A facility such as the above with five or less occupants is classified as a residential use group.

Use Group I-2: This use group includes buildings and structures used for medical, surgical, psychiatric, nursing or custodial care on a 24-hour basis of six or more persons who are not capable of self-preservation. Where accommodating persons of this description, the following types of facilities are classified as I-2 facilities: hospitals, nursing homes (both intermediate care facilities and skilled nursing facilities), mental hospitals and detoxification facilities. A facility such as the above with five or less occupants is classified as a residential use group.

Use Group I-3: This use group includes buildings and structures which are inhabited by six or more persons who are under some restraint or security. An I-3 facility is occupied by persons who are generally incapable of self-preservation due to security measures which are not under the occupants' control. Where accommodating persons of this description, the following types of facilities are classified as I-3 facilities: prisons, jails, reformatories, detention centers, correctional centers and prerelease centers.

Mercantile Use Group

All buildings and structures which are occupied for display and sales purposes involving stocks of goods, wares or merchandise incidental to such purposes, and are open to the public, are classified as Use Group M. Such occupancies include retail stores, automotive service stations, shops, salesrooms and markets.

Residential Use Groups

Use Group R-1 Structures: This use group includes all hotels, motels, boarding houses and similar buildings arranged for shelter and sleeping accommodations for more than five occupants who are primarily transient in nature, occupying the facilities for a period of less than 30 days.

Use Group R-2 Structures: This use group includes all multiple-family dwellings having more than two dwelling units, except as provided for in Use Group R-3 for multiple single-family dwelling units, and includes all boarding houses and similar buildings arranged for shelter and sleeping accommodations in which the occupants are primarily not transient in nature.

Use Group R-3 Structures: This use group includes all buildings arranged for occupancy as one- or two-family dwelling units, including not more than five lodgers or boarders per family, and multiple single-family dwellings where each unit has an independent means of egress and is separated by a 2-hour fire separation assembly.

Use Group R-4 Structures: This use group shall include all detached one- or two-family dwellings not more than three stories in height, and the accessory structures. All such structures are designed in accordance with the requirements applicable to Use Group R-3.

Storage Use Groups

All structures which are primarily used for the storage of goods, wares or merchandise are classified as Use Groups S-1 or S-2.

Use Group S-1: Buildings occupied for the storage of moderate-hazard contents which are likely to burn with moderate rapidity, but which do not produce either poisonous gases, fumes or explosives are classified as Use Group S-1. A motor vehicle repair garage is that portion of a property wherein major repairs, such as engine overhauls, painting or body work, are performed on motorized vehicles and is a part of this use group.

Use Group S-2: Low-hazard storage occupancies include buildings occupied for the storage of noncombustible materials and low-hazard wares that do not ordinarily burn rapidly, such as products on wood pallets or in paper cartons without significant amounts of combustible wrappings, but with a negligible amount of plastic trim such as knobs, handles or film wrapping. Such occupancies are classified as Use Group S-2.

Utility and Miscellaneous Occupancies

Buildings and structures of an accessory character and miscellaneous structures not classified in any specific use group, fall under Group U. Some of the buildings that fall under this group are listed in the following table.

Utility and Miscellaneous Occupancies	
Agricultural buildings	Livestock shelters
Barns	Detached private garages
Carports	Greenhouses
Grain silos	Sheds having a building area less than 2500 sq. ft.
Stables	

Building code requirements are specific and exact for each type of occupancy.

12-1   If a fire protection system is installed in a building for which a fire protection system is not required, what standards and installation regulations apply?

A) All building code regulations apply

B) No code regulations apply

C) Only minimum code regulations apply

D) Exact requirements are left to the discretion of the authority having jurisdiction

Answer: A

Even if a fire protection system is not required in a specific building, all code-specified regulations must be observed, including equipment, installation and use.

12-2   Which of the following is the best description of a standpipe system?

A) A standby alarm system

B) A secondary fire-suppression system

C) Piping and valves for use as a fire protection system

D) A dry-chemical extinguishing system

Answer: C

A standpipe system is a fire protection system that consists of a network of piping, valves, and hose connections that provides fire-water supply.

12-3   A multiple-station smoke detector, as shown in Figure 12-1 on the next page, provides which of the following?

A) Two or more detectors for a single fire incidence

B) Activation of several sprinkler heads

C) Both smoke and heat detection

D) Interconnection between separate detectors

Answer: D

Multiple-station smoke detectors are single-station smoke detectors that can be interconnected so that when any one alarm is sounded, all connected device alarms are sounded.

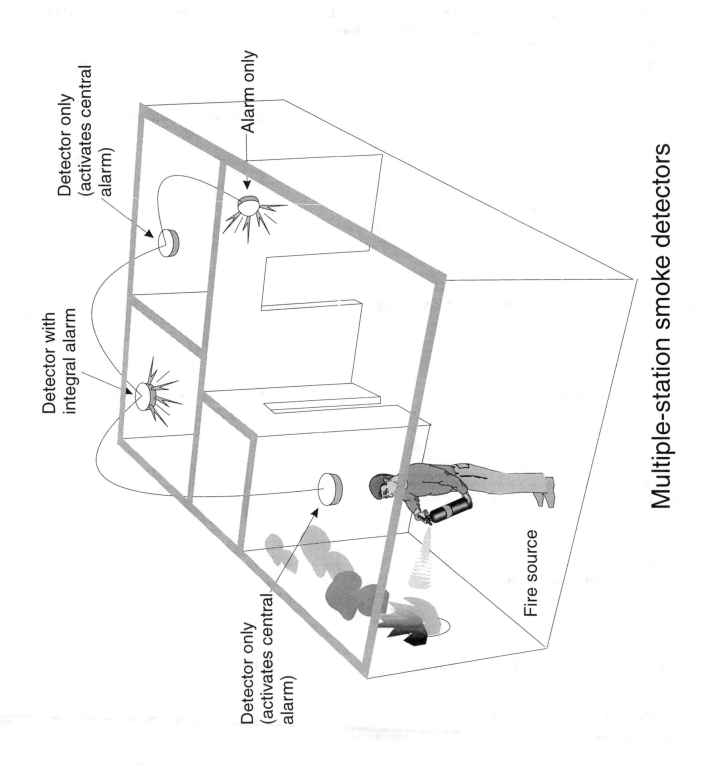

Figure 12-1: Typical installation of multiple-station smoke detectors.

12-4   Who is responsible for the inspection of fire protection systems for proper maintenance?

A) The building inspector

B) The fire department

C) The owner of the building

D) The system's manufacturer

Answer: B

The fire department inspects fire protection systems regularly to see that such systems are being adequately maintained.

12-5   What do most building codes consider a use group?

A) A group of buildings or building complex

B) A category describing how a building will be used

C) The construction type of a group of buildings

D) The particular people who will use a building

Answer: B

Use groups are categories of occupancy that describe the use to which a building will be put. For instance, an assembly use means that a building will be used primarily for a congregation of people in one or more rooms; a dance hall or theater are assembly uses.

12-6   Which of the following is not included in a residential occupancy (use group R)?

A) Apartment buildings

B) A dormitory

C) Rest or nursing homes

D) Motels

Answer: C

Most codes categorize nursing homes as an institutional occupancy (use group I). The occupants are in a residential setting but are under the care of others.

12-7   A standard water-sprinkler fire protection system can be used in areas housing all except which of the following?

A) Paper

B) Quicklime

C) Wooden furniture

D) Dining rooms

Answer: B

Extinguishing systems must be compatible with the agents being stored or housed. Quicklime is incompatible with a water extinguishing system.

12-8   The actuation of water-sprinkler systems is best described by which of the following?

A) Fire department actuation

B) Central panel control actuation

C) Automatic actuation

D) Actuation by trained personnel

Answer: C

Normally, most codes require water sprinklers to be automatically actuated.

12-9   Which of the following does not require specific fire protection by most codes?

A) Commercial kitchen exhaust hoods

B) Commercial linen chutes

C) Bathroom exhaust fans

D) Hazardous exhaust ducts

Answer: C

Exhausted air from bathrooms is not considered to be a fire hazard by most codes.

12-10   Which of the following are required by most codes for limited area sprinkler systems?

A) Alarms

B) Automatic actuation

C) At least 30 sprinkler heads

D) A minimum 6-inch water supply main

Answer: B

Limited area sprinkler systems must be automatically actuated, requiring no manual assistance.

12-11   Which of the following standpipe systems is approved by most codes and is the best choice for use in open parking structures?

A) A wet system utilizing antifreeze compounds

B) An automatically actuated system

C) A wet standpipe system

D) A dry standpipe system

Answer: D

A dry standpipe system is approved by most codes for use in open parking structures because it can be protected from freezing.

12-12   At what height above the floor level are standpipe hose connections required to be located?

A) The centerline to the hose connection must be 5 feet above the floor

B) Not more than 5 feet above the floor

C) At least 5 feet above the floor

D) Between 5 and 6 feet above the floor

Answer: B

Hose connections must be no more than 5 feet above the floor level.

12-13   Which of the following standpipe specifications must be compatible with the local fire department?

A) The hose connection diameter

B) The hose threads

C) The hose valves

D) The height of the hose connection

Answer: B

Most codes require that the threads on the hose connections of standpipes be compatible with the hose threads of the local fire department. Hose connections are required to be 2½-inches in diameter.

12-14   Making a smoke vent operational, or the actuation of a smoke vent, must comply with which of the following?

A) Manual operation only

B) Automatic actuation by a smoke detector

C) Manual and automatic operation

D) Only be automatic operation

Answer: C

Most codes require smoke vents to have an automatic activation that is initiated by a heat-responsive device. Smoke vents must also be capable of manual operation.

12-15   Which of the following does not apply to portable fire extinguishers?

A) They must be installed in accordance with NFPA 10

B) They must be installed at commercial kitchen exhaust hoods

C) They are required in lecture halls

D) They are not required in buildings that are equipped with sprinkler systems

Answer: D

Most codes have requirements for portable fire extinguishers that are separate from any requirements for sprinklers. Many areas that are required to have sprinkler systems also have requirements for portable fire extinguishers.

Chapter 13

Related Trades

A contractor is a person or firm that furnishes supplies and performs work at a given price or wage, usually based on a contract. There are many types of contractors — from the small builder or remodeler to huge organizations with offices and projects around the world.

General Contractors

Most construction projects are handled by a general contractor who is responsible for the overall construction of the entire project and coordinates the work schedules of all specialty contractors (also called subcontractors).

When a construction project is put out for bid, the general contractor requests bids from specialty contractors — electrical, mechanical, painting, structural, and others. These bids are combined to form the overall bid or price for the entire project. Consequently, most construction projects use both a general contractor and several subcontractors.

Construction Workers

Much time and expense are involved in any building project before the actual work begins. However, all the contract negotiations and planning would be in vain were it not for the skilled worker. The trades are the backbone, arms, and legs of the construction industry. No building could ever be constructed without them.

It takes excavators to dig the foundation; carpenters to construct forms for the footings; masons, concrete finishers, and ironworkers to construct foundations; masons and carpenters to erect the walls; roofers to finish the roof; electricians to install the electrical system; plumbers to install the plumbing; and HVAC workers to install heating, cooling, and ventilation systems.

Other specialty trades may also be required, such as millwrights, pipefitters, floor finishers, painters, and instrumentation personnel. It takes a close working team of skilled professionals to complete a building accurately and on time.

Organization and Structure

The building construction industry is organized into three sectors:
- Residential
- Commercial
- Industrial

The residential sector supports construction of single- and multifamily dwellings. Projects range from home alterations and improvements to the construction of modular homes, land-tract developments, and townhouses.

The commercial section supports construction of nonresidential buildings including stores, high-rise offices, churches, schools, and shopping complexes.

The industrial general contractor normally constructs warehouses, industrial complexes, automobile assembly plants, pharmaceutical manufacturing plants, oil refineries, and so on.

Most large industrial contractors keep key workers from each trade on their staff. When a new project begins, these workers supervise their particular trade at the job site. The trade workers, however, are usually hired locally.

Heavy Construction Contractors

There is also a fourth group of general contractors who specialize in heavy construction projects such as highways, streets, railroads, sewer systems, airport runways, bridges, tunnels, and elevated highways. These contractors fall into two major groups:

- Highway and street construction
- All other heavy construction projects

Special Trade Contractors

The general contractor subcontracts work when it is cost-effective to do so, or when the general contractor does not have the required expertise. Consequently, specialized trade workers are called on throughout the different phases of the construction project.

As subcontractors, specialized trade contractors report directly to the general contractor and must complete their work within a specified time. The general contractor is usually responsible for the entire project, including the work done by all subcontractors.

13-1   Which of the following trades is usually responsible for building the concrete forms for the foundation walls in Figure 13-1?

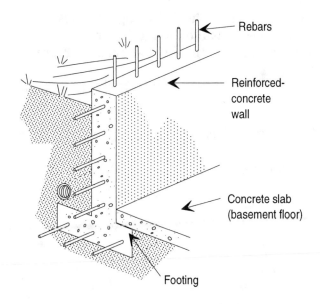

A) Carpenters

B) Drywall installers

C) Ironworkers

D) Concrete finishers

Figure 13-1: Building foundation, footings, and concrete slab.

Answer: A

Carpenters have traditionally been responsible for building wooden concrete forms. Even with newer steel and fiberglass forms, the carpentry trade is usually responsible for form erection and demolition, but the responsible trade also frequently depends upon local labor agreements.

13-2   Which of the following trades would normally be responsible for installing the rebars for the project in Figure 13-1?

A) Carpenters

B) Drywall installers

C) Ironworkers

D) Concrete finishers

Answer: C

The reinforcing steel used in the concrete footings and foundation walls in Figure 13-1 would normally be handled by ironworkers. Careful coordination is required between the carpenters who build the forms and the ironworkers who install and support the rebars at the same time.

13-3   Which of the following trades will be responsible for the concrete pour of the foundation walls and concrete slab of the project shown in Figure 13-1?

A) Carpenters

B) Drywall installers

C) Ironworkers

D) Concrete finishers

Answer: D

Concrete workers will assist in the concrete pour and also finish (smooth) the walls and floor once the concrete begins to set.

13-4   Which of the following trades is usually responsible for mixing the mortar for the concrete blocks and brick in Figure 13-2?

A) Masons

B) Concrete finishers

C) Ironworkers

D) Drywall finishers

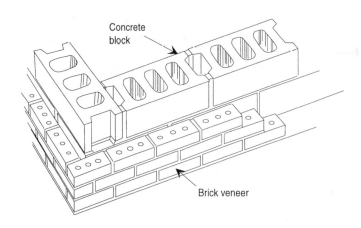

Figure 13-2: Masonry construction is used to some extent in nearly all types of building projects.

Answer: A

Masonry contractors provide a wide range of construction services including bricklayers, stone masons, concrete finishers, and plasterers. Masons or their helpers will be responsible for mixing the mortar for the masonry work in Figure 13-2.

13-5   Which of the following best describes the trade that will lay the concrete block for the project in Figure 13-2?

A) Concrete finishers

B) Stone masons

C) Bricklayers

D) Block masons

Answer: D

Block masonry is similar to bricklaying. On most projects, bricklayers lay both brick and concrete block, but a block mason is the best answer. The pay for both bricklayers and block masons is comparable.

13-6   Who is normally responsible for installing the metal wall ties between the concrete block wall and the brick veneer in Figure 13-2?

A) Metal building assemblers

B) Masons

C) Ironworkers

D) Concrete finishers

Answer: B

Masons will insert the metal wall ties into mortar joints of the concrete blocks as the wall is being constructed. The bricklayers, in turn, will fit these wall ties into the mortar joints of the brick as the veneer is installed.

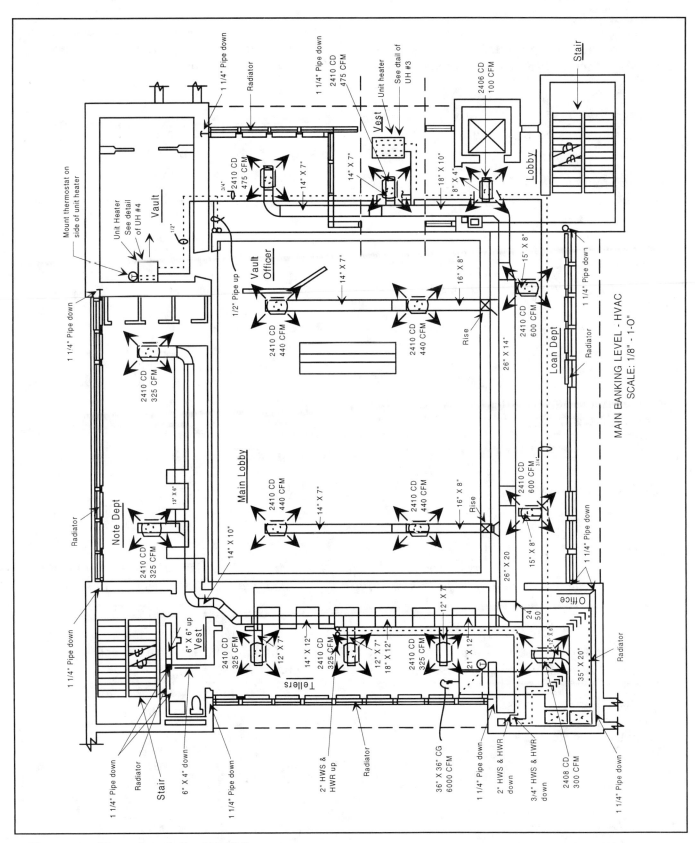

Figure 13-3: Floor plan of a bank building.

13-7   The floor plan in Figure 13-3 shows 4 devices in the main lobby, designated 2410 CD and 440 CFM. Which of the following answers best describes this type of device?

A) Certificate of Deposit number 2410 valued at $440

B) Catalog number 2410 ceiling diffuser with air velocity of 440 cu. ft. per minute

C) Catalog number 2410 ceiling damper with air resistance of 440 cu. ft. per minute

D) Compact disk intercom system with designated catalog number and operating voltage

Answer: B

The "2410 CD" designates a catalog number 2410 ceiling diffuser designed to deliver 440 cu. ft. of air per minute.

13-8   Which of the following trades would be responsible for installing the ductwork for the system in Figure 13-3?

A) Industrial coaters

B) Insulation workers

C) HVAC workers

D) Millwrights

Answer: C

Although sheet metal workers may fabricate the ductwork for the HVAC system, HVAC workers will be responsible for the installation of all ductwork, diffusers, grilles, dampers, turning vanes, etc.

13-9   Note the thermostat requirement in the vault area of the bank building in Figure 13-3. Which of the following trades is most likely to install this control?

A) Insulation workers

B) Pipefitters

C) Millwrights

D) Instrumentation workers

Answer: D

The instrumentation trade involves developing, installing, and repairing instruments and control devices that are used throughout the construction industry.

13-10   Which of the following best describes the trade that installs, transports, operates, and maintains heavy machinery?

A) Insulation workers

B) Millwrights

C) Glaziers

D) Pipefitters

Answer: B

Millwrights install, transport, operate, and maintain heavy machinery, such as rigging devices, hoists, and jacks. Millwrights are also usually skilled in several other trades in the construction industry, which is important to small construction firms.

13-11   Which of the following trades would be responsible for installing a fire-suppressor sprinkler system for the bank building in Figure 13-3?

A) Firefighters

B) Insulation workers

C) Pipefitters

D) Millwrights

Answer: C

Pipefitters design and install various types of piping systems such as hot water lines, sprinkler systems, lubricating systems, and heating and cooling systems — to name a few.

13-12   Which of the following trades would be responsible for installing plate glass windows for the bank building in Figure 13-3?

A) Insulation workers

B) Millwrights

C) Glaziers

D) Pipefitters

Answer: C

Glaziers cut and install glass for windows, doors, and other opening devices. These trade workers are found in glass production plants and large commercial installations. Very few residential projects require glaziers because most residential windows and doors are ready-made at the factory.

13-13 The harsh environments of many industrial establishments destroy certain materials — especially metal — if they are not properly treated. Which of the following trades is responsible for this treatment?

A) Insulation workers

B) Millwrights

C) Industrial coaters

D) Painters

Answer: C

Many specialized paints, fiberglass wrappings, and other coatings have been developed to protect industrial equipment and related systems that are exposed to harsh environments. The highly specialized industrial coater analyzes, designs, and installs such coatings.

13-14 Which of the following trades must design and make geometric shapes that require a good knowledge of math, including plane and solid geometry?

A) Welders

B) Sheet metal workers

C) Pipefitters

D) Millwrights

Answer: B

Sheet metal workers install and repair ventilation and air ducts for HVAC companies. Much time is spent cutting and molding sheets of metal into workable products of almost every conceivable shape and size.

13-15 Which of the following trades would be responsible for joining structural steel members using heat or pressure?

A) Ironworkers

B) Millwrights

C) Welders

D) Pipefitters

Answer: C

Welders unite pieces of steel and other metals using either arc, gas, or resistance welding methods. The skilled welder understands each type and knows what type is best to use on a specific project.

13-16   Which of the following trades would be responsible for the installation of dumbwaiters and escalators?

A) Insulation workers

B) Demolition workers

C) Roofers

D) Elevator constructors

Answer: D

Elevator workers construct and install elevators, dumbwaiters, and escalators. These workers also inspect, maintain, and repair elevators, as well as modify older elevator systems to keep up with changing technology, safety codes, and regulations.

13-17   Which of the following trades would most likely have a need for explosives in their line of work?

A) Demolition workers

B) Sheet metal workers

C) Pipefitters

D) Millwrights

Answer: A

When a building is no longer fit for use or renovation, it must be destroyed by a qualified demolition crew. These workers frequently use explosives and wrecking machines to do their job. Some demolition workers operate heavy machinery, while others handle explosives.

13-18   Which of the following trades would would normally be responsible for installing both metal and precast concrete decks?

A) Ironworkers

B) Concrete finishers

C) Welders

D) Roofers

Answer: D

Roofers install metal decks, asphalt shingles, slate shingles, and cedar shingles on residential and commercial projects. Industrial and heavy commercial projects often use precast concrete decks and poured lightweight concrete decks.

The Building and Construction Industry
Organization of Contractors

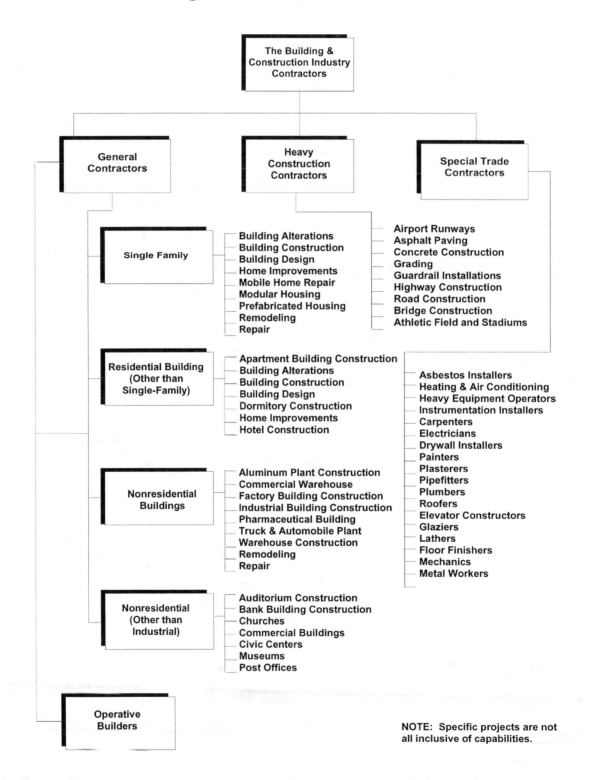

Figure 13-4: Organizational structure of contractors in the building and construction industry.

Chapter 14

Types of Construction

Building types, used to describe the type of occupancy, are covered in Chapter 12 – Fire Protection Systems. This chapter deals with construction material and the methods used to install them.

In general, six basic types of building construction are in common use:

- Wood frame
- Masonry
- Reinforced concrete
- Structural steel
- Steel frame
- Prefabricated structures

In many cases, two or more of the basic types of structures are incorporated into a building or sections of it. For example, most residential buildings, regardless of structure type, will have a masonry or reinforced concrete foundation. The remaining structure may consist of wood framing, masonry, brick veneer on wood framing or any of the other types of construction.

Wood-Frame Structures: The most common form of building structure for residential applications in the United States is the wood-frame building, with various types of outside finishes — including brick veneer, stone veneer, clapboard, and the like.

Masonry Structures: Probably the simplest form of building structure is masonry, which is erected by placing, one upon the other, small units of clay brick, clay tile, or cement blocks bonded together with cement mortar. However, except for ground-floor or basement slabs, the floor, ceiling, and roof construction of masonry structures is usually of wood frame. Masonry is used also in conjunction with reinforced concrete and structural steel to form portions of the exterior walls and interior partitions of buildings.

Reinforced Concrete Structures: Reinforced concrete construction is commonly used in many sections of the country for multifamily units; that is, apartment houses. Such construction requires the building of forms — either from plywood or prefabricated metal. Once the forms are erected, the necessary steel reinforcing rods are inserted within the forms for the foundations, walls, floor slabs, and the like. Concrete is poured into or onto the forms. When it has hardened or "set up" sufficiently (usually within 28 days), the forms are stripped off. Reinforced concrete is also used in conjunction with structural steel in buildings for the construction of floors, exterior walls, and some interior partitions.

Structural Steel: A framework of steel columns and beams is constructed with sections of various sizes of steel I-beams, angles, channels, and plates, which are usually bolted together. In some instances, particularly in the case of small-sized members, they may be welded together instead of bolted.

Steel-Frame Structures: Open steel-frame construction, usually with exterior walls of masonry or galvanized corrugated sheet steel, is sometimes used in garages and other outbuildings around residences — especially around farm dwellings. The floors are usually a concrete slab on the ground. The roofs are of the tar-and-gravel built-up type on wood sheathing or corrugated sheet steel.

Prefabricated Structures: Prefabricated construction has been used extensively in recent years for residential buildings. Such construction is usually of wood frame with plywood or plasterboard exterior and interior sheathing. Sections of floors, walls, and roofs are constructed at a central yard

and the proper sections shipped to the building site, where they are assembled by contractors. Many steel-frame structures are also prefabricated before delivery to the job site.

Wood Construction

Wood has been used for building homes for centuries. In some buildings, the first or ground floor consists of a concrete slab poured on the graded and prepared surface of the ground. In such cases a layer of crushed rock or gravel is usually spread on the graded ground surface, and wire mesh reinforcing is put in place, over which the concrete is poured. See Figure 14-1.

Wood-frame floor construction consists of horizontal floor joists of 2-inch-thick or larger timbers on edge, and of a width and length required by the length of the span between the supporting walls and the load to be carried by the floor. Such floors are usually rough-sheathed with plywood nailed to the topside of joists, with the finish floor placed over the rough sheathing. See Figure 14-2. Sound-deadening or insulating materials may be placed in the frame floor construction.

Walls: The walls of a building serve two purposes; primarily to enclose and subdivide the building into rooms, and also to support the roof structure or additional floor and wall structures of multifloor buildings. The type of construction de-

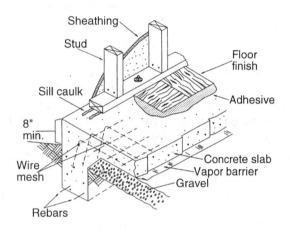

Figure 14-1: Details of a wood structure built on a concrete slab.

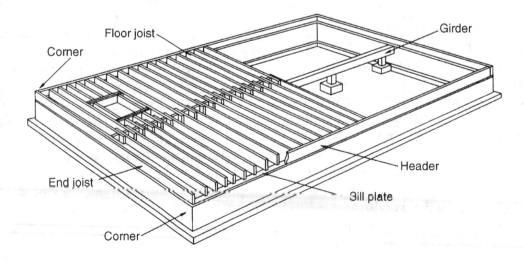

Figure 14-2: Floor framing details.

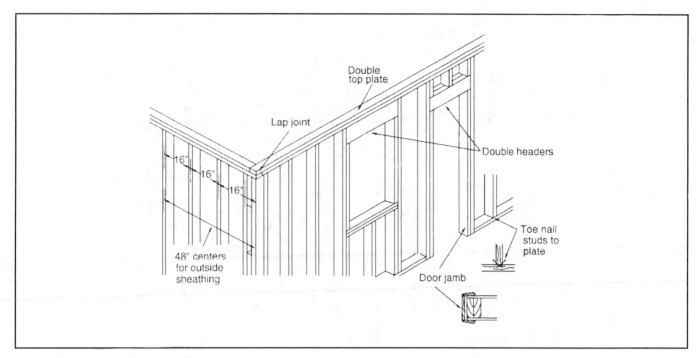

Figure 14-3: Principles of framing for door and window openings.

pends upon the purpose served and the weight to be supported.

In the case of frame construction, the walls consist of vertical wood studding to which the exterior sheathing is nailed and the interior wall surface applied. Diagonal wood bracing of one form or another is nailed or otherwise secured between the studs to keep the studs in a vertical position and also to make them less susceptible to twisting. Wood blocking is often secured between the studs to give the walls rigidity and, in the case of enclosed walls, to serve as fire blocking. The studding is usually nailed to a horizontal bottom or sole plate consisting of a 2-inch-thick board and to a horizontal top plate or partition cap consisting of two 2-inch-thick boards as shown in Figure 14-3.

Roofs: Wood-frame roof construction varies from flat roofs, with only a slight pitch, through hip roofs, gable roofs, gambrel roofs, and mansard roofs, to the relatively steep-pitched "A-frame" and similar designs. Special "sawtooth" construction and self-supporting wood-frame arch construction are adapted to some forms of construction. However, the majority of residential buildings use wood-truss supporting construction with wood purlins and plywood sheathing. Typical roof framing is shown in Figure 14-4 on the next page.

Types of Wood Structures

Wood structures are built in many different ways, ranging from pole construction to sophisticated, complex designs. Since wood structures are used far greater than any other type of residential building construction, let's take a look at some of the more popular designs.

Post and Beam Construction: This type of building system uses heavy posts and beams to form the base framework. The use of timbers creates a load-bearing system that allows an open arrangement. The wall areas, except for the posts, are nonbearing. Heavy planks are used on the floor and roof. This type is widely used for ultra-modern residential construction where cathedral ceilings are prevalent.

Pole Construction: This type of construction is popular for storage buildings, warehouses, temporary construction job shacks, and also for farm buildings. Poles are used as the main support members.

A-Frame Construction: An A-frame design is often used for summer or vacation homes, especially in the eastern United States. As the name implies, the house is constructed with an "A" shape when viewed from the ends.

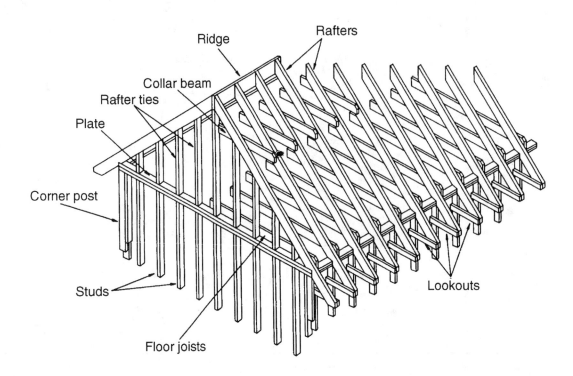

Figure 14-4: Typical roof framing.

Balloon Framing: This type of house framing was popular during the early part of this century. In this type of construction, the studs are continuous from the foundation sill to the roof line. Joists at each floor are nailed to the sides of the studs and rest on a ribbon or ledger board.

Platform Framing: This widely used framing method for residential construction utilizes a complete platform at each floor level. Walls are constructed separately and are then raised in place on the platform. Refer back to Figure 14-2.

Masonry Structures

Masonry construction of all types has proven its usefulness through the centuries. Bricks, concrete blocks, tiles, and other variations have been used for all types of construction from gate posts to huge office buildings.

For economy in most types of commercial construction, the standard 8 × 8 × 16-inch and 4 × 8 × 16-inch concrete blocks still dominate the field, but many new shapes and sizes are also available. Some, too, are colored, or they have polished or cut

faces which resemble stone. Large and small sizes with different shapes are also used to vary the pattern in walls. Lintel and jamb blocks for doors and windows are prefabricated, ready for use.

Concrete blocks are used mostly for foundation work in residential construction, or to provide fire-wall construction in town houses or multifamily developments. For interior basement walls, furring strips are often used over the blocks, and then some type of wallboard is used for the interior finish.

Standard bricks are frequently used to face concrete block when the block is above ground. Wood structures are often brick veneered and usually provide better insulation than when brick is used on concrete block walls.

Regardless of the type of masonry used, all are bonded together with mortar. To form a good bond between concrete blocks or bricks, mortar must have sufficient strength and be workable. Unless properly mixed and applied, the mortar will be the weakest part of any type of masonry. Both the strength and the waterproofing of masonry work depend largely on the strength of the mortar bond. Consequently, the home inspector must always check the mortar joints of masonry construction. Weak joints cause water leaks that will eventually weaken structures, and may jeopardize a lending institution's investment.

Bricks and Brickwork

Standard bricks manufactured in brick factories are usually $2\frac{1}{4} \times 2\frac{1}{4} \times 8$ inches. Handmade bricks, along with English and Roman bricks, are sometimes of other dimensions.

Brick Veneer: In brick veneer construction the brick is used only as a facing material, without utilizing its load bearing properties. The brick is applied over wood framing and sheathing on both old and new houses.

Veneered walls resist fire exposure better than frame walls. The brick can be laid in any type bond or pattern formed by the use of half-bricks as headers.

In new construction, the foundation walls should extend 5 inches outside the face of the wood sheathing to receive the brick veneer. On old buildings, the veneer should be started on the projecting portion of the footing.

The wood walls should be covered with waterproof building paper. The brick veneer is then anchored in place with one non-corroding metal tie for each two-foot square of brick area. The ties should be spaced not more than 24 inches apart horizontally and vertically.

Brick veneer can also be applied on concrete walls, or more commonly, cement block walls. A shelf angle secured by an anchor bolt imbedded in the concrete supports the brick veneer, or brick ties are embedded in the mortar joints of concrete block walls. Dovetail anchor slots are provided to hold the brick to the wall. The space between the brick and the concrete or concrete block wall is sluiced with mortar or grout.

Concrete Block Walls

Because of their strength and fireproofing qualities, concrete blocks are one of the most widely used materials in masonry work.

Blocks are available in colors that are durable and easily maintained. Concrete blocks can also be spray painted. A waterbase paint mixed with portland cement, or a paint with a latex-vinyl or acrylic-emulsion base, may be used. Before painting the wall, a sealer coat should be applied to close up all pores in the cement.

Prefabricated Structures

Prefabricated homes have become quite common over the past couple of decades. Sometimes called *industrialized buildings,* they use a high degree of prefabricated construction or building components or both. For example, a house may use partially prefabricated components such as windows, doors, trusses, and the like. In some cases, a whole section may be built at the factory and delivered to the job site. In many cases, whole houses — usually delivered in two sections — are built at the factory and then joined at the job site.

14-1   Why does heavy-timber wood framing have a relatively high fireresistant rating?

A) It is usually covered with noncombustible finishes

B) It produces smoke that is mainly vaporized water

C) Charred surfaces act as a fire insulator

D) Green timber that does not ignite easily is always used

Answer: C

Building codes acknowledge that heavy timber (8 inches minimum thickness or width) produces a charred surface when exposed to fire. This charred surface, in turn, protects the timber from further burning — similar to applied fireproofing materials.

14-2   The use of combustible piping materials is permitted in accordance with which of the following codes?

A) Electrical and plumbing

B) Electrical and mechanical

C) Piping and mechanical

D) Mechanical and plumbing

Answer: D

The use of combustible piping materials is permitted in accordance with the mechanical and plumbing codes listed in BOCA.

14-3   Buildings and structures of Types 1 and 2 construction are those in which the walls, partitions, floors and ceilings, etc., are constructed of what kind of materials?

A) Any material approved by the local building inspector

B) Approved noncombustible materials

C) Unapproved noncombustible materials

D) Heat-treated nonflammable materials

Answer: B

According to national building codes, Types 1 and 2 materials must be approved noncombustible materials.

14-4   What type of construction utilizes steel I-beams, angles, channels, etc. as the main structure?

A) Prefabricated construction

C) Modular construction

B) Structural steel construction

D) Wood-frame construction

Answer: B

Structural steel construction is a framework of steel columns and beams with sections of various sizes of steel I-beams, angles, channels, and plates, which are usually riveted together.

14-5   What is a more common name for industrialized buildings?

A) Prefabricated structures

C) All metal office buildings

B) Portable homes

D) Reinforced concrete buildings

Answer: A

Sections of prefabricated structures are constructed at a central yard and shipped to the building site where they are assembled by contractors.

14-6   What must be used in conjunction with concrete when reinforced concrete is used for the structural support?

A) Welded wire mesh

C) Reinforcing bars

B) Rivets

D) Nuts and bolts

Answer: C

Reinforced concrete construction is commonly used in many sections of the country for apartment houses. Such construction requires the building of forms which have been reinforced with steel bars before the concrete is poured to give it added strength.

14-7   Why is it important to use steel column top plates when steel columns are used to support heavy wood beams?

A) To help level the beam

B) For adequate connection from beam to column

C) The unit-bending stresses in the wood beam are reduced

D) The unit stress perpendicular to the wood grain is reduced

Answer: D

Building code requirements are based on the fact that the relatively thin steel column walls will punch into the wood grain to an unacceptable depth. With the addition of a steel column top bearing plate, the load is evenly distributed from the wood beam to the column.

14-8   Figure 14-5 shows a construction detail drawing (vertical section) of floor joists framed into a wood stud wall. What type of framing is shown?

A) Ledgered

B) Balloon

C) Platform

D) Heavy timber

Answer: B

Balloon framing was once very popular in the United States. This type of framing can be found in many older buildings. The wall studs are continuous from floor to roof with a wooden ribbon inletted into the studs to act as a bearing level.

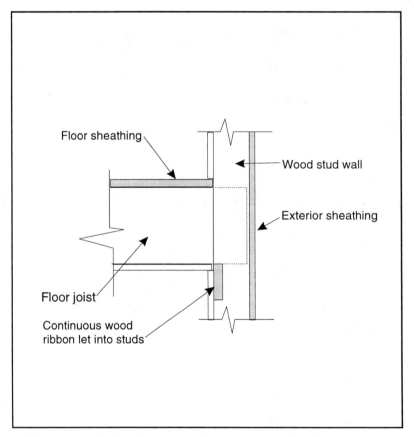

Figure 14-5: Vertical cross section of structure framing.

14-9   Prefabricated wood roof trusses (gang-nailed) are kept in a vertical position to prevent bowing out, horizontally, under full-load stress by which of the following types of bracing?

A) Winding

B) Staggered

C) Continuous

D) Lateral

Answer: D

Lateral bracing uses horizontal wood members to brace individual web members of a truss. Sometimes, such wooden members are installed diagonally in continuous horizontal rows.

14-10   What are the actual cross-sectional dimensions of standard commercially dressed 2 × 10 lumber?

A) $1\frac{1}{2} \times 10\frac{1}{4}$ inches

B) $1\frac{1}{2} \times 9\frac{1}{4}$ inches

C) $1\frac{1}{2} \times 9$ inches

D) 2×10 inches

Answer: B

Commercially produced and graded lumber in the United States is cut to exact standard dimensions. A 2 × 10 (nominal dimensions) board is cut to exactly $1\frac{1}{2} \times 9\frac{1}{4}$ inches.

14-11   Which of the following best describes the structural conditions when using brick facing over wood-stud wall construction as shown in Figure 14-6?

A) The structural load on the stud wall is doubled

B) The structural dead load on the foundation remains the same with or without the brick facing

C) The structural load on the foundation must support the load of the stud wall as well as the brick facing

D) The structural load of the brick facing increases the load on the stud wall by approximately 20%

Answer: C

Building codes do not allow masonry facing or veneer to contribute any structural capability to the walls upon which they are applied. However, the additional weight of the veneer's dead load must be supported by the foundation and related footing.

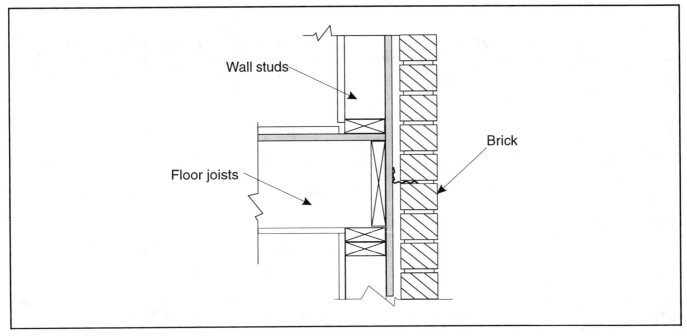

Figure 14-6: Wall section of wood-frame construction with brick veneer.

14-12   Why are vertical joints normally installed in long lengths of masonry walls?

A) For crack control

B) For aesthetic purposes only

C) To provide stops for different runs of block

D) To provide nailing access to wood backing

Answer: A

Vertical joints, called "control joints," are installed to help control vertical wall cracks in masonry construction.

14-13   What is the maximum allowable wall height for a one-story exterior masonry bearing wall, laterally braced by the roof, that is built using standard hollow core 10-inch concrete block?

A) 10 feet

B) 15 feet

C) 17 feet

D) 18 feet

Answer: B

Hollow core exterior block walls must have lateral bracing at intervals not exceeding 18 times the nominal block thickness. Since standard concrete block has a nominal thickness of 10 inches, 10 × 18 = 180 inches or 15 feet.

14-14   Which one of the following dimensions is an accurate description of 1 course of standard concrete block as shown in Figure 14-7?

A) 8½ inches

B) 7½ inches

C) 8 inches

D) 7¾ inches

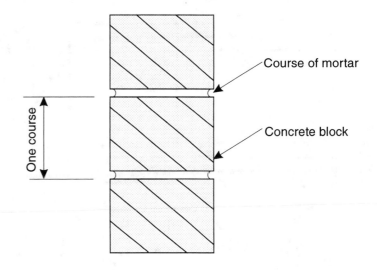

Answer: C

The block is actually 7¾ inches high and the mortar joint is ¼ inch high. Consequently, a course of concrete block includes the block and one mortar joint for a total height of 8 inches.

Figure 14-7: Cross-sectional view of a concrete block wall.

14-15   The diagrams in Figure 14-8 represent cross-sectional views through a simple-span reinforced concrete beam in 4 different positions. Which diagram shows the correct design orientation of the beam?

A) **a**   C) **c**

B) **b**   D) **d**

Answer: D

Reinforced concrete beams are designed with the bulk of the reinforcing steel (rebars) located in the bottom or lower half of the beam because the greatest tension stresses occur at this location. Steel reinforcing provides resistance to tension stress, which in turn, adds to the structural strength of the beam. Concrete alone does not have this advantage.

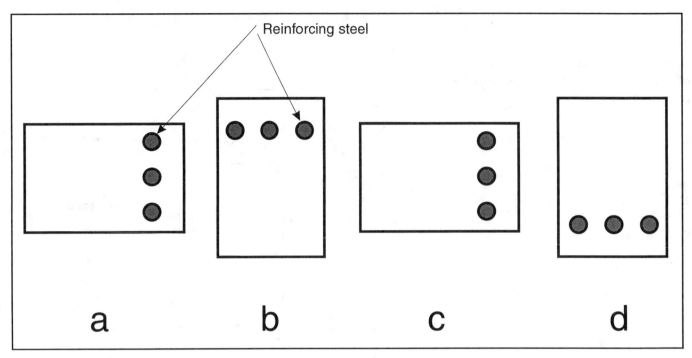

Figure 14-8: Reinforced concrete beams.

14-16   What is the minimum allowable thickness for a concrete floor slab supported directly by the ground?

A) $2\frac{1}{2}$ inches

B) 3 inches

C) $3\frac{1}{2}$ inches

D) 4 inches

Answer: C

Building codes require floor slabs, poured directly on grade, to be at least $3\frac{1}{2}$ inches thick.

14-17   Special mixes for concrete are sometimes required when exposed to certain concrete-damaging substances. Which of the following is particularly damaging to concrete?

A) Water and acidic soil

B) Salts and sulfates

C) Hail and ice

D) Oil and gasoline

Answer: B

Chlorides and sulfates are particularly damaging to concrete surfaces. Sulfates may exist in various types of soil, and chlorides may be in the form of deicing salt or sea water.

14-18   Which of the following best describes precast construction?

A) Concrete that is mixed and poured to obtain high strength

B) Concrete cast at a location away from the building site

C) Concrete formwork that is designed to be removed earlier than usual

D) Building framework installed prior to most other types of construction

Answer: B

Precast concrete is cast at a location away from the building site under controlled design conditions.

14-19   Why do the columns in most prefabricated metal buildings gradually increase in thickness from the floor to the roof?

A) Bending stresses are higher at the top of the column

B) More surface area is needed at the top of the column for attachments

C) The roof purling need additional support at the column top

D) Additional room is needed for welding

Answer: A

Many types of pre-engineered buildings make use of rigid structural frames that use columns and roof beams as a single component. Such components join together at the junction of the wall and roof in a widened "knee" where most of the bending stresses occur.

14-20   Which of the following is an accurate description of prefabricated wood wall panels?

A) Bracing is not required on prefabricated wood structures

B) Bracing for prefabricated wood structures is identical to conventional structures

C) Bracing is handled solely by the sheathing on prefabricated structures

D) Bracing is required only from the top of the foundation to the first floor line

Answer: B

Building codes require the walls in both conventional and prefabricated structures to be braced according to the same code requirements.

14-21   Why is it usually necessary to install reinforcing steel in both the top and bottom of footings for prefabricated metal building columns?

A) Roof loads are greater than when using conventional framing

B) Footing must be extremely large for prefabricated metal buildings

C) Construction loads place greater stress on the footings

D) Uplift loads may be as great as downward structural loads

Answer: D

Roof loading, due to wind and snow, may cause one side of a rigid frame-type building to compress down onto a footing, while at the same time, the other side may tend to pull out of the ground — taking the footing with it. This condition necessitates placing reinforcing steel in both the top and bottom of footings used for prefabricated metal buildings.

14-22   What type of wood framing is shown in Figure 14-9?

A) Balloon

B) Pole

C) Platform

D) Multistory

Answer: C

Platform framing is the most common type currently used for wood-frame construction in the United States.

14-23   What is the main reason for the 3-stud arrangement at the corners of the building in Figure 14-9?

A) For added support where most roof stress will occur

B) To provide a nailing surface for the exterior sheathing

C) To provide a nailing surface for the corner bracing

D) To provide a nailing area for the interior wall finish

Answer: D

While the 3 studs at the corners provide a nailing surface for the exterior sheathing, the main reason for the stud arrangement is to provide a nailing surface for the interior drywall, gypsum board, or other interior finish.

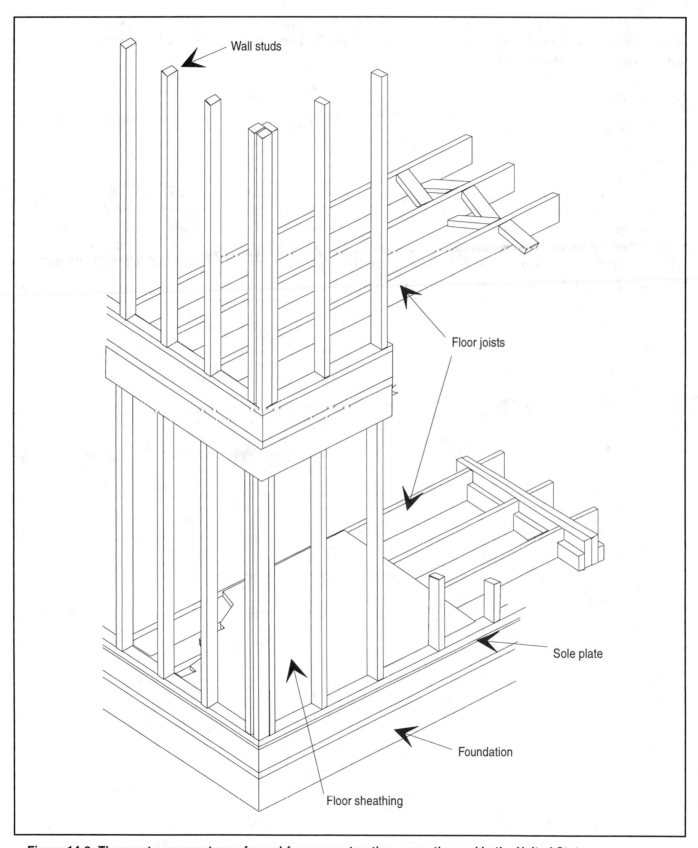

Figure 14-9: The most common type of wood-frame construction currently used in the United States.

14-24   What is the name given to the diagonally-installed braces between the floor joists supporting the second floor?

A) Bridging

B) Crowning

C) Firestops

D) Top plates

Answer: A

One method of bracing floor joists is by using short strips of 1- × 3-inch lumber nailed diagonally between the joists from top to bottom. However, most building codes no longer require bridging between residential floor joists; that is, for spans not exceeding 15 feet and where the joist depth is no greater than 12 inches. Recent studies have found that no significant transfer of loads occur after the subfloor and finish floor are installed. The studies also showed that bridging increases the likelihood of squeaking floors if the subfloor is not glued to the joists.

Chapter 15

Special Construction

Besides conventional residential, commercial, institutional, and industrial building, there are other types of construction that fall under the category of "special construction." Construction projects falling under this group include:

- Signs
- Membrane structures
- Temporary structures
- Canopies and awnings
- Pedestrian walkways
- Floor-resistant construction
- Radio and television towers and antennas
- Window-cleaning safeguards

Signs: Any fabricated sign or outdoor display structure, including its support members, consisting of any letter, figure, character, mark, point, plane, marquee sign, design, poster, pictorial, picture, stroke, stripe, line, etc. is considered by building codes to be a *sign* and falls under the special construction category.

Membrane structures: Any air-supported, air-inflated, membrane-covered cable and membrane-covered frame structures, are collectively known as *membrane structures*, and are regulated by most building codes if they are erected for a period of 90 days or longer.

Temporary structures: Any membrane structures erected for less than 90 days, or other type of structures erected for a period of less than 180 days, are known as *temporary structures* and are regulated under this category by building codes.

Canopies and awnings: These coverings are governed by most building codes and include structures that are supported in whole or in part by members resting on the ground, and used for patio covers, car ports, summer houses or other similar use. Building codes further cover awnings which are architectural projections that provide weather protection, identify or decorate and are wholly supported by the building to which they are attached.

Pedestrian walkways: An exterior elevated pedestrian walkway that connects buildings is covered under special construction by most building codes, and is regulated accordingly.

Flood-resistant construction: All buildings and structures erected in areas prone to flooding must be constructed and elevated as required by national and local building codes.

Radio and television towers: These towers must be designed and constructed for the prevailing wind load and if located atop a building, must have the same fireresistant rating as the building.

Antennas: A building permit is normally not required for radio and television antennas that are not more than 12 feet in height. Permits, however, are usually required if the antennas are more than 12 feet in height above the roof of the building on which they are erected.

15-1   When are window-cleaning safeguards required on multistory buildings?

A) When buildings are more than 2 stories

B) When buildings are more than 3 stories

C) When buildings are more than 4 stories

D) When buildings are more than 5 stories

Answer: C

All buildings and structures over 50 feet or 4 stories in height, in which the windows are cleaned from the outside, must be provided with safeguards for all window openings.

15-2   Which of the following is not an approved window-cleaning safeguard?

A) Anchors

B) Belt terminals

C) Awnings

D) Motorized vertical scaffold with guard rails

Answer: C

Awnings are not safeguards; the remaining answers are safeguards that are approved by most building codes.

15-3   Which of the following dish antennas are subject to the structural provisions of building codes?

A) Antennas over 1 foot in diameter

B) Antennas over 14 inches in diameter

C) Antennas over 18 inches in diameter or 2 sq. ft., whichever is greater

D) Antennas over 2 feet in diameter

Answer: D

Dish antennas larger than 2 feet in diameter are subject to the structural provisions of most building codes, including snow-load provisions, unless the antenna system has a heater to melt falling snow.

15-4   What provisions must be made during the design and construction of radio and television towers to resist wind uplift?

A) Towers must resist 2 times the calculated wind uplift

B) Towers must resist 3 times the calculated wind uplift

C) Towers must resist 4 times the calculated wind uplift

D) Towers must resist 5 times the calculated wind uplift

Answer: A

Building codes require adequate foundations and anchorage must be provided to resist 2 times the calculated wind uplift.

15-5   Which of the following methods are approved for providing ready access to television towers for inspection purposes?

A) 6-foot step ladders

B) Step bolts and ladders

C) Chain hoists

D) 24-foot extension ladder

Answer: B

Towers must be located and equipped with step bolts and ladders so as to provide ready access for inspection purposes.

15-6   Which of the following is an accurate statement regarding structural loads on radio and television towers?

A) Towers must be designed for the dead load, wind loads, plus the ice load in regions where ice formation occurs.

B) Only live loads are considered in the design of radio and television towers

C) Towers must be designed for the dead load plus the ice load in regions where ice formation occurs.

D) Only wind loads are considered in the design of radio and television towers

Answer: A

The structural provisions of building codes require radio and television towers to be designed for the deal load plus 2 times the calculated wind uplift, and the ice load in regions where ice formation occurs.

15-7   Which of the following is the best definition of an *open sign*?

A) A sign in which at least 20% of the enclosed area is open to the transmission of wind

B) A sign in which at least 30% of the enclosed area is uncovered or open to the transmission of wind

C) A sign in which at least 40% of the enclosed area is open to the transmission of wind

D) A sign in which at least 50% of the enclosed area is open to the transmission of wind

Answer: D

Building codes classify an open sign as one in which at least 50% of the enclosed area is uncovered or open to the transmission of wind.

15-8   Which of the following is the best definition of a projecting sign?

A) A sign that extends more than 12 inches from the building wall to which it is attached

B) A sign that extends more than 15 inches from the building wall to which it is attached

C) A sign that extends more than 24 inches from the building wall to which it is attached

D) A sign that extends more than 36 inches from the building wall to which it is attached

Answer: B

Any display sign that is attached directly to a building wall, and which extends more than 15 inches from the face of the wall, is known as a projecting sign.

15-9   Which of the following takes precedence over building codes in regard to the erection of display signs?

A) The owner of the property

B) The owner of the sign

C) The authority having jurisdiction

D) Zoning laws

Answer: D

The limitations of zoning laws that affect the requirements and occupancy of land takes precedence over the regulations of building codes.

15-10   In most areas, who may order the removal of any display sign that is not maintained in accordance with the provisions of building codes?

A) Any law-enforcement officer

B) The city or county Board of Supervisors

C) The code official having jurisdiction

D) The city or county Board of Trustees

Answer: C

Most building codes and local ordinances allow the code officials in the area to order the removal of any sign that is not maintained in accordance with the local code.

15-11   Wall signs with an area of over 40 sq. ft. must be constructed of which of the following materials?

A) Metal or other approved noncombustible material

B) The same material used to construct the wall to which the sign is attached

C) California redwood, red cedar, or locust wood

D) Any material that is easily and readily removed without harm to the building's finish

Answer: A

Wall signs must not extend beyond the ends of the wall to which they are attached and must be made of metal or other approved noncombustible material, except for nailing rails and as otherwise provided in the building codes.

15-12   What is the maximum allowable height that a closed roof sign may project above the roof of a building with Types 1 and 2 construction?

A) 25 feet

B) 50 feet

C) 75 feet

D) 100 feet

Answer: B

A closed roof sign must not be erected to a height greater than 50 feet above the roof of buildings with Types 1 or 2 construction. A sign may project to a maximum height of 35 feet above the roof of buildings with Types 3, 4, and 5 construction.

15-13   Whenever an auxiliary inflation system is required for a membrane structure, which of the following must be provided?

A) Not less than 3 separate electric services

B) An approved standby power-generating system

C) A 12-volt battery with a connected inverter to change dc to ac

D) At least one spare motor of the proper horsepower rating and motor code number

Answer: B

An approved emergency standby power-generating system must be provided and the system must be equipped with a suitable means for automatically starting the generator set upon failure of the normal electrical power.

15-14   What is the classification of buildings that are connected by pedestrian walkways?

A) All connected buildings are considered to be one structure

B) All connected buildings are considered to be one structure if all are owned by one individual or the by the same corporation

C) Connected buildings are considered to be separate structures

D) Connected buildings are considered to be separate structures only when designated as such by the architect or consulting engineer

Answer: C

Except where buildings are located on the same lot in accordance with building code specifications, buildings connected by pedestrian walkways are considered to be separate structures.

15-15   Walkways must be separated from the interior of buildings by fire separation walls. What must the fireresistance rating of these walls be?

A) 1 hour

B) 2 hours

C) 3 hours

D) 4 hours

Answer: B

Separation assemblies between walkways and building interiors must have a fireresistance rating of not less than 2 hours. Furthermore, they must extend vertically from a point 10 feet above the walkway roof surface to 10 feet below the walkway and horizontally 10 feet from each side of the walkway.

15-16   When designing or constructing flood-resistant structures, which of the following agencies is considered to be the authority in establishing the official flood-hazard map?

A) National Fire Protection Association

B) American Institute of Structural Steel

C) Federal Emergency Management Agency

D) Occupational Health and Welfare

Answer: C

The most recent Flood Insurance Rate Map published by the Federal Emergency Management Agency is considered in establishing the official flood-hazard map that is used by building codes.

15-17   Which of the following building code regulations apply to structural enclosures below the base flood elevation?

A) The enclosure may not be used as a bedroom

B) The enclosure may be used only as a recreation or storage room

C) The enclosure must not contain any combustible materials

D) The enclosure must not be used for human occupancy

Answer: D

Such enclosures must not be used for human occupancy except as a means of egress from the structure, entrance foyers, stairways or incidental storage.

15-18   Which of the following conditions would classify an area of tidal influence to be in a high-hazard (V) zone?

A) Subject to wave heights in excess of 12 feet

B) Subject to wave heights in excess of 9 feet

C) Subject to wave heights in excess of 6 feet

D) Subject to wave heights in excess of 3 feet

Answer: D

Areas of tidal influence that have been determined to be subject to wave heights in excess of 3 feet, or subject to high-velocity wave run-up or wave-induced erosion, are classified as high-hazard zones.

15-19   Which of the following is an accepted foundation for structures erected in high-hazard zones?

A) Reinforced concrete footings and columns

B) Pilings or columns

C) Precast concrete footings

D) Structural steel wide-flange beams

Answer: B

All buildings or structures erected in high-hazard zones must be supported on pilings or columns and must be adequately anchored to such pilings or columns.

15-20   Which of the following is *not* a building code requirement for mobile homes?

A) A mobile unit on a permanent foundation shall comply with code requirements for on-site and prefabricated construction

B) Parking spaces for mobile units must provide anchoring for such units

C) Compliance of a mobile unit with the building code automatically provides zoning approval

D) Mobile units shall not be mounted on permanent foundations

Answer: C

A zoning ordinance and the building code are two different entities with entirely different agendas. Zoning is more of a localized form of land control — it determines if the use of the land for a mobile home or factory, etc. is acceptable. Zoning approval of a particular land use is usually required before a building permit will be issued.

15-21   Which of the following codes is used to enforce new and replacement water supply systems in high hazard zones?

A) The National Electrical Code

B) The National Plumbing Code

C) The National Mechanical Code

D) CABO

Answer: B

Most building codes recognize the National Plumbing Code as the authority on all plumbing systems, including water supply and waste removal systems.

15-22   When a walkway serves as a required exit, what is the maximum allowable length of exit access travel if an automatic sprinkler system is not present?

A) 50 feet

B) 100 feet

C) 150 feet

D) 200 feet

Answer: D

The length of exit access travel must not exceed 200 feet. If the walkway is equipped throughout with an automatic sprinkler system, it may extend up to 250 feet.

15-23   What is the minimum allowable unobstructed width of a pedestrian walkway?

A) 3 feet

B) 4 feet

C) 5 feet

D) 6 feet

Answer: A

See explanation to Question 15-24.

15-24   What is the maximum allowable width of a pedestrian walkway with or without an automatic sprinkler system?

A) 10 feet

B) 20 feet

C) 30 feet

D) 50 feet

Answer: C

The unobstructed width of pedestrian walkways must not be less than 36 inches and must not exceed 30 feet.

15-25   When exterior walls of walkway-connected buildings are required to have a fireresistance rating of more than 2 hours, which of the following is a building code requirement for walkways?

A) The walls of the walkway must have the same fireresistant rating

B) The walkway must be equipped throughout with an automatic sprinkler system

C) Both A and B

D) Neither A or B

Answer: B

Where exterior walls of connected buildings are required by national and local building codes to have a fireresistance rating greater than 2 hours, the walkway must be equipped throughout with an automatic sprinkler system installed in accordance with the national and local building codes.

Chapter 16

Special Equipment

Items falling under the category of special equipment usually include the following:

- Elevators
- Dumbwaiters
- Moving walks
- Escalators
- Special hoisting equipment
- Special conveying

Contractors installing special equipment also frequently inspect, maintain, troubleshoot, and repair the equipment as well. Furthermore, these same contractors modify existing systems to keep up with changing technology, safety codes, and regulations. Figure 16-1 on the next page shows the basic elevator construction process.

Definitions

The following words and terms are used for questions in this chapter and should be understood before proceeding.

Dumbwaiter: A hoisting and lowering mechanism with a car of limited capacity and size which moves in guides in a substantially vertical direction and is used exclusively for carrying materials, not people.

Elevators: A hoisting and lowering mechanism equipped with a car or platform to transport individuals or freight in a substantially vertical direction.

- *Freight elevator:* Primarily used for carrying freight and on which only the operator and the persons necessary for loading or unloading are permitted to ride.
- *Hand elevator:* A manually-driven freight elevator.
- *Hydraulic elevator:* A power elevator in which the motion of the car is obtained through the application of force from liquid under pressure.
- *Passenger elevator:* Used for the transportation of individuals.
- *Power elevator:* The motion of the car is obtained through the application of force other than by hand or gravity.
- *Sidewalk elevator:* A freight elevator which operates between a sidewalk or other area exterior to the building and floor levels inside the building below such area, and which does not have a landing opening into the building at its upper limit of travel.

Elevator Repairs: All work necessary to maintain elevator equipment in a safe and serviceable condition, including troubleshooting malfunctions

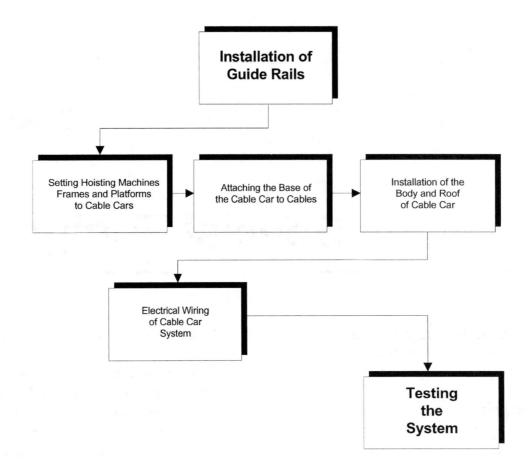

Figure 16-1: Elevator construction process.

and adjusting or replacing defective, broken or worn parts.

Escalator: A power-driven, inclined, continuous stairway used for raising and lowering passengers.

Hoist, Material: A nonpermanent mechanism and its hoistway for use in conjunction with the construction, alteration or demolition of a building or structure. It is equipped with a suspended platform, car, cage or bucket that moves vertically and is used exclusively for raising or lowering materials. It is controlled from a point outside the conveyance.

Hoist, Personnel: A nonpermanent mechanism and its hoistway for utilization in conjunction with the construction, alteration or demolition of a structure. It is utilized for the raising and lowering of people or materials.

Hoisting and Conveying Equipment, Special: Manually or power-operated hoisting, lowering or conveying mechanisms — other than elevators, es-

calators or dumbwaiters — for the transport of persons or freight in a vertical, inclined or horizontal direction on one floor or in successive floors. Types include:

- Automotive lift
- Conveyors
- Freight lift

Hoisting and Elevating Equipment, Miscellaneous: All power-operated hoisting and elevating equipment for raising, lowering and moving persons or merchandise from one level to another, such as inclined elevators, slings and hooks, and tiering and piling machines not permanently located in a fixed position.

Moving Walk: A type of passenger-carrying device on which passengers stand or walk, and in which the passenger-carrying surface remains parallel to its direction of motion and is uninterrupted.

16-1   How frequently must manlifts be tested to ensure that the installation is operating safely?

A) At intervals of not more than 6 months

B) At intervals of not more than 3 months

C) Monthly

D) Weekly

Answer: A

Building codes require that manlifts be periodically inspected at intervals of not more than six months, and at intervals not exceeding those set forth in ASME A17.1 for elevators, escalators, dumbwaiters and moving walks.

16-2   Which of the following personnel is allowed to operate a passenger elevator prior to obtaining a certificate of compliance from the local code official?

A) Only the owner of the building

B) The architect

C) Only the installer

D) The consulting engineer

Answer: C

It is unlawful for any persons other than the installer to operate passenger elevators until such equipment has been inspected, tested and approved for a certificate of compliance issued by the local code official.

16-3   Which of the following is required by the building code to be installed in each elevator lobby at each floor and associated machine/equipment room?

A) An ash tray

B) A sand bucket to enable smokers to safely extinguish cigars and cigarettes

C) A cellular phone

D) Smoke detectors

Answer: D

Smoke detectors must be installed in accordance with national and local building codes.

16-4   If an automatic sprinkler system is installed in elevator hoistways or elevator equipment rooms, what other devices must be installed in these same areas?

A) Standpipe system

B) Heat detectors

C) A cutoff valve

D) Exact requirements are left to the discretion of the authority having jurisdiction

Answer: B

Where an automatic sprinkler system is installed in hoistways or elevator equipment rooms, heat detectors must be installed in the same areas in accordance with national and local building codes. The heat detectors must be designed to initiate power disconnect to the affected elevator.

16-5   If the same conditions exist as described in Question 16-4, when should the sprinkler system be designed to activate?

A) Before the heat detectors disconnect the electrical power to the affected elevator

B) Before and after the heat detectors sense excessive heat

C) 10 minutes after the heat detectors are activated

D) After the heat detectors disconnect the electrical power to the affected elevator(s)

Answer: D

Sprinkler systems must be designed to activate after the actuation of heat detectors which in turn, must be designed to initiate power disconnection to the affected elevators.

16-6   Where 4 or more elevators all serve the same portion of a building, what are the minimum number of hoistways allowed?

A) 1

B) 2

C) 3

D) 4

Answer: B

Building codes require a minimum of 2 hoistways if 4 or more elevators serve the same portion of a building.

16-7   What are the maximum number of passenger elevators allowed in a single hoistway?

A) 1

B) 2

C) 3

D) 4

Answer: D

No more than 4 elevators are allowed in any one hoistway.

16-8   A pictograph sign, of an approved standardized type, must be posted over each elevator call station on all floors. What must this sign indicate?

A) Minors are not allowed to operate automatic elevator systems unless accompied by an adult

B) Cigar and pipe smoking are not allowed on elevators, only cigarettes

C) In case of fire, occupants must not use the elevators; stairways are the approved method of exit

D) Only certified elevator operators are allowed to operate nonautomatic systems

Answer: C

An emergency sign must be present to indicate to occupants that elevators must not be used in case of fire. This sign is not required, however, for elevators that are part of an accessible means of egress that complies with building code requirements.

16-9   What is the required fire protection rating of hoistway doors that open into vestibule openings which are protected with assemblies having a fire protection rating of not less than 1 hour ?

A) 15 minutes

B) 30 minutes

C) 45 minutes

D) 1 hour

Answer: C

Building codes require that hoistway doors used in the described situations must have a fire protection rating of not less than $^3/_4$ hour.

16-10   Which of the following must be constructed of approved noncombustible and fireretardant materials when used on escalators and moving walks?

A) Electrical equipment

B) Wiring

C) Handrails

D) Backing for wood veneers on balustrades

Answer: D

Escalators and moving walks must be constructed of approved noncombustible and fireretardant materials except electrical equipment, wiring, wheels, and handrails. The wood veneers used on balustrades must be backed up with noncombustible materials.

16-11   Escalators must be equipped with a power-operated automatic shutter at every floor pierced by the apparatus and the shutter must be constructed of approved noncombustible materials with a fire protection rating. What must this rating be?

A) Not less than 30 minutes

B) Not less than 45 minutes

C) Not less than 60 minutes

D) Not less than 90 minutes

Answer: D

Automatic fire shutters for escalator systems must have a fire protection rating of not less than $1\frac{1}{2}$ hours.

16-12   Where must hoistway vents for passenger elevators be located?

A) In the side of the hoistway enclosure directly below the floor at the top of the hoistway

B) In the side of the hoistway enclosure directly above the floor at the top of the hoistway

C) In the side of the hoistway enclosure directly above the floor at the bottom of the hoistway

D) In the bottom of the hoistway enclosure directly below the floor at the bottom of the hoistway

Answer: A

Hoistways of elevators serving more than 3 stories must be provided with a means for venting smoke and hot gases to the outer air in case of fire. These vents must be located in the hoistway enclosure directly below the floor at the top of the hoistway.

16-13   Which elevator type below is the best answer to the following definition? A power elevator in which the motion of the car is obtained through the application of force from liquid under pressure.

A) Power elevator

B) Freight elevator

C) Hydraulic elevator

D) Sidewalk elevator

Answer: C

A hydraulic elevator is the best answer for this definition.

16-14   What type of equipment would you use to lift an automobile to a showroom on the top floor of a building?

A) Special hoisting and conveying equipment

B) Dumbwaiter

C) Material hoist

D) Miscellaneous hoisting and elevating equipment

Answer: A

This equipment group includes manual or power-operated hoist mechanisms, other than elevators, escalators or dumbwaiters. One type is an automotive lift.

16-15   Which of the following are the main types of equipment used to transport individuals in a building?

A) Sidewalk elevator, hand elevator and conveyor

B) Passenger elevator, escalator and moving walk

C) Sidewalk elevator, moving walk and conveyor

D) Dumbwaiter, passenger elevator and moving walk

Answer: B

The passenger elevator, escalator and moving walk are principally for use in transporting individuals. The other types of conveyances are for freight or materials.

16-16   Which of the following best describes a sidewalk elevator?

A) A freight elevator that operates between the exterior sidewalk level and floor levels within a building

B) A hand elevator that operates between the interior of the building at sidewalk level and other floor levels within a building

C) A passenger elevator that operates between the exterior sidewalk level and floor levels within a building

D) A freight elevator that operates between the interior of the building at sidewalk level and other floor levels within a building

Answer: A

Building codes define sidewalk elevator as a freight elevator that operates between a sidewalk or other area exterior to the building and floor levels inside the building below such area, which does not have a landing opening into the building at its upper limit of travel.

Chapter 17

Safety Codes

Every building contractor has the responsibility to provide a safe and healthy working environment for employees.

Federal OSHA

The Federal Occupational Safety and Health Act (OSHA) consists of several volumes: OSHA Safety and Health Standards for the Construction Industry, 29 CFR 1926/1910, contains the minimum safety standards that apply to the construction industry. These standards must be strictly followed. The document is available from the district or state Office of Occupational Safety and Health or from the Superintendent of Documents, U.S. Government Printing Office, Washington, D.C. 20402.

OSHA establishes the safety and health obligations of employers toward their employees. In general, the Act requires that employers provide an accident prevention plan and that the employment place is free of harmful and lethal hazards.

State Safety Requirements

Most states have adopted federal safety standards. However, there are several state standards that regulate activities not presently covered by federal OSHA. There are also a number of state standards that are substantially different from federal standards covering the same subject matter. Consequently, candidates for the building contractor's exam should obtain a copy of the local safety requirements. The agencies listed in Appendix I of this book should either be able to furnish state and local safety requirements for building contractors, or else be able to give the name and address of another agency to contact for such information.

General Requirements

Each employer must investigate all work-related injuries and occupational diseases, and any sudden or unusual occurrence or change of conditions that pose an unsafe or unhealthy exposure to employees.

Within 48 hours of an occurrence, each employer must notify the nearest office of the Area Director of the Occupational Safety and Health Administration to report any:

- Work-related fatalities
- Disabling, serious, or significant injury
- Occupational disease

Employers with 11 or more employees are not only subject to OSHA safety requirements, but also must maintain records of all occupational injuries and illnesses regardless of severity, including:

- Cuts, fractures, sprains, or amputations that result from work-related activity
- Abnormal conditions caused by inhalation, absorption or ingestion

- Injuries which result in death, lost work-days, restriction of work or motion, loss of consciousness, job transfer, or medical treatment other than first aid

Generally, an accident is not recordable if only first-aid treatment is required.

Each employer must maintain a log and summary of all recordable occupational injuries and illnesses for his establishment. These records are maintained on a calendar year basis and kept for five years. The information should be entered on the log and summary as early as possible, but not later than six working days after receiving the information. For this purpose, Federal OSHA Form 200 or any private equivalent form may be used.

The log and summary should be available for inspection at each establishment plus a supplementary record for that establishment. Federal OSHA Form 101 or an acceptable alternative form may be used, but the record must be completed in the detail prescribed in the instructions with Form 101. The supplementary record also should be completed within six working days after receiving information that a recordable case has occurred.

Safety Standards

Federal OSHA safety standards contained in 29 CFR 1926/1910 are requirements that contractors must be familiar with and follow. The following paragraphs briefly describe sections from these safety standards which deal with contractor-related subjects. However, contractors should be aware that these sections are not all-inclusive. Each contractor is responsible for determining standards of safety for each of his or her projects.

Safety Training: Employers must instruct their employees to recognize and avoid unsafe conditions.

Medical Services and First Aid: Employers must ensure, before starting a project, that prompt medical service is available if a serious injury should occur. First-aid kits must be easily accessible to employees.

Sanitation: A supply of drinking water in an approved container and drinking cups shall be provided for employees. Approved toilet facilities must be provided for employees.

Head Protection: In areas where there is a possible danger from falling or flying objects, protective helmets are to be provided for employees.

Ear Protection: When levels and duration of noise are above permissible limits, employers must provide ear protection devices for their employees. Plain cotton is not an acceptable protective device.

Eye Protection: The employer must provide protective equipment when employees must work around machinery or chemicals that present potential eye or face injury.

Fire Protection: Employers shall develop fire protection programs and provide firefighting equipment. Access to firefighting equipment must always be available. Firefighting equipment is to be periodically inspected and maintained in good operating condition. Fire extinguishers shall be provided and maintained in good operating condition.

Tools: All hand and power tools shall be maintained in a safe condition. When guards are available for power tools, the guards must be used.

Scaffolds: Scaffolds must be erected so they are sound, rigid, and can carry the maximum intended load. Guardrails and toeboards must be installed on platforms that are more than 10 feet above ground.

Motor Vehicles: Strict standards exist for vehicles that are operated within an off-highway jobsite. Some of the subjects in this section include requirements for:

- Braking systems: service, parking, and emergency brakes.
- Lighting systems: headlights, taillights, and brake lights.
- Reverse signal alarms or observers to assist in backing a vehicle.
- Windshields, wipers, and defrosting devices.
- Protective shields if the vehicle is loaded by cranes, shovels, etc.
- Adequate seats if employees are transported in the vehicle.

17-1   According to the Occupational Safety and Health Act, which of the following work accidents does not have to be recorded?

A) An injury that requires medical treatment other than first aid

B) An injury that involves loss of consciousness

C) An injury that involves only first-aid treatment

D) An injury that requires a transfer to a different job

Answer: C

An injury to an employee, such as a small cut or abrasion, that involves only first aid does not have to be recorded under the current OSHA regulations.

17-2   What is the maximum height that a working platform may be before guardrails and toe boards are required to be installed on all open sides and ends?

A) 10 feet

B) 12 feet

C) 14 feet

D) 16 feet

Answer: A

OSHA standard 1926.451 — Scaffolding requires guardrails and toe boards on all platforms which are more than 10 feet above the ground or finished floor.

17-3   How much weight over the maximum intended load must scaffolding and its components be capable of supporting?

A) The maximum intended load

B) Twice the maximum intended load

C) 3 times the maximum intended load

D) 4 times the maximum intended load

Answer: D

OSHA standard 1926.451(7) — requires that scaffolding must be capable of supporting 4 times the maximum intended load without failure.

17-4   If full-thickness 2- × 10-inch, undressed, scaffold-grade scaffold planking is used to support a working load of 25 pounds per sq. ft., what is the maximum allowable span?

A) 4 feet

B) 6 feet

C) 10 feet

D) 12 feet

Answer: C

OSHA standard 1926.451(7) — Scaffolding(10) states that all planking must be scaffold grade, or equivalent, as recognized by approved grading rules for the species of wood used. The maximum spans allowed are given in Table L-3 — Materials. For the conditions stated in Question 17-4, this table permits a maximum span of 10 feet.

17-5   In the absence of an infirmary, clinic, hospital, or physician, who may treat an employee in an emergency?

A) The foreman

B) A co-worker

C) Anyone who knows CPR

D) A certified EMT

Answer: D

According to OSHA standard 1926.50(c), a person who has a valid certificate in first-aid training from the U.S. Bureau of Mines, the American Red Cross, or equivalent training, must be available at the worksite to render first aid.

17-6   Some employees are required to enter into "confined and enclosed spaces" as part of their job. Which of the following best describes this phrase?

A) A clothes closet

B) Storage tanks, boilers or tunnels

C) A crawl space under a refinery

D) An underground room smaller than 4 × 6 feet

Answer: B

OSHA standard 1926.21(6ii) states that this phrase includes, but is not limited to, storage tanks, process vessels, bins, boilers, ducts, sewers, underground utility vaults, tunnels, pipelines and open top spaces more than 4 feet in depth.

17-7   When temporary sleeping quarters are necessary on a construction job, what must be provided?

A) Heat, ventilation and lights

B) A bed with clean linen

C) A sink and tub

D) A vending machine

Answer: A

OSHA 1926.51 states that temporary sleeping quarters must be heated, ventilated, and lighted.

17-8   What is the employer's responsibility in relation to a fire-protection program?

A) A lookout tower must be provided

B) Everyone must be taught how to call the local fire department

C) Firefighting equipment, a water supply and training must be provided

D) A separate hose and a suitable water supply must be provided for everyone

Answer: C

OSHA standard 1926.150 states that firefighting equipment, a water supply and trained personnel must be on the job site.

17-9   When power operated tools are designed to accommodate guards, which of the following is an accurate statement?

A) It is up to the worker to make the decision whether or not to use the guards

B) The tools must have the guards attached when in use

C) Guards are only necessary when ground-fault circuit-interrupters are not available

D) Guards apply only to cutting tools

Answer: B

OSHA Section 1926.300(b) requires guarded tools to have the guards attached when in use.

17-10   Which of the following machines do not require point of operation guarding?

A) Portable ¼-inch hand drill

C) Milling machines

B) Alligator shears

D) Power saws

Answer: A

Portable ¼-inch hand drills are not normally designed to accommodate guards. Consequently, OSHA Section 1926.300(iv) does not require these tools to be used with guards.

17-11   When would a wrench be considered an "unsafe" tool?

A) When the jaws are too tight to adjust comfortably

C) When any amount of chrome begins to flake

B) When the first sign of rust occurs

D) When the jaws are sprung to the point that slippage occurs

Answer: D

OSHA Section 1926.301 requires that employers not issue or permit the use of unsafe hand tools. Wrenches, including adjustable pipe, end, and socket wrenches, must not be used when the jaws are sprung to the point that slippage occurs.

17-12   Which of the following must be provided on pneumatic impact (percussion) tools to prevent attachments from being accidentally expelled?

A) Safety pins

C) Safety clips or retainers

B) 1-inch staples

D) Paper clips are sufficient for the purpose

Answer: C

OSHA Section 1926.302 requires safety clips or approved retainers to be securely installed and maintained on pneumatic impact tools to prevent any attachments from being accidentally expelled.

17-13   Vehicles that are operated on the jobsite only must be equipped with which of the following combinations of lighting equipment?

A) Fog lights and headlights

B) Signal lights and brake lights

C) Headlights, taillights and brake lights

D) Signal lights, fog lights and headlights

Answer: C

According to OSHA safety regulations, 1926.601, vehicles used on the job site must be equipped with two working headlights, two working taillights and brake lights.

17-14   Are safety belts required in vehicles that are used only on the job site?

A) No

B) Yes, but for the driver only

C) Yes, but only for front-seat passengers

D) Everyone riding in the vehicle must have a safety belt

Answer: D

Seat belts and anchorages meeting the requirements of 49 CFR part 571, Federal Motor Vehicle Safety Standards shall be installed in all motor vehicles.

17-15   Employees working in areas where there is a possible danger of injury from a falling object must wear which of the following?

A) A helmet

B) Ear plugs

C) Goggles

D) A cap with the company's logo on it

Answer: A

Safety standard 1926.100 states that a protective helmet must be worn when there is possible danger of head injury due to falling or flying objects.

17-16   Which of the following best describes a jobsite warning sign that has white lettering in a red oval on a black rectangular background?

A) Caution sign

B) Safety First sign

C) Danger sign

D) No Smoking sign

Answer: C

A danger sign indicates machines or areas that pose immediate hazards to workers and equipment. When this sign is encountered, the instructions must be followed exactly to avoid injury.

Chapter 18

Final Examination

Now that you have gone through all the questions in this book (and reviewed supplemental material in areas where you were weak), you should be ready for the big event — the exam to test your ability to be a building contractor. But you just don't walk into the examiner's office and say you want to take the exam; it's not quite that simple. First of all, you have to get permission to take the examination. That normally requires filling out an application in advance and paying a fee. The examining board then reviews your application and either approves or disapproves it. If approved, you will then be notified of the time and place to take your examination. If your application is rejected, the board will usually tell you why. You may then reapply at a later date once the reasons for the rejection has been taken care of.

Qualifications

The exact qualifications for a building contractor will vary from state to state. Many areas require a minimum of 5 years experience before a candidate may apply for a contractor's license to bid commercial or industrial work. Furthermore, they need a letter of recommendation from an architect, engineer, banker, or similar person before their application is even considered. Those seeking a residential contractor's license are usually required to have a minimum of 3 years experience before applying.

At the other extreme, some areas only require, and I quote, "a pickup truck and a hammer" to become a contractor. If the contractor does not live in the state, he or she must provide a payment bond to become licensed.

Steps Required to Obtain a Contractor's License

1. Obtain an application for a contractor's license from the state in which you plan to work. See Appendix I of this book for names and addresses of licensing agencies in each state.

2. Complete the license application and submit it to the appropriate agency with the required financial information and application fee.

3. If a written examination is required, complete the exam registration form and submit it with the application fee to the appropriate testing agency.

Typical Applications

The application shown in Figures 18-1 through 18-9 on the following pages is typical of those

STATE OF TENNESSEE
DEPARTMENT OF COMMERCE AND INSURANCE
CONTRACTORS LICENSING BOARD
500 JAMES ROBERTSON PARKWAY / SUITE 110
NASHVILLE, TN 37243-1150
(615) 741-8307 / 1-800-544-7693 IN STATE
FAX# (615) 532-2868

_____ Original License

_____ Second License

_____ Merger / Reorganization

_____ Buy Out / Sale of Stock

_____ Reinstatement
License No. _____

CONTRACTORS LICENSE APPLICATION

APPLICATION FEE: $150.00 (NONREFUNDABLE)

_____

_____

BUSINESS NAME TO APPEAR ON LICENSE_____

_____

MAILING ADDRESS_____

_____

CITY_____STATE_____ZIP CODE_____

BUSINESS TELEPHONE ( )_____ FAX NO._____

WATTS NO. (800)_____ CONTACT PERSON_____

TO BE COMPLETED BY INDIVIDUALS:

Owner_____Social Security #_____

TO BE COMPLETED BY PARTNERSHIPS:

Partner_____Social Security #_____

Partner_____Social Security #_____

Partner_____Social Security #_____

TO BE COMPLETED BY CORPORATIONS:

Officer_____Title _____

Social Security #_____

Officer_____Title _____

Social Security #_____

Officer_____Title _____

Social Security #_____

LIST ALL MAJOR STOCKHOLDERS OWNING 20% OR MORE OF STOCK:

_____

_____

IN-0439 (Rev. 6/95)   1   RDA 1578

Figure 18-1: Page 1 of Contractor's License Application for the state of Tennessee.

SYNOPSIS

MANNER OF OPERATION:

_____ Individual   _____ Partnership   _____ Corporation   _____ LLC

(1). List the classification(s) you are requesting to be licensed for (Refer to page ii): _____

_____

_____

(All applicants requesting a (S) Specialty license for asbestos abatement, underground storage tanks or lead abatement, must attach a current certificate of training from an approved EPA course.)

(2). What is the monetary limit you are requesting? $_____

_____

(3). Do you currently hold a Tennessee contractor's license?_____

License Number_____   Expiration_____

(4). Have you ever held a Tennessee contractor's license?_____

License Number_____   Expiration_____

(5). Do you currently hold a contractor's license in another state?_____ If yes, provide the following information:

License Number_____   Expiration_____

Classification(s)_____

_____   Monetary Limit $_____

(6). Have you ever had a state contractor's license revoked or suspended? _____ If yes, provide the following information: License Number_____State_____

Action_____

_____   Date_____

(7). Have you or your organization ever failed to complete any construction contract(s)?_____

If yes, explain:_____

_____

(8). Are any of your assets or liabilities related to any parent, subsidiary or affiliated company?

_____ If yes, provide company's name and address, explain your connection with it and state where ownership lies and percentage of ownership: _____

_____

_____

(9). Have you or your organization ever had a complaint filed relative to construction?_____

If yes, explain: _____

_____

_____

Figure 18-2: Page 2 of Contractor's License Application for the state of Tennessee.

(10). Have you ever acted as a qualifying agent for a state licensed contractor?_____ If yes, provide the fcllowing:

Company's Name _____

License Number_____Exam(s) Taken_____

_____

(11). Are you still associated with the company? _____ If yes, explain your association: _____

_____

If no, provide the date your association with the company ended: _____Why?_____

_____

(12). List the qualifying agent(s) for your organization:

Name	Title	Exam(s) Taken	Date

If exam(s) have not been taken, provide the date exam(s) are scheduled to be taken and exam site.

_____

(13). In which city do you prefer to hold your Board interview?

_____ Nashville _____ Chattanooga _____ Memphis _____ Knoxville

(14). If you are a corporation, have you registered with the Tennessee Secretary of State?_____ If yes, a copy of either your charter or certificate of authority must be attached. If no, a license will not be granted until proof of registration is provided. **(CALL 615-741-2286 FOR FORMS)**

(15). If you are a Limited Liability Company (LLC), a copy of your articles of organization must be attached. Have you received them from the Tennessee Secretary of State? _____

EXPLAIN_____

> *Note:* A Limited Liability Company (LLC) is a type of buisness structure available only in a few states. In general, the LLC combines the many favorable characteristics of corporations, limited partnerships, and general partnerships. In simple terms, an LLC is a partnership that operates as a corporation. There is no personal liability or obligation and management is vested in its members. An LLC must file its Articles of Incorporation with the State Corporation Commission.

Figure 18-3: Page 3 of Contractor's License Application for the state of Tennessee.

CONTRACTOR'S STATEMENT OF EXPERIENCE

Business Name to Appear on License _____

_____

(1). How many years has your organization been in business under your present name?

_____ years

(2). How many years experience does your organization have as a

(a) prime contractor? _____ years

(b) subcontractor? _____ years

(3). What is the construction experience of the principal individuals of your organization?

_____ years total

INDIVIDUAL'S NAME	TITLE	YEARS EXPERIENCE

(4). List the major projects your organization has completed in the past three (3) years.

YEAR	TYPE OF CONSTRUCTION WORK	CONTRACT AMOUNT	LOCATION

(5). If your organization has not completed any construction projects in the past three years, provide the construction experience of the owners and qualifying agents:

NAME	EXPERIENCE

4

Figure 18-4: Contractor's Statement of Experience form.

(6). (To be completed by highway contractors only) Are you familiar with the Standard Specifications for road and bridge construction adopted by the State of Tennessee, Department of Highways and Public Works, and approved by the U.S. Bureau of Public Roads which form the basis of proposals which are submitted?_____

REMARKS _____

_____

_____

(7). Provide names and addresses of all banks and/or financial institutions with whom you are currently doing business:

NAME	BUSINESS ADDRESS	CONTACT PERSON

(8). List the construction equipment you own, lease or rent:

EQUIPMENT	RENT	LEASE	OWN

YOU MAY ATTACH A DEPRECIATION SCHEDULE OR OTHER LISTING

(9). Has your organization established a line of credit with a supplier or furnisher of material?

_____yes _____no

(10). Have you or any member of your organization ever been convicted of a felony? (Refer to T.C.A. 62-6-118 (2) (h))

_____YES _____NO   EXPLAIN: _____

_____

_____

_____

_____
(PREPARER'S SIGNATURE)

_____
(SOCIAL SECURITY NUMBER)

_____
(DATE)

5

Figure 18-4: Contractor's Statement of Experience form. *(Cont.)*

THIS AFFIDAVIT MUST BE SIGNED AND NOTARIZED

STATE OF: _____

COUNTY OF: _____

_____, being first duly sworn, hereby deposes and
(Applicant)

says as follows:

1. I am the _____ of _____
   (Title)   (Name of Firm)
   which has applied to the Tennessee Board for Licensing Contractors for a license to engage in contracting in the State of Tennessee.

2. To the best of my knowledge, information, and belief, a petition in bankruptcy (___) **has** (___) **has not** been filed within seven (7) years preceding the filing of this application from any person who is an officer, owner, or partner of this form. If such a petition has been filed, an accurate explanation of the proceedings is attached hereto as part of this affidavit.

3. As owner/proprietor, partner, officer, director, major stockholder with this company, firm, or corporation, do hereby swear and affirm that during my association with this company, firm, or corporation, ***(___) **have** (___) **have not** been convicted of a felony, or any other conduct which constitutes improper, fraudulent, or dishonest dealing, or violation of TCA 62-6-118. (If there has been such a conviction, please attach an explanation including the name(s) and title of the person convicted.)

4. Firm (___) **has** (___) **has not** bid or performed any construction work in the State of Tennessee where the amount of the contract would require a license to engage in contracting.

   **(If you have bid in the last six months, please attach an explanation. Please note, part four (4) of this affidavit is not applicable to projects financed with Federal funds let by the Bureau of Highways with the Tennessee Department of Transportation.)

(over)

Figure18-5: Affidavit that is attached to the Contractor's License Application.

5. The foregoing statement of experience and all statements therein are true and correct. The foregoing financial statement, taken from the books is a true and accurate statement of the firm's condition as of the date thereof, and all information provided in this application is true. Further, the foregoing statements are submitted to the Board for Licensing Contractors for the express purpose of inducing the Board to license the applicant as a contractor in the State of Tennessee, and that any depository, vendor, or other agency herein named is hereby authorized to supply such Board with any information necessary to verify these statements.

THIS SECTION IS TO BE SIGNED BY EITHER THE OWNER, PARTNERS, CORPORATE OFFICERS, OR MAJORITY STOCKHOLDERS OF THE ORGANIZATION. AFFIDAVIT MUST BE NOTARIZED.

_____	_____
(Signature)	(Title)
_____	_____
(Signature)	(Title)
_____	_____
(Signature)	(Title)
_____	_____
(Signature)	(Title)
_____	_____
(Signature)	(Title)
_____	_____
(Signature)	(Title)

Sworn to me this _____ day of _____ , 19 _____

_____
Notary Public

My Commission expires: _____

SEAL

Figure18-5: Affidavit that is attached to the Contractor's License Application. *(Cont.)*

POWER OF ATTORNEY

Know all that I, _____ , of _____

County, State of _____ , major stockholder/owner of

_____ (company), do hereby appoint:

_____   _____
NAME   TITLE

to act as the qualifying agent by interviewing on the company's behalf and taking the examination(s) required for a Tennessee contractors license.

I understand that should the qualifying agent leave the company, pursuant TCA-6-115, another individual will be designated by the company to pass the examination(s), within three months.

_____   _____
Signature   Title

Sworn and subscribed to me this _____ day of _____ , 19 _____.

_____
Notary Public

My Commission Expires: _____

(To be completed by corporations and partnerships
appointing qualifying agents for testing and interview)

Figure18-6: Power of Attorney form that is attached to the Contractor's License Application in case a corporation or partnership appoints qualifying agents for testing and interviews.

REFERENCE FROM: _____ Past Client   **T.C.A. 62-6-111(b)(2)**

_____ Employer

_____ Codes Administration Official

This form is being completed by:

_____
(NAME)

_____
(MAILING ADDRESS)

_____
(CITY)   (STATE)   (ZIP CODE)

Inquiry Relating To:_____
(BUSINESS NAME TO APPEAR ON LICENSE)

Mailing Address: _____

Prior to granting a license certificate, the Board requires that a license application containing certain information relative to finances, equipment, experience, etc. be completed by the prospective applicant and submitted to the State Board for Licensing Contractors. All applicants understand that statements will be verified. The verification pertaining to the individual, partnership or corporation whose identity appears above is now in process. You can greatly assist both the applicant and the Board by furnishing information requested on this form.

How long have you known the owners/principals of the above mentioned company, firm or corporation?_____

What has been your general experience with the above?_____
_____
_____

Are you aware of any pending claims or suits against the above that are relative to construction?
_____EXPLAIN_____
_____
_____

What is your business opinion of the above?_____
_____
_____

Do you recommend that a state license be granted to the above?_____ EXPLAIN _____
_____
_____
_____

_____   _____
(SIGNATURE)   (DATE)

Figure18-7: Reference form attached to the Contractor's License Application. Your bank, a former employer, architect, engineer, and former customers are likely candidates from whom to obtain references.

issued at the state level in many areas. However, you should obtain the actual application from the state in which you plan to work to find out the exact requirements.

Financial Statements

Most applicants applying for a state contractor's license will be required to submit a financial statment. A financial statement gives an overview of the applicant's financial condition (net worth) and is arrived at by using the following equation:

$$\text{Assets} - \text{Liabilities} = \text{Net Worth}$$

Individuals applying for a contractor's license as a sole proprietor are usually required to submit the company's financial statement as well as their personal financial statement.

Partnerships applying for a contractor's license are usually required to submit a financial statement for the partnership as well as personal financial statements from each partner.

Sometimes the Contractor's Licensing Board will accept financial statements prepared by the applicant, but the Board has the option of requiring financial statements to be audited and attested to by a licensed public accountant (PA) or certified public accountant (CPA).

A financial statement can be a short one-page form as shown in Figure 18-8, or a more detailed balance sheet as shown in Figure 18-9.

It is recommended that the applicant make copies of both of these forms and practice inserting the requested information.

BALANCE SHEET			
Assets		**Liabilities**	
Checking Accounts and Cash	$	Balance on Mortgage	$
Savings and Money Mkt. Accts.		Balance on Auto Loans	
Accounts Receivable		Balance on Credit Cards	
Loans Owned		Balance on Education Loans	
Insurance Cash Value		Balance on Personal Loans	
Pension/Profit-Sharing Plans		Balance on Other Loans	
Marketable Securities		Accounts Payable	
Bonds		Other Liabilities (Please List)	
Saving Bonds/SPDAs			
IRA/Keogh Accounts			
Metals and Collectibles			
Real Estate			
Other Assets (Please List)			
Total Assets			$
		Total Liabilities	–
Net Worth			$

Figure 18-8: Short form for determining the net worth of an individual or a business.

Contractors Audited or Reviewed FINANCIAL STATEMENT—BALANCE SHEET
Audited Statements are required for license over 1,000,000.00—TCA 62-6-111-(3)
Audited or Reviewed Statements are required for licenses 1,000,000 or below—TCA 62-6-111-(4)

SUBMITTED BY_____

☐ Corporation
☐ Partnership
☐ Individual
☐ LLC

PRINCIPAL OFFICE_____

CONDITION AT CLOSE OF BUSINESS_____, 19____ ACCOUNTING YEAR END:

ASSETS	DOLLARS ONLY		
1. Cash: (a) On hand $_____ (b) In bank $_____ (c) Elsewhere $_____			
2. Notes Receivable: (a) Amounts due within one year_____			
(b) Past due_____			
3. Accounts receivable from completed contracts exclusive of claims not approved for payment_____			
4. Sums earned on incomplete contracts as shown by Engineer's or Architect's estimate:			
(a) Amount receivable after deducting amounts retained_____			
(b) Amounts retained to date, due upon completion of contracts_____			
5. Accounts receivable from sources other than construction contracts_____			
6. Deposits for bids or other guarantees: (a) Recoverable within 90 days_____			
(b) Recoverable after 90 days_____			
7. Other Current Assets_____			
8. Stocks and Bonds: Current (a) Listed____ at cost_____			
(b) Unlisted____at cost_____			
9. Materials in stock not included in Item 4: (a) For incomplete contracts (inventory value)_____			
(b) Other materials (inventory value)_____			
TOTAL CURRENT ASSETS_____			
10. Real Estate: (a) Used for business purposes_____			
(b) Not used for business purposes_____			
11. Construction Plant and Equipment, net book value_____			
12. Furniture and Fixtures, net book value_____			
13. Stocks and Bonds: Long Term (a) Listed____ at cost_____			
(b) Unlisted____ at cost_____			
14. Other Assets (Non-Current)_____			
TOTAL ASSETS_____			

LIABILITIES AND EQUITY			
17. Notes Payable (Amounts due within 1 year EXCLUSIVE of Real Estate and Equipment obligations)_____			
18. Due Sub-Contractors (retained percentage and current estimates)_____			
19. Accounts Payable: (a) Not past due_____			
(b) Past due_____			
20. Real Estate Encumbrances due within one year_____			
21. Equipment Encumbrances due within one year_____			
22. Other Current Liabilities_____			
TOTAL CURRENT LIABILITIES_____			
23. Notes Payable (Amounts due after 1 year EXCLUSIVE of Real Estate and Equipment obligations)_____			
24. Real Estate Encumbrances due after one year_____			
25. Equipment Encumbrances due after one year_____			
26. Other Liabilities due after one year_____			
TOTAL LIABILITIES_____			
27. PROPRIETOR'S OR PARTNERS' EQUITY_____			

27. SHAREHOLDERS' EQUITY:			
Capital Stock paid up — Preferred: $_____			
— Common: $_____			
Capital Surplus: $_____			
Retained Earnings: $_____			
Less Treasury Stock at cost: $_____			
SHAREHOLDERS' EQUITY_____			
TOTAL LIABILITIES AND EQUITY_____			

CONTINGENT LIABILITIES — Listed and Described on Separate Schedule _____ $____

SHOW MONEY VALUES IN EVEN DOLLARS

Figure18-9: Contractor's audited or reviewed detailed financial statement — balance sheet.

Contractors Audited or Reviewed FINANCIAL STATEMENT—DETAILS RELATIVE TO ASSETS

1★ CASH:
(a) On hand _____ $ _____
(b) Deposited in banks named below _____ _____
(c) Elsewhere—(state where) _____

NAME OF BANK	LOCATION	DEPOSIT IN NAME OF	AMOUNT

2★ NOTES RECEIVABLE:
(a) Amounts due within one year _____ $ _____
(b) Amounts past due _____

RECEIVABLE FROM: NAME AND ADDRESS	FOR WHAT	DATE OF MATURITY	HOW SECURED	AMOUNT

Have any of the above been discounted or sold? _____ If so, state amount, to whom, and reason _____

3★ ACCOUNTS RECEIVABLE FROM COMPLETED CONTRACTS exclusive of claims not approved for payment: $ _____

NAME AND ADDRESS OF OWNER	NATURE OF CONTRACT	AMOUNT OF CONTRACT	AMOUNT RECEIVABLE

Have any of the above been assigned, sold or pledged? _____ If so, state amount, to whom, and reason _____

4★ SUMS EARNED ON INCOMPLETE CONTRACTS as shown by Engineer's or Architect's estimate:
(a) Amount receivable after deducting amounts retained _____ $ _____
(b) Amounts retained to date, due upon completion of contract _____

NAME AND ADDRESS OF OWNER	NATURE OF CONTRACT	AMOUNT OF CONTRACT	% COMP.	AMOUNT RETAINED	AMOUNT DUE EXCLUSIVE OF AMOUNT RETAINED

Have any of the above been assigned, sold or pledged? _____ If so, state amount, to whom, and reason _____

*List separately each item amounting to 10 per cent or more of the total and combine the remainder.

Figure18-9: Contractor's audited or reviewed detailed financial statement — balance sheet. *(Cont.)*

Contractors Audited or Reviewed FINANCIAL STATEMENT—DETAILS RELATIVE TO ASSETS (Continued)

5★ ACCOUNTS RECEIVABLE NOT FROM CONSTRUCTION CONTRACTS: _____ $ _____

RECEIVABLE FROM: NAME AND ADDRESS	FOR WHAT	WHEN DUE	AMOUNT

What amount, if any, is past due _____ $ _____
Assigned, sold or pledged _____ $ _____

6 DEPOSITS WITH BIDS OR OTHERWISE AS GUARANTEES: _____ $ _____

DEPOSITED WITH: NAME AND ADDRESS	FOR WHAT	WHEN RECOVERABLE	AMOUNT

What amount, if any, has been assigned, sold or pledged _____ $ _____

7 OTHER CURRENT ASSETS: _____ $ _____

DESCRIPTION	AMOUNT

What amount, if any, has been assigned, sold or pledged _____ $ _____

8 STOCKS and BONDS:

13

	8	13
(a) Listed — Total Amount at cost _____	$_____	$_____
(b) Unlisted — Total Amount at cost _____	$_____	$_____
	CURRENT	LONG TERM

	DESCRIPTION	ISSUING COMPANY	NO. SHARES	UNIT COST	AMOUNTS (AT COST)	AMOUNTS (AT COST)
1						
2						
3						
4						
5						
6						
7						

	WHO HAS POSSESSION	IF ANY ARE PLEDGED OR IN ESCROW, STATE FOR WHOM AND REASON	AMOUNT PLEDGED OR IN ESCROW
1			
2			
3			
4			
5			
6			
7			

*List separately each item amounting to 10 per cent or more of the total and combine the remainder.

Figure18-9: Contractor's audited or reviewed detailed financial statement — balance sheet. *(Cont.)*

Contractors Audited or Reviewed FINANCIAL STATEMENT—DETAILS RELATIVE TO ASSETS (Continued)

9 MATERIALS IN STOCK — not included in Item 4:
(a) For use on incomplete contracts (inventory value) _____ $ _____
(b) Other materials (inventory value) _____ $ _____

| DESCRIPTION OF MATERIALS | QUANTITY | PRESENT VALUE | |
		FOR UNCOMPLETED CONTRACTS	OTHER MATERIALS

10 REAL ESTATE } Book Value }
(a) Used for business purposes _____ $ _____
(b) Not used for business purposes _____ $ _____

| DESCRIPTION OF PROPERTY | IMPROVEMENTS | | TOTAL BOOK VALUE |
	NATURE OF IMPROVEMENTS	BOOK VALUE	
1			
2			
3			
4			
5			
6			

LOCATION	HELD IN WHOSE NAME	ASSESSED VALUE	AMOUNT OF ENCUMBRANCES
1			
2			
3			
4			
5			
6			

11 CONSTRUCTION EQUIPMENT at net book value: _____ $ _____
Items may be combined by type. (List separately all items of quarries, gravel pits, warehouses and similar plants which are not included under Item 10—Real Estate)

| QUAN-TITY | DESCRIPTION | ENTER MONEY VALUE FOR EACH OF 4 COLUMNS BELOW. | | | |
		PURCHASE PRICE	DEPRECIATION CHARGED OFF	BOOK VALUE	ENCUM-BRANCES

12 FURNITURE and FIXTURES at net book value: _____ $ _____

14 OTHER ASSETS (NON-CURRENT): _____ $ _____

DESCRIPTION	AMOUNT

TOTAL ASSETS $ _____

Figure 18-9: Contractor's audited or reviewed detailed financial statement — balance sheet. *(Cont.)*

Contractors Audited or Reviewed FINANCIAL STATEMENT—DETAILS RELATIVE TO ASSETS (Continued)

15 Total value of other contracts awarded or pending award and NOT INCLUDED in foregoing statement of assets _____ $ _____

DESCRIPTION OF CONTRACT AND FOR WHOM TO BE PERFORMED	ESTIMATED DATE OF COMPLETION	AMOUNT

16 List two of largest bonds supplied in each of last three years:

OWNER	SURETY COMPANY	AMOUNT

DETAILS RELATIVE TO LIABILITIES

17
23 NOTES PAYABLE (Amounts due EXCLUSIVE of Real Estate and Equipment obligations)

	17	**23**

TOTAL AMOUNTS _____ $ _____ $ _____

TO WHOM: NAME AND ADDRESS	WHAT SECURITY	CURRENT Amounts due within one year	LONG TERM Amounts due after one year

18 DUE SUB-CONTRACTORS:
(a) Account of retained percentage _____ $ _____
(b) Current estimates _____ $ _____ $ _____ TOTAL AMOUNT

19★ ACCOUNTS PAYABLE:
(a) Not past due _____ $ _____
(b) Past due _____ $ _____

TO WHOM: NAME AND ADDRESS	FOR WHAT	WHEN DUE	AMOUNT

*List separately each item amounting to 10 per cent or more of the total and combine the remainder.

Figure18-9: Contractor's audited or reviewed detailed financial statement — balance sheet. *(Cont.)*

Contractors Audited or Reviewed FINANCIAL STATEMENT—DETAILS RELATIVE TO ASSETS (Continued)

20★ 24	REAL ESTATE ENCUMBRANCES:		**20**	**24**
		TOTAL AMOUNTS $	$	
			CURRENT	LONG TERM
	TO WHOM: NAME AND ADDRESS	FOR WHAT	Amounts Due Within One Year	Amounts Due After One Year

21★ 25	EQUIPMENT ENCUMBRANCES:		**21**	**25**
		TOTAL AMOUNTS $	$	
			CURRENT	LONG TERM
	TO WHOM: NAME AND ADDRESS	FOR WHAT	Amounts Due Within One Year	Amounts Due After One Year

22	OTHER CURRENT LIABILITIES:	$	
	DESCRIPTION	WHEN DUE	AMOUNT

26	OTHER LIABILITIES DUE AFTER ONE YEAR:	$	
	DESCRIPTION	WHEN DUE	AMOUNT

27	PROPRIETOR'S—PARTNERS'—SHAREHOLDERS' EQUITY	$

*List separately each item amounting to 10 per cent or more of the total and combine the remainder.

TOTAL LIABILITIES AND EQUITY _____ $ _____

Figure 18-9: Contractor's audited or reviewed detailed financial statement — balance sheet. *(Cont.)*

If a financial statement is required by the state in which you are applying for your contractor's license, but the Contractor's Licensing Board does not provide forms, the forms in this book may be used to send in with your application and required fee.

Registering for Examinations

Sometimes it is necessary for the applicant to register separately for the contractor's examination, especially if the exam is handled by the National Assessment Institute. The exam registration form and fee must be received by the testing agency within an alotted time before the exam. Late applications are usually returned to the applicant, and he or she must reapply for the next available exam date.

In some areas, however, if the registration deadline has passed, the applicant may prefer to register as a walk-in candidate at the exam site. Candidates who have not preregistered for the contractor's exam may register as "walk-ins" at a scheduled exam site on the date of the exam. While there are usually sufficient extra exam booklets and seating spaces to accommodate all walk-ins, acceptance is based on availability and is not guaranteed. In addition to the regular exam fees, there is a walk-in fee of approximately $25 or more per exam.

Candidates with Disabilities

If you have a disability, handicap, or other special need that prevents you from taking the exam under normal conditions, attach documentation of your handicap to your registration form and indicate in writing what special arrangements are required. You will be contacted by the testing agency.

Admissions Letters

Admissions letters are usually mailed to all pre-registered candidates ten days before the exam date. You should receive your letter approximately 1 week before the exam. The letter tells you where the exam will be given, what time you should arrive, and what you should bring with you. If you haven't received your admission letter 3 days before the exam, you should call the testing agency.

Rescheduling

If you need to reschedule your examination, notify the examining agency in writing prior to the original exam date. Indicate the new date when you wish to take your exam and include a check or money order for the rescheduling fee. Most areas do not refund examination fees.

On Examination Day

The exact schedule for contractor's exams will vary from locale to locale. However, the following is typical of states giving contractor's exams:

- 7:30 a.m.   Examinee reports to the examination center; seats are assigned.
- 8:00 a.m.   Examination orientation begins.
- 8:30 a.m.   Examination session begins.
- 12:30 p.m.   Examination session ends.

To ensure that all examinees are examined under equally favorable conditions, the following regulations and procedures are observed at most examination sites:

- Each examinee must present proper identification, preferably his/her driver's license, before he/she will be permitted to take the examination.
- Each examinee will be assigned to a seat specifically designated by name and number when admitted to the examination room, and this seat will remain his/her seat assignment for the entire examination. Once you enter the examination room, locate your assigned seat and be seated.
- Each examinee should bring a watch. No one will be permitted to work beyond the established time limits.

- Examinees should not, in most cases, bring books or other reference materials to the examination center unless instructed to do so by your state's examining agency. Many states will not allow the examinee to take the exam if notes or other reference material are brought to the exam center.

- In most states, examinees will be furnished with two #2 black lead pencils and copies of any reference material that is allowed for open-book exams. Other states have no open-book exams at all.

- Most states will allow the examinees to use noiseless, nonrecording, battery-operated calculators and/or slide rules during the examination.

- All scratch work is usually permitted only on the blank spaces included in the examination booklet, NOT in the margins of the answer sheet(s). Answer sheets should contain only the required identifying information and responses to the examination questions.

- Permission of an examination proctor must be obtained before leaving the room while the examination is in progress.

- Any examinee engaging in any kind of irregular conduct (such as giving or receiving help, conveying to others information about any questions appearing on the examination, using any materials not permitted, taking part in an act of impersonation, or removing examination materials or notes from the examination room) will be subject to disqualification and will be reported to the State Board of Examiners.

Description of the Examination

Business and law exams, along with contractor's trade exams can be open-book, multiple-choice or a combination of open-book and closed-book multiple-choice. Some testing areas have no open-book exams. You are tested solely on what you know without referring to any reference material. Some questions may refer to a drawing, table or chart located either in the text booklet or in the reference material.

Testing agencies also try to divide their questions into certain categories to ensure that most of the contracting field will be covered. The following categories appear on one state's contractor's exam. Most areas will have similar coverage.

CONTENTS OF CONTRACTOR'S EXAM	
Subject	Percentage of Total Exam
Carpentry	30%
Concrete	5%
Masonry	14%
Structural Steel and Rebar	12%
Roofing	10%
Associated Trades	10%
Excavation and Site Work	6%
Drywall	5%
Insulation	4%
Safety	4%

Please be aware that the above categories and percentages represent some testing agencies, but these vary from state to state.

Taking the Examination

In most states, the examination consists entirely of multiple-choice questions. Read all of the instructions carefully before attempting to answer any question. Reading the instructions too fast, or skipping over any part, may cause you to miss something important and possibly arrive at an incorrect answer.

Keep track of time: Do not spend too much time on any one question. If a question is difficult for you, mark the answer on the answer sheet that you think is correct and place a check by that question in the examination booklet. Then go on to the next question; if you have time after finishing the rest of the examination you can go back to the questions you have checked.

Your answers to the questions on the examination are usually recorded on separate answer sheets provided for you. See Figure 18-10. Answer spaces on the answer sheets are lettered to correspond with the letters of the possible answers printed in the examination booklet. For each question, you are to decide which one of the four possible answers is best and blacken the appropriate lettered space on your answer sheet. The following example illustrates how answers are usually marked on your qualifying examination answer sheet.

Which of the following is the easiest type of business organization to form?

A) Sole proprietorship

B) General partnership

C) Limited partnership

D) Corporation

Since choice A) is the best answer, the A) space should be blackened.

When marking answers, follow these instructions:

- Do not use ink or ballpoint pen
- Use black lead #2 pencil only
- Make heavy marks that fill the circle completely
- Erase cleanly any answer you wish to change
- Make no stray marks on the answer sheet

If you mark more than one answer to any question by darkening more than one lettered space, it will be graded as incorrect. Therefore, if you change an answer, be sure that any previous marks for that question are erased completely.

Your grade on the examination will be determined by the total number of questions you answer correctly. Do the best you can. Since very few examinees answer all questions correctly, do not be concerned if there are a few you cannot answer.

If you have some knowledge of a question, even though you are uncertain about the answer, you may be able to eliminate one or more of the answer choices that are wrong. In such cases, it is better to guess at the correct answer than leave the answer space blank.

Sample Questions

All of the questions appearing in this book are designed to illustrate the type of questions that appear on contractor's exams throughout the country. But let's review the exact process of answering questions. Keep in mind that most questions will not have supplemental illustrations; other questions will have illustrations to refer to when answering the question. In this case, make sure you look at the correct illustration, as they appear in different locations in the exam booklet; that is, the illustration might appear above the question, or it might appear below it.

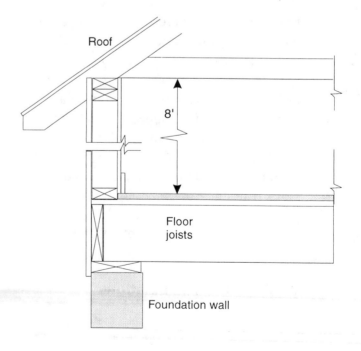

Figure 18-11: Cross-sectional view of a frame building.

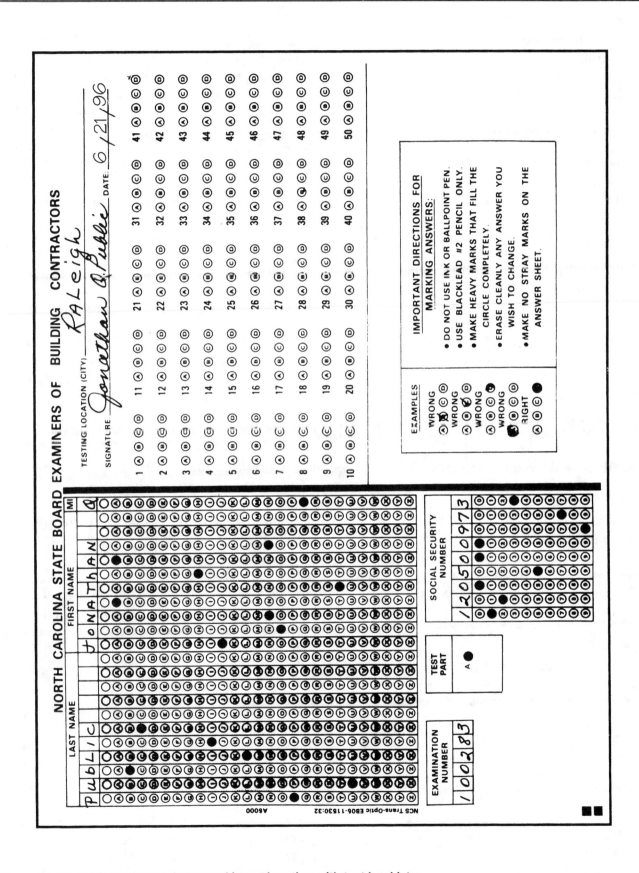

Figure 18-10: Typical answer sheet used in conjunction with test booklets.

Example 1: In Figure 18-11, what are the characteristics of the ceiling insulation?

A) It has an R-factor of 30

B) No specifications are shown

C) The insulation is to be blown in

D) The insulation has an R-factor of 20

Here you are asked to examine the drawing and then select the correct answer concerning the insulation. Since no specifications for insulation are shown, you would select answer B). This is the one that best describes the situation.

Example 2: AASHTO sets standards for:

A) Plywood

B) Steel

C) Highway bridges

D) Refrigeration piping

Here the "question" is in the form of an incomplete statement. Your task is to select the choice that best completes the statement. In this case, you should have selected C) since the Association of State Highway and Transportation Officials (AASHTO) sets standards for highways and related construction work, such as highway bridges, and their standards are incorporated into many building codes.

Example 3: The state of California has licensing requirements for all commercial, residential and public works construction *except* when the:

A) Contractor presents a performance bond to the Contractor's State License Board

B) Project exceeds $25,000 in total costs

C) Total cost of construction is less than $25,000

D) Total cost of construction is less than $300

Again the "question" is in the form of an incomplete statement and your task is to select the choice that best completes the statement. In this case, you are to find an exception. You have to select the condition that does not require a contractor's license in the state of California. You should have selected D) because a contractor's license is required only on construction projects of $300 or more.

Example 4: Regardless of the type or requirements of residential windows, no window may be selected whose air infiltration exceeds what amount?

A) 0.25 cubic feet per minute per linear foot

B) 0.50 cubic feet per minute per linear foot

C) 0.75 cubic feet per minute per linear foot

D) 1.00 cubic feet per minute per linear foot

Here you are asked to determine the code requirement for residential window infiltration. The Council of American Building Officials (CABO), in Section 608.2, states the maximum amount to be 0.50 cubic feet per minute. Therefore, your answer should be B).

Example 5: Which of the following factors makes preparing accurate estimates a challenge to every contractor and estimator? I. Each construction job is different; it is difficult to standardize the measurement and pricing of construction costs. II. Conditions such as weather, location, and other unforeseen factors can complicate the estimating process.

A) I only

B) II only

C) Both I and II

D) Neither I nor II

Here you are asked to determine which of two conditions best answers the question. Since both I and II are valid answers, you would select answer C) as the correct one.

Final Examination

The examinations to follow are meant to test your understanding of law and business organization, as applied to the building contracting industry, as well as your knowledge of the building trades. The questions are representative of typical contractor's examinations given throughout the United States for both city and state licenses. Complete solutions to all examination problems are contained in Appendix III.

Before taking these exams, however, make sure you have thoroughly studied the questions and answers in the previous 17 chapters. Answer the questions in the following exams as if you were actually taking an exam to obtain your contractor's license. This might be the only chance you have to take a sample exam prior to taking the real thing.

Instructions: Obtain several pieces of blank lined paper such as a legal pad. Write "Law and Business Organization Exam" at the top of one page, and then number the lines 1 through 50. This sheet of paper will be for your answers to the questions. Or you can photocopy the computer answer form in this book (Figure 18-12). Do not write your answers in this book. The Law and Business Organization exam should not take you longer than 3 hours to complete. To simulate an actual situation, you might want to wake up on your day off from work (like on Saturday morning), eat a good breakfast, have your numbered papers and several pencils handy, and start the exam as if you are at your state licensing location. Find a quiet location in your home and ask your family to cooperate. Then complete the exam without any references.

If you cannot spend a full 3 hours on the exam at one sitting, keep account of the time actually spent, and then return to the exam later. But do not spend more than a total of 3 hours on the Law and Business Organization exam. Once completed, put the answers to this exam in a safe place. Do not grade your exam yet.

Now take another sheet of paper and write "Contractor's Exam" at the top of the page and again number the lines 1 to 50 for the answers to the Contractor's exam. When time permits, answer the questions on the Contractor's exam as you did for the Law and Business Organization exam.

While taking either of these two examinations, if you don't know the answer to a question, don't stop taking the exam; remember you are working under a time limit. Go on to the next question. If you have time when you have gone through all the questions, go back to ones you did not answer and try to think of the solution. However, don't look up the answer. Sure, you can cheat now and score high on this sample exam, but you won't have that opportunity when the actual examination day comes.

When both exams are completed, have someone else grade your answer sheets, if possible. Remember, 70% is the lowest passing grade in most states. This means you must correctly answer 35 out of a total of 50 questions to pass each exam.

The person grading your exam should also write the reference notes to those questions missed. This will give you a quick-reference for further study in the fields you find that you are the weakest.

Now, let's assume that you made, say, 74% on one of the sample exams, which is a passing grade. Are you ready for the real thing? You might be, but I wouldn't chance it. You will not have these same questions on the real exam, and there might be more questions on the real exam in your weakest area. Therefore, it is recommended that you do further study in the field or fields in which you are the weakest. Wait a few days and then take the exam again — following the same procedure as before. Make sure you keep the answers from your previous attempt out of sight.

If you score 90% or more on this sample test, you stand a good chance of passing the real contractor's exam. But do you want to stop there? Remember, virtuoso musicians always practice techniques more difficult or beyond their performance range. By doing so, the ranges in which they actually perform in public come easier. By the same token, the closer you can score to 100% on this sample exam, the better your chances of passing the real examination, and passing the real examination is the reason you have this book. So be serious, and good luck!

Law and Business Organization Exam Answer Sheet

Name _____
Please print   (last)   (first)   (middle)

Address _____

_____

Signature _____

1 Ⓐ Ⓑ Ⓒ Ⓓ Ⓔ	26 Ⓐ Ⓑ Ⓒ Ⓓ Ⓔ	51 Ⓐ Ⓑ Ⓒ Ⓓ Ⓔ	76 Ⓐ Ⓑ Ⓒ Ⓓ Ⓔ
2 Ⓐ Ⓑ Ⓒ Ⓓ Ⓔ	27 Ⓐ Ⓑ Ⓒ Ⓓ Ⓔ	52 Ⓐ Ⓑ Ⓒ Ⓓ Ⓔ	77 Ⓐ Ⓑ Ⓒ Ⓓ Ⓔ
3 Ⓐ Ⓑ Ⓒ Ⓓ Ⓔ	28 Ⓐ Ⓑ Ⓒ Ⓓ Ⓔ	53 Ⓐ Ⓑ Ⓒ Ⓓ Ⓔ	78 Ⓐ Ⓑ Ⓒ Ⓓ Ⓔ
4 Ⓐ Ⓑ Ⓒ Ⓓ Ⓔ	29 Ⓐ Ⓑ Ⓒ Ⓓ Ⓔ	54 Ⓐ Ⓑ Ⓒ Ⓓ Ⓔ	79 Ⓐ Ⓑ Ⓒ Ⓓ Ⓔ
5 Ⓐ Ⓑ Ⓒ Ⓓ Ⓔ	30 Ⓐ Ⓑ Ⓒ Ⓓ Ⓔ	55 Ⓐ Ⓑ Ⓒ Ⓓ Ⓔ	80 Ⓐ Ⓑ Ⓒ Ⓓ Ⓔ
6 Ⓐ Ⓑ Ⓒ Ⓓ Ⓔ	31 Ⓐ Ⓑ Ⓒ Ⓓ Ⓔ	56 Ⓐ Ⓑ Ⓒ Ⓓ Ⓔ	81 Ⓐ Ⓑ Ⓒ Ⓓ Ⓔ
7 Ⓐ Ⓑ Ⓒ Ⓓ Ⓔ	32 Ⓐ Ⓑ Ⓒ Ⓓ Ⓔ	57 Ⓐ Ⓑ Ⓒ Ⓓ Ⓔ	82 Ⓐ Ⓑ Ⓒ Ⓓ Ⓔ
8 Ⓐ Ⓑ Ⓒ Ⓓ Ⓔ	33 Ⓐ Ⓑ Ⓒ Ⓓ Ⓔ	58 Ⓐ Ⓑ Ⓒ Ⓓ Ⓔ	83 Ⓐ Ⓑ Ⓒ Ⓓ Ⓔ
9 Ⓐ Ⓑ Ⓒ Ⓓ Ⓔ	34 Ⓐ Ⓑ Ⓒ Ⓓ Ⓔ	59 Ⓐ Ⓑ Ⓒ Ⓓ Ⓔ	84 Ⓐ Ⓑ Ⓒ Ⓓ Ⓔ
10 Ⓐ Ⓑ Ⓒ Ⓓ Ⓔ	35 Ⓐ Ⓑ Ⓒ Ⓓ Ⓔ	60 Ⓐ Ⓑ Ⓒ Ⓓ Ⓔ	85 Ⓐ Ⓑ Ⓒ Ⓓ Ⓔ
11 Ⓐ Ⓑ Ⓒ Ⓓ Ⓔ	36 Ⓐ Ⓑ Ⓒ Ⓓ Ⓔ	61 Ⓐ Ⓑ Ⓒ Ⓓ Ⓔ	86 Ⓐ Ⓑ Ⓒ Ⓓ Ⓔ
12 Ⓐ Ⓑ Ⓒ Ⓓ Ⓔ	37 Ⓐ Ⓑ Ⓒ Ⓓ Ⓔ	62 Ⓐ Ⓑ Ⓒ Ⓓ Ⓔ	87 Ⓐ Ⓑ Ⓒ Ⓓ Ⓔ
13 Ⓐ Ⓑ Ⓒ Ⓓ Ⓔ	38 Ⓐ Ⓑ Ⓒ Ⓓ Ⓔ	63 Ⓐ Ⓑ Ⓒ Ⓓ Ⓔ	88 Ⓐ Ⓑ Ⓒ Ⓓ Ⓔ
14 Ⓐ Ⓑ Ⓒ Ⓓ Ⓔ	39 Ⓐ Ⓑ Ⓒ Ⓓ Ⓔ	64 Ⓐ Ⓑ Ⓒ Ⓓ Ⓔ	89 Ⓐ Ⓑ Ⓒ Ⓓ Ⓔ
15 Ⓐ Ⓑ Ⓒ Ⓓ Ⓔ	40 Ⓐ Ⓑ Ⓒ Ⓓ Ⓔ	65 Ⓐ Ⓑ Ⓒ Ⓓ Ⓔ	90 Ⓐ Ⓑ Ⓒ Ⓓ Ⓔ
16 Ⓐ Ⓑ Ⓒ Ⓓ Ⓔ	41 Ⓐ Ⓑ Ⓒ Ⓓ Ⓔ	66 Ⓐ Ⓑ Ⓒ Ⓓ Ⓔ	91 Ⓐ Ⓑ Ⓒ Ⓓ Ⓔ
17 Ⓐ Ⓑ Ⓒ Ⓓ Ⓔ	42 Ⓐ Ⓑ Ⓒ Ⓓ Ⓔ	67 Ⓐ Ⓑ Ⓒ Ⓓ Ⓔ	92 Ⓐ Ⓑ Ⓒ Ⓓ Ⓔ
18 Ⓐ Ⓑ Ⓒ Ⓓ Ⓔ	43 Ⓐ Ⓑ Ⓒ Ⓓ Ⓔ	68 Ⓐ Ⓑ Ⓒ Ⓓ Ⓔ	93 Ⓐ Ⓑ Ⓒ Ⓓ Ⓔ
19 Ⓐ Ⓑ Ⓒ Ⓓ Ⓔ	44 Ⓐ Ⓑ Ⓒ Ⓓ Ⓔ	69 Ⓐ Ⓑ Ⓒ Ⓓ Ⓔ	94 Ⓐ Ⓑ Ⓒ Ⓓ Ⓔ
20 Ⓐ Ⓑ Ⓒ Ⓓ Ⓔ	45 Ⓐ Ⓑ Ⓒ Ⓓ Ⓔ	70 Ⓐ Ⓑ Ⓒ Ⓓ Ⓔ	95 Ⓐ Ⓑ Ⓒ Ⓓ Ⓔ
21 Ⓐ Ⓑ Ⓒ Ⓓ Ⓔ	46 Ⓐ Ⓑ Ⓒ Ⓓ Ⓔ	71 Ⓐ Ⓑ Ⓒ Ⓓ Ⓔ	96 Ⓐ Ⓑ Ⓒ Ⓓ Ⓔ
22 Ⓐ Ⓑ Ⓒ Ⓓ Ⓔ	47 Ⓐ Ⓑ Ⓒ Ⓓ Ⓔ	72 Ⓐ Ⓑ Ⓒ Ⓓ Ⓔ	97 Ⓐ Ⓑ Ⓒ Ⓓ Ⓔ
23 Ⓐ Ⓑ Ⓒ Ⓓ Ⓔ	48 Ⓐ Ⓑ Ⓒ Ⓓ Ⓔ	73 Ⓐ Ⓑ Ⓒ Ⓓ Ⓔ	98 Ⓐ Ⓑ Ⓒ Ⓓ Ⓔ
24 Ⓐ Ⓑ Ⓒ Ⓓ Ⓔ	49 Ⓐ Ⓑ Ⓒ Ⓓ Ⓔ	74 Ⓐ Ⓑ Ⓒ Ⓓ Ⓔ	99 Ⓐ Ⓑ Ⓒ Ⓓ Ⓔ
25 Ⓐ Ⓑ Ⓒ Ⓓ Ⓔ	50 Ⓐ Ⓑ Ⓒ Ⓓ Ⓔ	75 Ⓐ Ⓑ Ⓒ Ⓓ Ⓔ	100 Ⓐ Ⓑ Ⓒ Ⓓ Ⓔ

Figure 18-12: Answer sheet for use with the Law and Business Management Exam.

LAW AND BUSINESS EXAMINATION

TIME: 3 HOURS

---

1. What is the main advantage of a sole proprietorship contracting business?

A) The owner is liable for debts only to the amount of his or her investment

B) It is a separate legal entity created under the laws of a specific state

C) It is the easiest type of business to form

D) The ability to raise outside working capital is increased

---

2. A separate legal entity created under the laws of a specific state to engage in building contracting is what type of business organization?

A) Corporation

B) Sole proprietorship

C) General partnership

D) Limited partnership

---

3. If a contracting business is operating under a limited partnership with one general partner and two limited partners, what is the amount of the limited partners' liability?

A) They have unlimited personal liability

B) They are not responsible for any debt created by the business

C) The limited partners will always be liable for 50% of the firm's debts

D) Their liability is limited to the amount of their investment in the business

---

4. The most important element of a contract is the agreement of both parties to the method of delivery and intended result of the project. Which of the following best describes this element?

A) A handshake

B) A signature

C) An oath

D) Mutual agreement

---

5. Which of the following best describes the contract phrase, "time is of the essence in this agreement?"

A) Specified completion dates must be met

B) All laborers' time must be kept

C) Specified completion dates must be met within a reasonable time limit

D) All subcontractor's time must be recorded and submitted to the general contractor

---

6. When the construction documents specify a lump-sum bid, to which of the following is the contract usually awarded?

A) Highest bidder

B) Most popular contractor

C) Lowest bidder

D) The contractor located nearest the job site

7. Which of the following is the best definition of construction estimating?

A) The analysis of all elements involved in the cost of a building construction project

B) A list of all material used on the job

C) Calculating overhead and profit

D) Adding all labor units and multiplying by an hourly rate

8. On most construction projects, who assumes responsibility for the subcontractor's work?

A) The owner

B) The architect

C) The consulting engineer

D) The general contractor

9. Which of the following best describes "front-end loading" when dealing with construction contracts?

A) The practice of contractors underpricing items of work at the beginning of a construction job

B) The practice of using an earth-moving machine at the beginning of a project

C) The practice of contractors overpricing items of work at the beginning of a construction job

D) Applying more building weight to the front of a building than to any other area of the same building

10. What is the name of the accounting or bookkeeping document that gives the financial condition of a business at a point in time — indicating the assets, liabilities, and owners' equity of a business?

A) General ledger

B) Payroll journal

C) Balance sheet

D) Disbursement journal

11. What is a document called that insures that the bidder of a construction project will enter into a contract if an award is made to the bidder?

A) Performance bond

B) Bid bond

C) Payment bond

D) Liability insurance

12.   Which of the following best defines "addendum" as applied to contracts and construction documents?

A) The request for progress payments when a certain portion of the contract has been completed

B) An issued modification to the contract documents issued prior to bidding

C) A change order to the original contract amount

D) An issued modification to the contract after the work is in progress

13.   When a conflict exists in a construction contract, which of the following is true?

A) Specific provisions of the contract prevail over general provisions

B) Typed provisions prevail over handwritten provisions

C) Printed provisions prevail over typed provisions

D) Printed provisions prevail over handwritten provisions

14.   Which of the following is not necessary in a contractor's proposal to the owner of a construction project?

A) The contractor's name, address, and license number

B) Date of the proposal

C) Date of birth of the contractor and the contractor's key employees

D) The title, description, and address of the project

15.   When the owner of a construction project accepts a contractor's proposal, what should the letter of acceptance contain?

A) A specific reference to the contractor's proposal

B) A clear and unqualified acceptance of the offer

C) Both A and B

D) Neither A or B

16.   Which of the following is usually not included in a set of contract documents? Note: Contract documents are also referred to as "construction documents."

A) Bidding documents

B) Drawings

C) Written specifications

D) IRS Form 941 for the bidder's quarterly tax returns

17. Which of the following best describes a Mechanics' Lien?

A) A legal claim to take or hold property as payment or security for payment of a debt

B) The amount of revenues of a business remaining after costs, expenses, and taxes on income have been deducted

C) Obligations of, or claims against the assets of, a business

D) Work that does not fulfill the requirements of the contract documents

18. The maximum amount allowed to be claimed when filing for a Mechanics' Lien is:

A) 50% of the total contract price

B) 80% of the total contract price

C) 40% of the total contract price

D) An amount equal to the unpaid portion of the contract or agreed-upon price

19. Which of the following statements is true concerning a Mechanics' Lien?

A) Only the building itself is subject to a lien; never any land

B) Only land is subject to a lien; never any buildings

C) The land upon which the building is constructed is also subject to the lien

D) Answers A, B, and C are all incorrect

20. How is a Mechanics' Lien normally ranked if the property which the lien is against must be sold to satisfy debts?

A) All persons other than the original contractors and subcontractors receive their money first

B) Subcontractors receive their money first

C) Subcontractors are always paid last

D) General contractors are always paid first

21. Which insurance coverage is not required by federal law for building contractors?

A) Workers' Compensation

B) Medicare insurance

C) Employer's liability insurance

D) Social Security

22. The Miller Act is a federal statute passed in 1935 that requires contractors to furnish performance and payment bonds on contracts involving public buildings or public works if the project costs exceed:

A) $25,000

B) $50,000

C) $100,000

D) $1 million

23. Which insurance policy protects the contractor against any physical loss or damage to the construction project or project materials, except for listed exclusions such as damage caused by natural disasters?

A) Fire insurance

B) All-risk builder's insurance

C) Motor truck and cargo insurance

D) Burglary insurance

24. Which of the following insurance policies is used to protect the contractor against claims brought by third parties who are not employees of the contractor?

A) Contractual liability insurance

B) An equipment floater policy

C) Contractor's public liability and property damage insurance

D) Completed operations liability insurance

25. Which of the following guarantees that the construction project will be completed according to the plans and terms specified in the contract?

A) Bid bond

B) Performance bond

C) Payment bond

D) Lien bond

26. Which of the following is not an OSHA safety standard?

A) Employers must instruct their employees to recognize and avoid unsafe working conditions

B) Approved toilet facilites must be provided for employees

C) A supply of safe drinking water in an approved container and drinking cups must be provided for employees during any and all work hours

D) When guards are available for power tools, the guards must always be removed before putting the tools to use on the job site

27. Which of the following is not an OSHA safety standard relating to the operation of vehicles within an off-highway jobsite?

A) The vehicle's body must be free of dents and be washed at least once a week

B) The vehicle must be equipped with windshields, wipers, and defrosting devices

C) The vehicle must be equipped with service, parking, and emergency brakes

D) Adequate seating must be provided if employees are transported in the vehicle

28.   Which of the following best defines "Hours of Work" as stipulated in the Fair Labor Standards Act (FLSA)?

A) The time during the workweek that the employee is required to be on the employer's premises, on duty, or at a prescribed workplace

B) The time during which employees opt to put in their 8 hours

C) The time between dawn and dusk

D) The time during which employees are actually performing productive labor

29.   If a contractor hires an employee on the basis of a 30-hour workweek at the pay rate of $11.75 per hour, and this employee works 37 hours one week, what should the employee's gross wages be for the week, based on FLSA regulations?

A) $434.75

B) $527.65

C) $475.88

D) $490.70

30.   If the same employee in Question 29 works 39 hours one week and 45 hours the next week, what should this employee's total gross pay be for the 2-week period?

A) $956.78

B) $1123.45

C) $976.85

D) $1016.38

31.   When a reverse-signal alarm is not present on a vehicle used on the job site, what steps must the contractor take to comply with OSHA safety standards?

A) The loads being hauled on the vehicle must be reduced to not more than 2 tons

B) The vehicle may be used only to haul personnel

C) Observers must be posted to assist in backing the vehicle

D) The vehicle must be removed from the job site immediately upon discovering the defect

32.   Which of the following is not an OSHA safety requirement?

A) Employers must develop fire-protection programs

B) A standpipe system is required on all construction projects over 2 stories in height

C) Employers must provide firefighting equipment on all job sites

D) Access to firefighting equipment must always be available

33.   The process of analyzing each of the tasks that must be performed to complete a construction project and determining the most effective means of performing the task is called:

A) Scheduling

B) Estimating and bidding

C) Project planning

D) Supervision and project control

34.   The process of assigning each of the tasks in Question 33 to a time slot so that the requirements of the plan can be met is called:

A) Scheduling

B) Estimating and bidding

C) Project planning

D) Supervision and project control

35.   What is the title of the contractor's key employee who directs the various trades, checks daily production, coordinates the subcontractors, and in general, keeps the construction project running smoothly?

A) Project estimator

B) Project superintendent

C) Project engineer

D) Project inspector

36.   Which of the following situations would be the least damaging to a contractor if there is a slack in the construction business?

A) The contractor keeps a maximum inventory

B) The contractor always keeps 20% more materials on hand than is needed for present work

C) The contractor always keeps twice the amount of materials on hand than is needed for present work

D) The contractor keeps the minimum inventory

37.   Which of the following makes cost estimating a challenge to every contractor and estimator?

A) Each construction job is different, making it difficult to standardize take-off, assign labor units, and price construction costs

B) Conditions such as weather, location, employee scarcity, and other factors can complicate the estimating process

C) Neither A or B

D) Both A and B

MARRIED Persons- WEEKLY Payroll Period

If the wages are-		And the number of withholding allowances claimed is-										
At least	But less than	0	1	2	3	4	5	6	7	8	9	10
		The amount of income tax to be withheld is-										
$740	$750	93	85	77	69	61	53	45	37	29	20	12
750	760	95	87	78	70	62	54	46	38	30	22	14
760	770	96	88	80	72	64	56	48	40	32	23	15
770	780	98	90	81	73	65	57	49	41	33	25	17
780	790	99	91	83	75	67	59	51	43	35	26	18
790	800	101	93	84	76	68	60	52	44	36	28	20
800	810	102	94	86	78	70	62	54	46	38	29	21
810	820	104	96	87	79	71	63	55	47	39	31	23
820	830	105	97	89	81	73	65	57	49	41	32	24
830	840	107	99	90	82	74	66	58	50	42	34	26
840	850	108	100	92	84	76	68	60	52	44	35	27
850	860	110	102	93	85	77	69	61	53	45	37	29
860	870	111	103	95	87	79	71	63	55	47	38	30
870	880	113	105	96	88	80	72	64	56	48	40	32
880	890	114	106	98	90	82	74	66	58	50	41	33
890	900	116	108	99	91	83	75	67	59	51	43	35
900	910	117	109	101	93	85	77	69	61	53	44	36
910	920	119	111	102	94	86	78	70	62	54	46	38
920	930	120	112	104	96	88	80	72	64	56	47	39
930	940	122	114	105	97	89	81	73	65	57	49	41
940	950	125	115	107	99	91	83	75	67	59	50	42
950	960	128	117	108	100	92	84	76	68	60	52	44
960	970	131	118	110	102	94	86	78	70	62	53	45
970	980	133	120	111	103	95	87	79	71	63	55	47
980	990	136	121	113	105	97	89	81	73	65	56	48
990	1,000	139	124	114	106	98	90	82	74	66	58	50
1,000	1,010	142	127	116	108	100	92	84	76	68	59	51
1,010	1,020	145	130	117	109	101	93	85	77	69	61	53
1,020	1,030	147	132	119	111	103	95	87	79	71	62	54
1,030	1,040	150	135	120	112	104	96	88	80	72	64	56
1,040	1,050	153	138	123	114	106	98	90	82	74	65	57
1,050	1,060	156	141	126	115	107	99	91	83	75	67	59
1,060	1,070	159	144	128	117	109	101	93	85	77	68	60
1,070	1,080	161	146	131	118	110	102	94	86	78	70	62
1,080	1,090	164	149	134	120	112	104	96	88	80	71	63
1,090	1,100	167	152	137	122	113	105	97	89	81	73	65
1,100	1,110	170	155	140	125	115	107	99	91	83	74	66
1,110	1,120	173	158	142	127	116	108	100	92	84	76	68
1,120	1,130	175	160	145	130	118	110	102	94	86	77	69
1,130	1,140	178	163	148	133	119	111	103	95	87	79	71
1,140	1,150	181	166	151	136	121	113	105	97	89	80	72
1,150	1,160	184	169	154	139	123	114	106	98	90	82	74
1,160	1,170	187	172	156	141	126	116	108	100	92	83	75
1,170	1,180	189	174	159	144	129	117	109	101	93	85	77
1,180	1,190	192	177	162	147	132	119	111	103	95	86	78
1,190	1,200	195	180	165	150	135	120	112	104	96	88	80
1,200	1,210	198	183	168	153	137	122	114	106	98	89	81
1,210	1,220	201	186	170	155	140	125	115	107	99	91	83
1,220	1,230	203	188	173	158	143	128	117	109	101	92	84
1,230	1,240	206	191	176	161	146	131	118	110	102	94	86
1,240	1,250	209	194	179	164	149	134	120	112	104	95	87
1,250	1,260	212	197	182	167	151	136	121	113	105	97	89
1,260	1,270	215	200	184	169	154	139	124	115	107	98	90
1,270	1,280	217	202	187	172	157	142	127	116	108	100	92
1,280	1,290	220	205	190	175	160	145	130	118	110	101	93
1,290	1,300	223	208	193	178	163	148	133	119	111	103	95
1,300	1,310	226	211	196	181	165	150	135	121	113	104	96
1,310	1,320	229	214	198	183	168	153	138	123	114	106	98
1,320	1,330	231	216	201	186	171	156	141	126	116	107	99
1,330	1,340	234	219	204	189	174	159	144	129	117	109	101
1,340	1,350	237	222	207	192	177	162	147	131	119	110	102
1,350	1,360	240	225	210	195	179	164	149	134	120	112	104
1,360	1,370	243	228	212	197	182	167	152	137	122	113	105
1,370	1,380	245	230	215	200	185	170	155	140	125	115	107
1,380	1,390	248	233	218	203	188	173	158	143	128	116	108

$1,390 and over — Use Table 1(b) for a **MARRIED person** on page 34. Also see the instructions on page 32.

Figure 18-13: Sample table in IRS Circular E, Employer's Tax Guide.

38. How much withholding tax should be withheld from a married employee claiming 4 dependents if his gross pay is $919 per week? Use the chart on the opposite page as a guide.

A) $76

B) $86

C) $92

D) $107

39. What is the required withholding tax of the employee in Question 38 if he gets a pay raise and his total weekly gross wages are now $995?

A) $98

B) $95

C) $87

D) $85

40. How much withholding tax should be withheld from a married employee claiming 2 dependents if his gross pay is $889 per week? Use the chart on the opposite page as a guide.

A) $83

B) $90

C) $96

D) $98

41. If the working hours of the employee in Question 40 are cut, making his weekly gross pay $840, what is the amount of withholding tax that should be withheld?

A) $86

B) $90

C) $92

D) $98

42. Which of the following best describes the Child Labor Act as set forth in the Fair Labor Standard Act?

A) It prohibits employers from hiring persons under the age of 18

B) It sets limits on the types and hours of work for persons between the ages of 14 – 18

C) If the minor has a work permit, no restrictions apply

D) No employer may hire a person under 21 years of age, unless they have a work permit

43. According to the FLSA definition, which of the following is the best description of a "workweek?"

A) A fixed and regularly recurring period of 40 hours, beginning at 7 a.m. on Monday of each week

B) A fixed and regularly recurring period of 40 hours begining at any hour of the day

C) The period of time between 8 a.m. Monday and 5 p.m. Friday

D) A fixed and regularly recurring period of 168 hours beginning at any hour of the day

44. Workers' Compensation is a type of insurance policy that is handled:

A) At the federal level

B) At the state level

C) At the county level

D) At the city or town level

45. In general, which of the following best describes the reason for Workers' Compensation?

A) To guarantee employees their full wages and benefits in the event of an injury

B) To provide a fair and just method of determining compensation to an injured employee based on wages paid and the extent of the injury

C) To protect employees against law suits from the contractor

D) To provide complete medical coverage to an employee and his or her dependents

46. What are the main requirements of the Davis-Bacon Act?

A) It limits the amount of an individual's income that may be garnished for a debt

B) It sets daily or weekly overtime standards on federal contracts

C) It requires payment of prevailing wage rates and fringe benefits on federally financed or assisted construction projects

D) It requires payment of minimum wage rates and fringe benefits on contracts which provide goods to the federal government

47. Which of the following Acts (abbreviated) require payment of minimum wage and overtime payments?

A) NEMA

B) FLSA

C) NFPA

D) ANSI

48. Which of the following equations gives a description of a contractor's gross profit for a construction project?

A) Amount of contract – direct costs – indirect costs = gross profit

B) Amount of contract – direct cost – indirect costs – general overhead – income taxes = gross profit

C) Amount of contract – labor – materials = gross profit

D) Amount of contract – indirect costs = gross profit

49. What is the first step in determining an accurate cost of a construction project?

A) Determining the amount of labor required

B) Pricing the materials

C) Making a complete material takeoff

D) Calculating the contractor's required overhead and profit

50. After a complete material takeoff, the unit prices are normally inserted and the material prices extended to reach a total cost of material for the job. What is usually the next step in a construction estimate?

A) Labor units (usually in worker hours) are calculated

B) Indirect costs are calculated

C) Subcontractors are approached for estimates

D) Building permits are obtained

What to Expect on the Contractor's Exam

Building contractor examinations will vary from state to state. Most, however, will last for 4 hours and are based on code requirements, OSHA standards, and trade-specific information on materials, tools, equipment, terminology, and practices.

Candidates for contractor's examination should bring the following items with them:
- Your admission letter
- Appropriate reference (if allowed)
- Two sharpened #2 pencils
- A silent, nonprinting, nonprogrammable calculator
- An official photo ID, such as a driver's license

See the Introduction at the beginning of this book for helpful hints on taking the contractor's examination. Then complete the following practice exam using the answer sheet on the following page to record your answers. Again, make a photocopy of the answer sheet so you can repeat the test for study purposes.

Contractor's Exam Answer Sheet

Name _____

Please print   (last)   (first)   (middle)

Address _____

_____

Signature _____

1 Ⓐ Ⓑ Ⓒ Ⓓ Ⓔ	26 Ⓐ Ⓑ Ⓒ Ⓓ Ⓔ	51 Ⓐ Ⓑ Ⓒ Ⓓ Ⓔ	76 Ⓐ Ⓑ Ⓒ Ⓓ Ⓔ
2 Ⓐ Ⓑ Ⓒ Ⓓ Ⓔ	27 Ⓐ Ⓑ Ⓒ Ⓓ Ⓔ	52 Ⓐ Ⓑ Ⓒ Ⓓ Ⓔ	77 Ⓐ Ⓑ Ⓒ Ⓓ Ⓔ
3 Ⓐ Ⓑ Ⓒ Ⓓ Ⓔ	28 Ⓐ Ⓑ Ⓒ Ⓓ Ⓔ	53 Ⓐ Ⓑ Ⓒ Ⓓ Ⓔ	78 Ⓐ Ⓑ Ⓒ Ⓓ Ⓔ
4 Ⓐ Ⓑ Ⓒ Ⓓ Ⓔ	29 Ⓐ Ⓑ Ⓒ Ⓓ Ⓔ	54 Ⓐ Ⓑ Ⓒ Ⓓ Ⓔ	79 Ⓐ Ⓑ Ⓒ Ⓓ Ⓔ
5 Ⓐ Ⓑ Ⓒ Ⓓ Ⓔ	30 Ⓐ Ⓑ Ⓒ Ⓓ Ⓔ	55 Ⓐ Ⓑ Ⓒ Ⓓ Ⓔ	80 Ⓐ Ⓑ Ⓒ Ⓓ Ⓔ
6 Ⓐ Ⓑ Ⓒ Ⓓ Ⓔ	31 Ⓐ Ⓑ Ⓒ Ⓓ Ⓔ	56 Ⓐ Ⓑ Ⓒ Ⓓ Ⓔ	81 Ⓐ Ⓑ Ⓒ Ⓓ Ⓔ
7 Ⓐ Ⓑ Ⓒ Ⓓ Ⓔ	32 Ⓐ Ⓑ Ⓒ Ⓓ Ⓔ	57 Ⓐ Ⓑ Ⓒ Ⓓ Ⓔ	82 Ⓐ Ⓑ Ⓒ Ⓓ Ⓔ
8 Ⓐ Ⓑ Ⓒ Ⓓ Ⓔ	33 Ⓐ Ⓑ Ⓒ Ⓓ Ⓔ	58 Ⓐ Ⓑ Ⓒ Ⓓ Ⓔ	83 Ⓐ Ⓑ Ⓒ Ⓓ Ⓔ
9 Ⓐ Ⓑ Ⓒ Ⓓ Ⓔ	34 Ⓐ Ⓑ Ⓒ Ⓓ Ⓔ	59 Ⓐ Ⓑ Ⓒ Ⓓ Ⓔ	84 Ⓐ Ⓑ Ⓒ Ⓓ Ⓔ
10 Ⓐ Ⓑ Ⓒ Ⓓ Ⓔ	35 Ⓐ Ⓑ Ⓒ Ⓓ Ⓔ	60 Ⓐ Ⓑ Ⓒ Ⓓ Ⓔ	85 Ⓐ Ⓑ Ⓒ Ⓓ Ⓔ
11 Ⓐ Ⓑ Ⓒ Ⓓ Ⓔ	36 Ⓐ Ⓑ Ⓒ Ⓓ Ⓔ	61 Ⓐ Ⓑ Ⓒ Ⓓ Ⓔ	86 Ⓐ Ⓑ Ⓒ Ⓓ Ⓔ
12 Ⓐ Ⓑ Ⓒ Ⓓ Ⓔ	37 Ⓐ Ⓑ Ⓒ Ⓓ Ⓔ	62 Ⓐ Ⓑ Ⓒ Ⓓ Ⓔ	87 Ⓐ Ⓑ Ⓒ Ⓓ Ⓔ
13 Ⓐ Ⓑ Ⓒ Ⓓ Ⓔ	38 Ⓐ Ⓑ Ⓒ Ⓓ Ⓔ	63 Ⓐ Ⓑ Ⓒ Ⓓ Ⓔ	88 Ⓐ Ⓑ Ⓒ Ⓓ Ⓔ
14 Ⓐ Ⓑ Ⓒ Ⓓ Ⓔ	39 Ⓐ Ⓑ Ⓒ Ⓓ Ⓔ	64 Ⓐ Ⓑ Ⓒ Ⓓ Ⓔ	89 Ⓐ Ⓑ Ⓒ Ⓓ Ⓔ
15 Ⓐ Ⓑ Ⓒ Ⓓ Ⓔ	40 Ⓐ Ⓑ Ⓒ Ⓓ Ⓔ	65 Ⓐ Ⓑ Ⓒ Ⓓ Ⓔ	90 Ⓐ Ⓑ Ⓒ Ⓓ Ⓔ
16 Ⓐ Ⓑ Ⓒ Ⓓ Ⓔ	41 Ⓐ Ⓑ Ⓒ Ⓓ Ⓔ	66 Ⓐ Ⓑ Ⓒ Ⓓ Ⓔ	91 Ⓐ Ⓑ Ⓒ Ⓓ Ⓔ
17 Ⓐ Ⓑ Ⓒ Ⓓ Ⓔ	42 Ⓐ Ⓑ Ⓒ Ⓓ Ⓔ	67 Ⓐ Ⓑ Ⓒ Ⓓ Ⓔ	92 Ⓐ Ⓑ Ⓒ Ⓓ Ⓔ
18 Ⓐ Ⓑ Ⓒ Ⓓ Ⓔ	43 Ⓐ Ⓑ Ⓒ Ⓓ Ⓔ	68 Ⓐ Ⓑ Ⓒ Ⓓ Ⓔ	93 Ⓐ Ⓑ Ⓒ Ⓓ Ⓔ
19 Ⓐ Ⓑ Ⓒ Ⓓ Ⓔ	44 Ⓐ Ⓑ Ⓒ Ⓓ Ⓔ	69 Ⓐ Ⓑ Ⓒ Ⓓ Ⓔ	94 Ⓐ Ⓑ Ⓒ Ⓓ Ⓔ
20 Ⓐ Ⓑ Ⓒ Ⓓ Ⓔ	45 Ⓐ Ⓑ Ⓒ Ⓓ Ⓔ	70 Ⓐ Ⓑ Ⓒ Ⓓ Ⓔ	95 Ⓐ Ⓑ Ⓒ Ⓓ Ⓔ
21 Ⓐ Ⓑ Ⓒ Ⓓ Ⓔ	46 Ⓐ Ⓑ Ⓒ Ⓓ Ⓔ	71 Ⓐ Ⓑ Ⓒ Ⓓ Ⓔ	96 Ⓐ Ⓑ Ⓒ Ⓓ Ⓔ
22 Ⓐ Ⓑ Ⓒ Ⓓ Ⓔ	47 Ⓐ Ⓑ Ⓒ Ⓓ Ⓔ	72 Ⓐ Ⓑ Ⓒ Ⓓ Ⓔ	97 Ⓐ Ⓑ Ⓒ Ⓓ Ⓔ
23 Ⓐ Ⓑ Ⓒ Ⓓ Ⓔ	48 Ⓐ Ⓑ Ⓒ Ⓓ Ⓔ	73 Ⓐ Ⓑ Ⓒ Ⓓ Ⓔ	98 Ⓐ Ⓑ Ⓒ Ⓓ Ⓔ
24 Ⓐ Ⓑ Ⓒ Ⓓ Ⓔ	49 Ⓐ Ⓑ Ⓒ Ⓓ Ⓔ	74 Ⓐ Ⓑ Ⓒ Ⓓ Ⓔ	99 Ⓐ Ⓑ Ⓒ Ⓓ Ⓔ
25 Ⓐ Ⓑ Ⓒ Ⓓ Ⓔ	50 Ⓐ Ⓑ Ⓒ Ⓓ Ⓔ	75 Ⓐ Ⓑ Ⓒ Ⓓ Ⓔ	100 Ⓐ Ⓑ Ⓒ Ⓓ Ⓔ

Figure 18-14: Answer sheet for use with Contractor's Exam.

BUILDING CONTRACTOR'S FINAL EXAMINATION

TIME: 4 HOURS

1.   Which of the following meets building code requirements for temporary construction loads, such as the storage of construction materials inside of a partially completed building, only during the time that a building is under construction?

A) All temporary construction loads must not exceed the designed structural capacity of the new building

B) A building, even during construction, must not be overloaded beyond its design capacity

C) Neither A or B

D) Both A and B

2.   Who is normally responsible for the foundation underpinning of an adjoining existing building to protect it from the effects of new construction?

A) The contractor who is responsible for the new construction project

B) The owner of the existing building

C) The local utility companies

D) The State Highway Department

3.   What is the minimum allowable clear width of straight stairways above and below the permitted handrail height and below the required headroom height?

A) 24 inches

B) 30 inches

C) 36 inches

D) 42 inches

4.   What is the minimum tread depth allowed for residential stairways?

A) 4 inches

B) 6 inches

C) 8 inches

D) 10 inches

5.   What is the minimum allowable headroom for a spiral stairway?

A) 6 feet 6 inches

B) 6 feet 8 inches

C) 6 feet 10 inches

D) 7 feet

6. Which of the following is a code requirement for all stairways?

A) A midway landing must be provided

B) Illumination must be provided

C) Handrails must be provided

D) Landings are required at both the top and bottom of stairways

7. Landings must be provided at the top and bottom of ramps where doors open onto the ramp and where the ramp changes direction. What is the minimum size allowed for such landings?

A) 3 feet by 3 feet

B) 3 feet by 4 feet

C) 4 feet by 4 feet

D) 3 feet by 5 feet

8. How many smoke detectors are required in a split-level home with the upper level less than one full story, and with no doors between levels?

A) 1

B) 2

C) 3

D) 4

9. How many smoke detectors are required in a split-level home with the upper level less than one full story, and with doors between levels?

A) 1

B) 2

C) 3

D) 4

10. Where commercial electric power is not available for a building, how must smoke detectors be powered?

A) Electric generator with a capacity of at least 1200 watts (volt-amperes)

B) Electric generator with an output capacity sufficient to carry the load of the required smoke detectors

C) Solar powered

D) Battery powered

11. What is the maximum flame-spread rating allowed for foam plastic insulation when used in residential construction?

A) 25

B) 50

C) 75

D) 100

12. **What is the maximum flame-spread classification of wall and ceiling finishes?**

A) 75

B) 100

C) 150

D) 200

13. **Which of the following woods is the least decay-resistant?**

A) Hemlock

B) Redwood heartwood

C) Black locust

D) Cedars

14. **At which of the following locations do most building codes require the use of pressure-treated preserved lumber?**

A) In areas where wood joists are closer than 24 inches to exposed ground, as in a crawl space

B) For wooden sleepers used on concrete basement slabs to which wooden flooring is attached, with an impervious moisture barrier separating the sleepers and the flooring

C) All sills and plates that rest on concrete or masonry exterior walls and that are less than 8 inches from exposed ground

D) Wood furring strips attached directly to the interior of above-grade exterior masonry or concrete walls

15. **When moisture vapor retarders are required on all frame walls, floors, and ceilings of a structure which is not ventilated to allow the escape of moisture, what is the maximum allowable perm rating of the moisture vapor retarders?**

A) 1.0

B) 2.0

C) 3.0

D) 3.5

16. **In areas favorable to termite damage, methods must be employed to protect structures. Which of the following is not a recognized method?**

A) Chemical treatment of the soil in and around the vicinity of the structure's footings and foundation

B) The use of natural (untreated) blue spruce lumber for all sills and plates that are less than 8 inches from the earth

C) Pressure-treated wood

D) Metal or plastic termite shields

17.   When a beam is purposely manufactured with a slight rise from the ends to the beam midpoint, what is this curvature called?

A) Rise

B) Camber

C) Reverse deflection

D) Converse deflection

18.   Which of the following stud-spacing arrangements is the maximum allowed for a frame structure supporting one floor, ceiling, and a roof?

A) 2 × 4s spaced at 18 inches on center

B) 2 × 6s spaced at 30 inches on center

C) 2 × 4s spaced at 16 inches on center

D) 2 × 4s spaced at 24 inches on center

19.   If a wood beam deflects too much under load, which of the following is certain to reduce deflection?

A) Replace the beam with a wider one of the same depth

B) Replace the beam with a deeper one of the same width

C) Replace the beam with a deeper one with less width

D) Replace the beam with a wider one with less depth

20.   How does a high or low moisture content in dimension lumber affect structural design values?

A) Moisture content does not affect structural design values

B) High-moisture content will lower allowable design values

C) Low-moisture content will lower allowable design values

D) High-moisture content rises the allowable design values

21.   Which of the following organizations provide standards and specifications for all structural steel construction in the United States?

A) NFPA

B) IBEW

C) AISC

D) NEMA

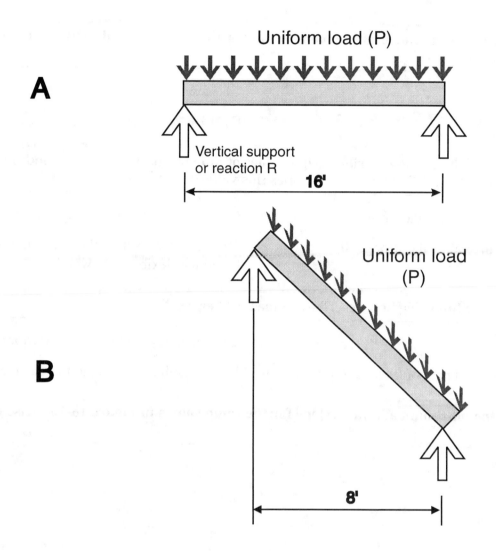

Figure 18-15: Uniform loads placed on a horizontal beam (A) and a sloped beam (B).

---

22. **The horizontal beam in Figure 18-15A is 16 feet long with load P distributed uniformly at an acceptable deflection. If this same beam is placed in a sloped position (as shown in B), how much of the same vertical load will it support?**

A) The same amount as when the beam was in the horizontal position

B) 10% less than when the beam was in the horizontal position

C) 20% less than when the beam was in the horizontal position

D) 30% less than when the beam was in the horizontal position

23. What percent of moisture still remains in lumber that is considered to have a high-moisture content?

A) 9%

B) 10%

C) 15%

D) 19%

24. A common unit used to describe design values of dimension lumber is the modulus of elasticity. Which of the following best describes this value?

A) The higher the value, the stronger the wood

B) The lower the value, the stronger the wood

C) This value is a measure of wood density

D) This value is not related to wood strength, but to the flexibility of wood

25. Which of the following best describes "a means of egress?"

A) An exit stair

B) An unobstructed path of travel out of a building

C) A hallway leading to an exterior door

D) A vestibule leading to the outside

26. What is the maximum allowable slope for the ramp shown in Figure 18-16 if rise E is 3 inches?

A) 1:20

B) 1:12

C) 1:10

D) 1:8

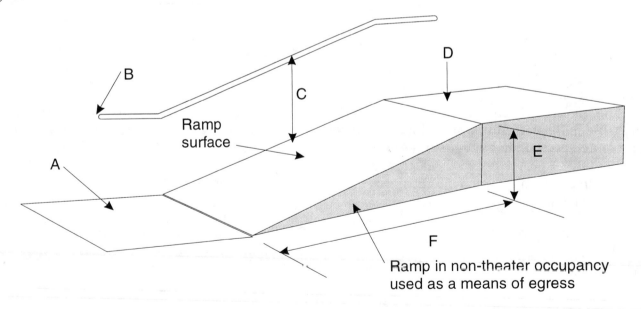

Figure 18-16: Typical ramp used for an accessible means of egress.

27. **What is the maximum distance that the handrail height (C) may be above the walking surface in Figure 18-16?**

A) 34 inches

B) 38 inches

C) 32 inches

D) 42 inches

28. **Referring again to Figure 18-16, under which of the following conditions are handrails not required?**

A) When dimension E is 6 inches or less and dimension F is 72 inches or less

B) When dimension F is no more than 74 inches

C) When dimension E is no more than 8 inches

D) When dimension E is 4 inches or less

29. **Handrails at stairs must have what amount of clear distance between the rail and the wall?**

A) $2\frac{1}{4}$ inches

B) $1\frac{1}{2}$ inches

C) 3 inches

D) $2\frac{3}{4}$ inches

30. **Which diagram in Figure 18-17 illustrates the most structurally-sound installation?**

A) A

B) B

C) C

D) D

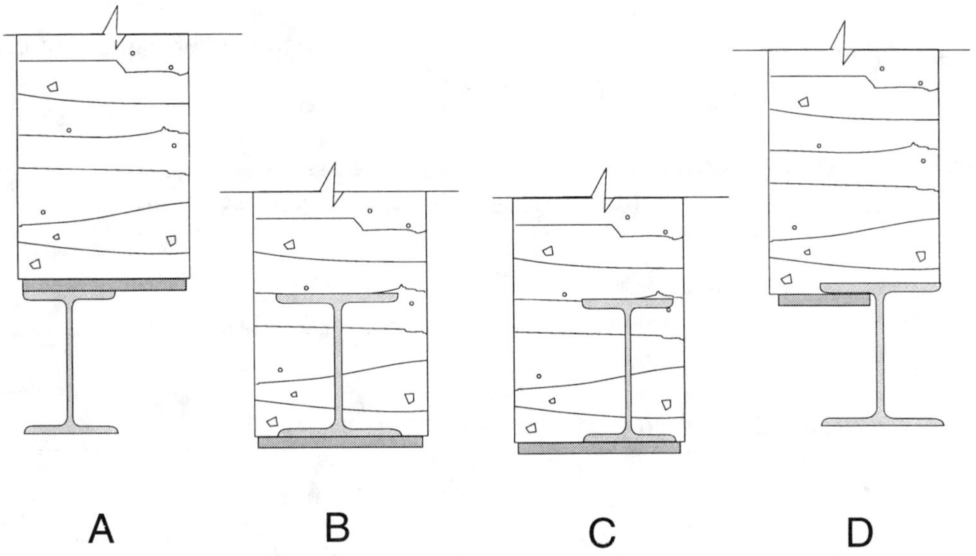

Figure 18-17: Cross-sectional views of steel beams supporting masonry walls.

31.   Even though steel is not considered a combustible substance, why do building codes require fireproofing around steel beams in buildings that must have a fireresistant rating?

A) Steel will burn at temperatures above 1200°F

B) Steel loses strength under high temperatures

C) Welded connections will eventually deteriorate when subjected to temperatures over 600° F

D) Toxic fumes are given off from steel under high temperatures

32.   Which of the following is one method of increasing the load-carrying capacity of a steel beam when used in conjunction with a concrete floor or roof system?

A) Composite slab design

B) Use a thinner, lighter-weight concrete slab

C) Use a wider steel beam

D) Use a thicker concrete slab

33.   Which of the following describes the best use for air-entrained cement?

A) Cement that will be mixed in the open air

B) Making cement frost-resistant

C) Mixing cement for underwater setting

D) Making cement moisture-resistant

34.   What is the purpose of a concrete slump test?

A) To verify the strength of concrete

B) To measure aggregate size

C) To measure the percentage of aggregate in the cement

D) To check the water content of cement

35.   What purpose does calcium chloride provide when it is mixed with concrete?

A) It acts as a restricter

B) It acts as a retarder

C) It acts as an accelerator

D) It acts as a hardener

36.   What is a concrete additive called that is used to delay setting time?

A) A retarder

B) A decreaser

C) A stiffener

D) A cooling agent

37.   Excessive water in concrete will normally cause:

A) A smoother, weaker finish

B) A rougher, stronger finish

C) Shrinkage cracks

D) Discoloration

38.   What test is used to guard against too much moisture in concrete?

A) Crunch test

B) Humidity test

C) Slump test

D) Slab test

39.   Which of the following is the minimum compression strength allowed for concrete used for footings?

A) 22,000 psi

B) 2,200 psi

C) 2,500 psi

D) 4,000 psi

40.   What is the diameter of a No. 5 reinforcing rod (rebar)?

A) ¼ inch

B) ½ inch

C) ⅝ inch

D) ¾ inch

41.   What is the diameter of a No. 6 reinforcing rod (rebar)?

A) ¼ inch

B) ½ inch

C) ⅝ inch

D) ¾ inch

42.   Which of the following best describes how rebars are sized?

A) According to their diameter in eights of an inch

B) According to their length in feet

C) According to their weight in ounces per foot

D) According to the diameter multiplied by their length

43.   Which of the following is the diameter of a No. 4 reinforcing bar (rebar)?

A) ⁴⁄₈ inch

B) ½ inch

C) Neither A or B

D) Both A and B

44. Which of the following best describes an automatic fire-suppression system like the one shown in Figure 18-18?

A) Heat detectors

B) A water sprinkler system

C) Smoke detectors

D) A fire-alarm master panel

45. What is the required fire rating of fireresistant separation partitions between a furnace room and adjacent areas?

A) 1 hour

B) 2 hours

C) 3 hours

D) 4 hours

46. Which of the following must be installed on a fireresistant door used to access a laundry room in a hotel?

A) A double lock

B) A self-closing apparatus

C) A security/fire-alarm foil-tape system

D) Automatic fire suppressors

47. Ground-fault circuit interrupter protection is required for all 125-volt, 15- or 20-ampere receptacles installed in the following dwelling-unit area:

A) Bedroom

B) Living room

C) Bath

D) Hallway

48. Electrical receptacle outlets in a dwelling must be installed in habitable rooms so that no point along the floor line is farther from an outlet than:

A) 3 feet

B) 6 feet

C) $41\frac{1}{2}$ feet

D) 5 feet

49. Besides forming a strong joint, what other characteristics are required of motar joints?

A) They should be porous

B) They should be flexible

C) They should be tooled according to local weather conditions

D) They should be water-resistant

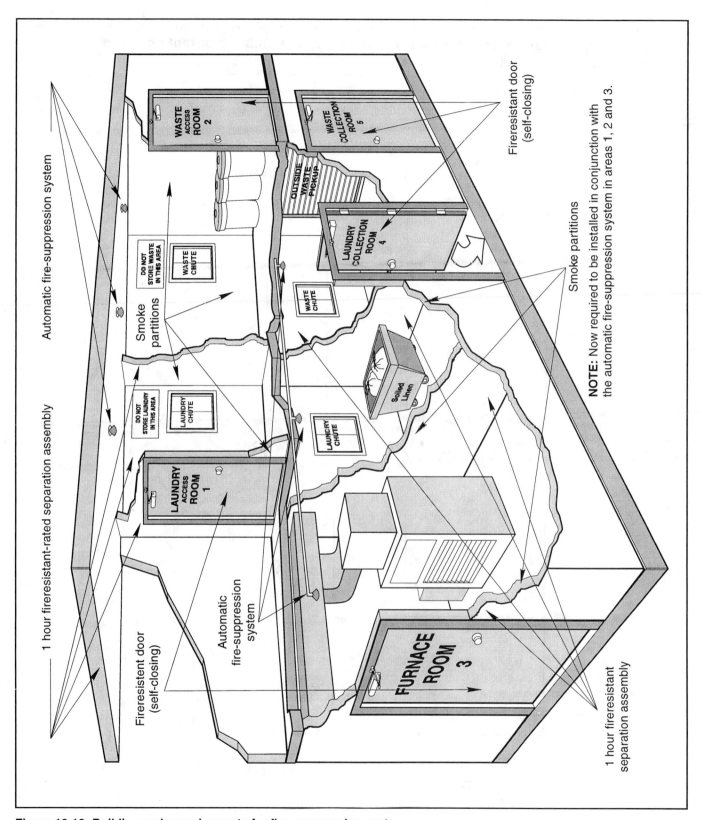

Figure 18-18: Building code requirements for fire-suppression systems.

50. Which of the diagrams in Figure 18-19 shows the most weather-resistant and durable exterior masonry mortar joint?

A) A

C) C

B) B

D) D

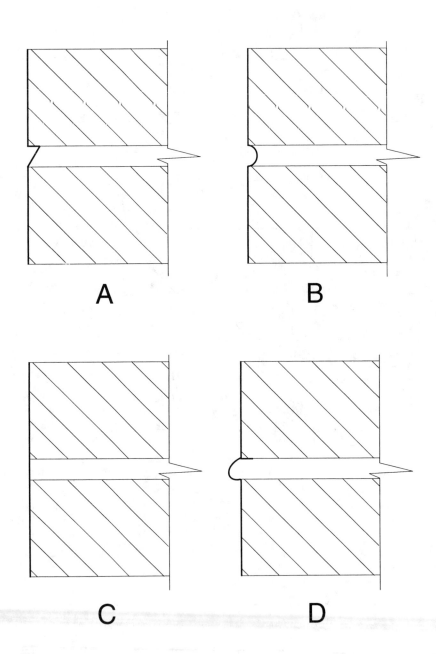

Figure 18-19: Four types of mortar joints used on brickwork.

State Contractor's Licensing Offices

Alabama

For residential builders:
Home Builders Licensure Board
400 S. Union Street, Suite 195
Montgomery, AL 36130
Phone: (334) 242-2230
Fax: (334) 263-1397
www.hblb.state.al.us

For commercial/industrial builders:
Licensing Board for General
  Contractors
2525 Fairlane Drive
Montgomery, Alabama 36116
Phone: (334) 272-5030
Fax: (334) 395-5336
www.genconbd.state.al.us

Alaska

Division of Occupational Licensing
Construction Contractor Section
P. O. Box 110806
Juneau, AK 99811-0806
Phone: (907) 465-8443
Fax: (907) 465-2974
www.dced.state.ak.us/occ/pcon.htm

Arizona

Registrar of Contractors
800 W. Washington Street, 6th Floor
Phoenix, AZ 85007
Phone: (602) 542-1525
Fax: (602) 542-1599
www.rc.state.az.us

Arkansas

Contractors Licensing Board
4100 Richards Road
North Little Rock, AR 72117
Phone: (501) 372-4661
Fax: (501) 372-2247
www.arkansas.gov/clb

California

Department of Consumer Affairs
Contractors State License Board
9821 Business Park Drive
P. O. Box 26000
Sacramento, CA 95826
Phone: 1-800-321-CSLB (2752)
Fax: (916) 366-9130
www.cslb.ca.gov

Colorado

The state of Colorado does not license
State General Contractor's Licenses.
Licensing is done on a local level.
Look in telephone directory under
"Town of," "City of," or "County of."

Connecticut

Department of Consumer Protection
Division of Occupational &
Professional Licensing
165 Capitol Avenue
Hartford, CT 06106
Phone: (860) 713-6050
Fax: (860) 713-7230
www.ct.gov/dcp

Delaware

Division of Professional Regulation
Board of Electrical Examiners
Cannon Building
861 Silver Lake Blvd., Suite 203
Dover, DE 19904
Phone: (302) 744-4500
Fax: (302) 739-2711
www.professionallicensing.state.de.us

District of Columbia

Department of Consumer and
  Regulatory Affairs
Occupational & Professional
Licensing Administration
941 North Capital Street, NE, 7th Floor
Washington, D.C. 20002
Phone: (202) 442-4400
Fax: (202) 442-9445
www.dcra.dc.gov/dcra/cwp

Florida

Dept. of Business and Professional
Regulation
Division of Professions
Construction Industry Licensing Board
1940 North Monroe Street
Tallahassee, FL 32399-1039
Phone: (850) 487-1395
Fax: (850) 488-8748
www.state.fl.us/dbpr/pro/cilb

Georgia

Construction Industry Licensing Board
237 Coliseum Drive
Macon, GA 31217-3858
Phone: (478) 207-1416
Fax: (478) 207-1425
www.sos.state.ga.us/plb/construct

Guam

Contractor's License Board
Department of Public Works
542 North Marine Drive, Suite A
Upper Tumon, Guam 96911
Phone: (671) 649-2211
Fax: (671) 649-2210
ns.gov.gu/government.html

Hawaii

Department of Commerce &
   Consumer Affairs
Div. of Professional & Vocational
Licensing
ATT: CLB
335 Merchant St., Room 301
P.O. Box 3469
Honolulu, HI 96801
Phone: (808) 586-3000
Fax: (808) 586-3031
www.hawaii.gov/dcca/pvl/
areas_contractor.html

Idaho

Public Works Contractors License
   Bureau
1090 E. Watertower St.
Meridian, ID 83642
Phone: (208) 334-4057
(800) 358-6895
Fax: (208) 855-9666
www.state.id.us/dbs

Illinois

The State of Illinois does not issue
State Contractor's Licenses. Licensing
is done on a local level. Look in the
telephone directory under "Town of,"
"City of," or "County of."
www.idfpr.com

Indiana

The State of Indiana does not issue
State Contractor's Licenses. Licensing
is done on a local level. Look in the
telephone directory under "Town of,"
"City of," or "County of."
www.ipla.in.gov

Iowa

The State of Iowa does not issue State
Contractor's Licenses. Licensing is
done on a local level. Look in the
telephone directory under "Town of,"
"City of," or "County of."
www.iowa.gov

Kansas

The State of Kansas does not issue
State Contractor's Licenses. Licensing
is done on a local level. Look in the
telephone directory under "Town of,"
"City of," or "County of."
www.accesskansas.org

Kentucky

Office of Housing, Buildings
   and Construction
101 Sea Hero Road, Suite 100
Frankfort, KY 40601
Phone: (502) 573-0382
Fax: (502) 573-1598
www.state.ky.us/agencies/cppr/dhbc

Louisiana

Licensing Board for Contractors
2525 Quail Drive
P. O. Box 14419
Baton Rouge, LA 70898-4419
Phone: (225) 765-2301
(800) 256-1392
Fax: (225) 765-2690
www.lslbc.louisiana.gov

Maine

The State of Maine does not issue
State Contractor's Licenses. Licensing
is done on a local level. Look in the
telephone directory under "Town of,"
"City of," or "County of."
www.state.me.us/pfr/olr

Maryland

Division of Occupational and
   Professional Licensing
500 N. Calvert Street, Room 302
Baltimore, MD 21202-6270
Phone: (410) 230-6270
Fax: (410) 333-6314
www.dllr.state.md.us

For home improvement contractors:
Home Improvement Commission
500 N. Calvert Street, Room 306
Baltimore, Maryland 21202
Phone: (410) 230-61760
Fax: (410) 333-08551
www.dllr.state.md.us/license/occprof/
homeim.html

New construction contractors must
register with:
Home Builder Registration Unit
Consumer Protection Division
Office of the Attorney General
200 St. Paul Place
Baltimore, MD 21202
Phone: (410) 576-6573
(877) 259-4525
Fax: (410) 576-6566
www.oag.state.md.us/Homebuilder/
index.htm

Massachusetts

Division of Professional Licensure
239 Causeway Street
Boston, MA 02114
Phone: (617) 727-3074
Fax: (617) 727-2197
www.mass.gov/reg/boards/el

Michigan

Dept. of Labor & Economic Growth
611 W. Ottawa
P. O. Box 30004
Lansing, MI 48909
Phone: (517) 373-1820
Fax: (517) 373-2129
http://michigan.gov/cis

Minnesota

Licensing Unit
Minnesota Department of Commerce
85 Seventh Place East, Suite 600
St. Paul, MN 55101-3165
Phone: (651) 296-6319
(800) 657-3978
www.commerce.state.mn.us

Mississippi

State Board of Contractors
215 Woodline Drive, Suite B
P. O. Box 320279
Jackson, MS 39232-0279
Phone: (601) 354-6161
(800) 880-6161
Fax: (601) 354-6715
www.msboc.state.ms.us

Missouri

The State of Missouri does not issue
State Contractor's Licenses. Licensing
is done on a local level. Look in the
telephone directory under "Town of,"
"City of," or "County of."
www.state.mo.us

Montana

Department of Labor & Industry
Employment Relations Division
Contractor Registration Unit
1805 Prospect Avenue
P.O. Box 8011
Helena, MT 59604-8011
Phone: (406) 444-7734
http://dli.state.mt.us

Nebraska

Contractors doing business in a county
with a population over 100,000 must
register with:
Nebraska Workforce Development
Department of Labor
Safety and Labor Standards
5404 Cedar Street
Omaha, NE 68106-2365
Phone: (402) 595-3189
Fax: (402) 471-5990
www.dol.state.ne.us/nwd

Nevada

State Contractors Board
9670 Gateway Drive, Suite 100
Reno, NV 89521
Phone: (775) 688-1141
Fax: (775) 688-12712
www.nscb.state.nv.us

New Hampshire

The State of New Hampshire does not
issue State Contractor's Licenses.
Licensing is done on a local level.
Look in the telephone directory under
"Town of," "City of," or "County of."
www.nh.gov/index.html

New Jersey

The State of New Jersey does not
issue State Contractor's Licenses.
Licensing is done on a local level.
Look in the telephone directory under
"Town of," "City of," or "County of."

Home improvement contractors must
be registered by December 31, 2005
with:
Division of Consumer Affairs
124 Halsey Street
Newark, New Jersey 07102
Phone: (973) 504-6200
Fax: (973) 273-8035
www.state.nj.us/lps/ca/home.htm

New Mexico

Construction Industries Division
2550 Cerrillos Road
P. O. Box 25101
Santa Fe, NM 87504-5101
Phone: (505) 476-4700
Fax: (505) 476-4685
www.rld.state.nm.us/cid

New York

The State of New York does not issue
State Contractor's Licenses. Licensing
is done on a local level. Look in the
telephone directory under "Town of,"
"City of," or "County of."
www.dos.state.ny.us

North Carolina

Licensing Board for General
  Contractors
3739 National Drive, Suite 225
P. O. Box 17187
Raleigh, NC 27619
Phone: (919) 571-4183
(800) 392-6102
Fax: (919) 733-6105
www.nclbgc.net

North Dakota

Secretary of State
Administrative/Licensing Division
600 E. Boulevard Ave., Dept 108
Bismarck, ND 58505-0500
Phone: (701) 328-3665
800-352-0867 ext. 8-3665
Fax: (701) 328-1690
http://www.state.nd.us/sec/licensing/

Ohio

The State of Ohio does not issue
State Contractor's Licenses. Licensing
is done on a local level. Look in the
telephone directory under "Town of,"
"City of," or "County of."
www.com.state.oh.us/dic

Oklahoma

The State of Oklahoma does not issue
State Contractor's Licenses. Licensing
is done on a local level. Look in the
telephone directory under "Town of,"
"City of," or "County of."
www.health.state.ok.us/cib

Oregon

Construction Contractors Board
700 Summer Street NE, Suite 300
PO Box 14140
Salem, OR 97309-5052
Phone: (503) 378-4621
Fax: (503) 373-2007
http://www.ccb.state.or.us/

Pennsylvania

The State of Pennsylvania does not
issue State Contractor's Licenses.
Licensing is done on a local level.
Look in the telephone directory under
"Town of," "City of," or "County of."
www.dli.state.pa.us

Rhode Island

Contractors' Registration Board
1 Capitol Hill
Providence, RI 02908
Phone: (401) 222-1268
Fax: (401)-222-2599
www.crb.state.ri.us/

South Carolina

Contractors' Licensing Board Synergy
Business Park Kingstree Building
110 Centerview Drive,
Suite 201
P.O. Box 11329
Columbia, SC 29211-1329
Phone: (803) 896-4686
Fax: (803) 896-4701
www.llr.state.sc.us/pol/contractors

South Dakota

The State of South Dakota does not
issue State Contractor's Licenses.
Licensing is done on a local level.
Look in the telephone directory under
"Town of," "City of," or "County of."

Contractors must have an excise tax
license:
SD Department of Revenue and
Regulation Business Tax Division
445 East Capitol Avenue
Pierre, SD 57501
Phone: 1-800-TAX-9188
www.state.sd.us/drr2/businesstax/
bustax.htm

Tennessee

Board of Licensing Contractors
500 James Robertson Parkway,
Suite 110
Nashville, TN 37243-1150
Phone: (615) 741-8307
(800) 544-7693
Fax: (615) 532-2868
www.state.tn.us/commerce/boards/
contractors

Texas

The State of Texas does not issue State
Contractor's Licenses. Licensing is
done on a local level. Look in the
telephone directory under "Town of,"
"City of," or "County of."
Also contact local building inspection
offices for more information.
www.license.state.tx.us

Utah

Division of Occupational and
Professional Licensing
160 East 300 South
P. O. Box 146741
Salt Lake City, UT 84114-6741
Phone: (801) 530-6628
(866) 275-3675 (UT)
Fax: (801) 530-6511
www.dopl.utah.gov/licensing/
contractor.html

Vermont

The State of Vermont does not issue
State Contractor's Licenses. Licensing
is done on a local level. Look in the
telephone directory under "Town of,"
"City of," or "County of."
www.state.vt.us/labind

Virginia

Department of Professional and
Occupational Regulation
Board for Contractors
3600 West Broad Street
P. O. Box 11066
Richmond, VA 23230-1066
Phone: (804) 367-8500
Fax: (804) 367-2475
www.dpor.virginia.gov

Washington

Department of Labor and Industries
Contractor Registration Section
7273 Linderson Way SW
Tumwater, WA 98501-5414
P. O. Box 44850
Olympia, WA 98504-4850
Phone: (360) 902-5799
Fax: (360) 902-5792
www.lni.wa.gov

West Virginia

Division of Labor
State Capitol Complex
Building 6, Room B749
Charleston, WV 25305
Phone: (304) 558-7890
Fax: (304) 558-3797
http://www.labor.state.wv.us/

Wisconsin

Department of Commerce
Safety and Buildings Division
201 West Washington Avenue
P. O. Box 2658
Madison, WI 53701
Phone: (608) 266-3151
Fax: (608) 283-7400
www.commerce.state.wi.us/SB/
SB-HomePage.html

Wyoming

The State of Wyoming does not issue
State Contractor's Licenses. Licensing
is done on a local level. Look in the
telephone directory under "Town of,"
"City of," or "County of."

Answers to Final Exam Questions

Law and Business Examination

1. C	11. B	21. C	31. C	41. C
2. A	12. B	22. A	32. B	42. B
3. D	13. A	23. B	33. C	43. D
4. D	14. C	24. C	34. A	44. B
5. A	15. C	25. B	35. B	45. B
6. C	16. D	26. D	36. D	46. C
7. A	17. A	27. A	37. D	47. B
8. D	18. D	28. A	38. B	48. A
9. C	19. C	29. A	39. A	49. C
10. C	20. A	30. D	40. D	50. A

Building Contractor's Examination

1. D	11. C	21. C	31. B	41. D
2. A	12. D	22. A	32. A	42. A
3. C	13. A	23. D	33. B	43. D
4. D	14. C	24. A	34. D	44. B
5. A	15. A	25. B	35. C	45. A
6. B	16. B	26. D	36. A	46. B
7. A	17. B	27. B	37. C	47. C
8. A	18. C	28. A	38. C	48. B
9. B	19. B	29. A	39. C	49. D
10. D	20. B	30. B	40. C	50. B

Index

Practical References for Builders

Estimating With Microsoft *Excel*

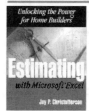

Most builders estimate with *Excel* because it's easy to learn, quick to use, and can be customized to your style of estimating. Here you'll find step-by-step instructions on how to create your own customized automated spreadsheet estimating program for use with *Excel*. You'll learn how to use the magic of *Excel* to create detail sheets, cost breakdown summaries, and links. You'll put this all to use in estimating concrete, rebar, permit fees, and roofing. You can even create your own macros. Includes a CD-ROM that illustrates examples in the book and provides you with templates you can use to set up your own estimating system. **148 pages, 7 x 9, $39.95**

Handbook of Construction Contracting

Volume 1: Everything you need to know to start and run your construction business; the pros and cons of each type of contracting, the records you'll need to keep, and how to read house plans and specs so you find any problems before the work begins. All aspects of construction are coveredl, including all-weather wood foundations, practical math for the job site, and elementary surveying. **416 pages, 8¹/₂ x 11, $32.75**

Volume 2: Everything you need to know to keep your construction business profitable; different methods of estimating, keeping and controlling costs, estimating excavation, concrete, masonry, rough carpentry, roof covering, insulation, doors and windows, exterior finishes, specialty finishes, scheduling work flow, managing workers, advertising and sales, spec building and land development, and selecting the best legal structure for your business. **320 pages, 8¹/₂ x 11, $33.75**

Contractor's Plain-English Legal Guide

For today's contractors, legal problems are like snakes in the swamp — you might not see them, but you know they're there. This book tells you where the snakes are hiding and directs you to the safe path. With the directions in this easy-to-read handbook you're less likely to need a $200-an-hour lawyer. Includes simple directions for starting your business, writing contracts that cover just about any eventuality, collecting what's owed you, filing liens, protecting yourself from unethical subcontractors, and more. For about the price of 15 minutes in a lawyer's office, you'll have a guide that will make many of those visits unnecessary. Includes a CD-ROM with blank copies of all the forms and contracts in the book. **272 pages, 8¹/₂ x 11, $49.50**

Markup & Profit: A Contractor's Guide

In order to succeed in a construction business, you have to be able to price your jobs to cover all labor, material and overhead expenses, and make a decent profit. The problem is knowing what markup to use. You don't want to lose jobs because you charge too much, and you don't want to work for free because you've charged too little. If you know how to calculate markup, you can apply it to your job costs to find the right sales price for your work. This book gives you tried and tested formulas, with step-by-step instructions and easy-to-follow examples, so you can easily figure the markup that's right for your business. Includes a CD-ROM with forms and checklists for your use. **320 pages, 8¹/₂ x 11, $32.50**

Moving to Commercial Construction

In commercial work, a single job can keep you and your crews busy for a year or more. The profit percentages are higher, but so is the risk involved. This book takes you step-by-step through the process of setting up a successful commercial business; finding work, estimating and bidding, value engineering, getting through the submittal and shop drawing process, keeping a stable work force, controlling costs, and promoting your business. Explains the design/build and partnering business concepts and  their advantage over the competitive bid process. Includes sample letters, contracts, checklists and forms that you can use in your business, plus a CD-ROM with blank copies in several word-processing formats for both Mac and PC computers. **256 pages, 8¹/₂ x 11, $42.00**

National Construction Estimator

Current building costs for residential, commercial, and industrial construction. Estimated prices for every common building material. Provides manhours, recommended crew, and gives the labor cost for installation. Includes a CD-ROM with an electronic version of the book with *National Estimator*, a stand-alone *Windows*™ estimating program, plus an interactive multimedia video that shows how to use the disk to compile construction cost estimates. **672 pages, 8¹/₂ x 11, $57.50. Revised annually**

How to Succeed With Your Own Construction Business

Everything you need to start your own construction business: setting up the paperwork, finding the work, advertising, using contracts, dealing with lenders, estimating, scheduling, finding and keeping good employees, keeping the books, and coping with success. If you're considering starting your own construction business, all the knowledge, tips, and blank forms you need are here. **336 pages, 8¹/₂ x 11, $28.50**

Construction Forms & Contracts

125 forms you can copy and use — or load into your computer (from the FREE disk enclosed). Then you can customize the forms to fit your company, fill them out, and print. Loads into *Word* for *Windows*™, *Lotus 1-2-3*, *WordPerfect*, *Works*, or *Excel* programs. You'll find forms covering accounting, estimating, fieldwork, contracts, and general office. Each form comes with complete instructions on when to use it and how to fill it out. These forms were designed, tested and used by contractors, and will help keep your business organized, profitable and out of legal, accounting and collection troubles. Includes a CD-ROM for *Windows*™ and Mac. **432 pages, 8¹/₂ x 11, $41.75**

Estimating & Bidding for Builders & Remodelers

This 4th edition has all the information you need for estimating and bidding new construction and home improvement projects. It shows you how to select jobs that will be profitable, do a labor and materials take-off from the plans, calculate overhead and figure your markup, and schedule the work. Includes a CD with an easy-to-use construction estimating program and a database of 50,000 current labor and material cost estimates for new construction and home improvement work, with area modifiers for every zip code. Price updates on the Web are free and automatic. **272 pages, 8¹/₂ x 11, $89.50**

QuickPass CD-ROM for the General Building (B) Examination

This CD-ROM has over 300 multiple choice questions covering all the points covered in the actual California State Contractor's Exam. You'll learn the right answer and a full explanation of the basic principles involved in that question. Even if you guess the right answer, the explanation is given, so you learn the material in the test. Originally designed for the California exam, this CD-ROM can help anyone in any state pass the general building examination in their state. **$99.00**

Rough Framing Carpentry

If you'd like to make good money working outdoors as a framer, this is the book for you. Here you'll find shortcuts to laying out studs; speed cutting blocks, trimmers and plates by eye; quickly building and blocking rake walls; installing ceiling backing, ceiling joists, and truss joists; cutting and assembling hip trusses and California fills; arches and drop ceilings — all with production line procedures that save you time and help you make more money. Over 100 on-the-job photos of how to do it right and what can go wrong. **304 pages, 8¹/₂ x 11, $26.50**

Peerless Inst. Contractor's Law & Business for the California Contractor's Exam

This gigantic book is filled with everything you need to pass the California Contractor Law & Business exam: Lien law, workers' comp, CAL-OSHA requirements, California unemployment insurance act, state sales and use tax, business management, and basic bookkeeping and accounting practices. There are even 1,000 questions and answers included — just like the actual state tests, to make sure you pass with high marks. **402 pages, 8¹/₂ x 11, $99.95**

Basic Engineering for Builders

If you've ever been stumped by an engineering problem on the job, yet wanted to avoid the expense of hiring a qualified engineer, you should have this book. Here you'll find engineering principles explained in non-technical language and practical methods for applying them on the job. With the help of this book you'll be able to understand engineering functions in the plans and how to meet the requirements, how to get permits issued without the help of an engineer, and anticipate requirements for concrete, steel, wood and masonry. See why you sometimes have to hire an engineer and what you can undertake yourself: surveying, concrete, lumber loads and stresses, steel, masonry, plumbing, and HVAC systems. This book is designed to help the builder save money by understanding engineering principles that you can incorporate into the jobs you bid.
400 pages, 8¹/₂ x 11, $36.50

Illustrated Guide to the *International Plumbing & Fuel Gas Codes*

A comprehensive guide to the *International Plumbing* and *Fuel Gas Codes* that explains the intricacies of the code in easy-to-understand language. Packed with plumbing isometrics and helpful illustrations, it makes clear the code requirements for the installation methods and materials for plumbing and fuel gas systems. Includes code tables for pipe sizing and fixture units, and code requirements for just about all areas of plumbing, from water supply and vents to sanitary drainage systems. Covers the principles and terminology of the codes, how the various systems work and are regulated, and code-compliance issues you'll likely encounter on the job. Each chapter has a set of self-test questions for anyone studying for the plumber's exam, and tells you where to look in the code for the details. Written by a former plumbing inspector, this guide has the help you need to install systems in compliance with the *IPC* and the *IFGC*.
312 pages, 8¹/₂ x 11, $37.00

National Contractor's Exam Study Guide

This book is not state-specific, but it is code-specific. It's guaranteed to help you obtain the knowledge and confidence needed to pass your contractor's exam on the first try. It lists 1,500 questions and answers — presented in the same format used on the actual exam — plus numerous references to the 2006 International Building Code. You'll find detailed illustrations that help clarify complicated code issues. Covers administration, definitions, use and occupancy classifications, special detailed requirements based on use and occupancy, general building heights and areas, types of construction, fire-resistant-rated-construction, interior finishes, fire-protection systems, means of egress, accessability, energy effeciency, exterior walls, roof assemblies and rooftop structures, structural design and tests, soils and foundations, concrete, special construction, encroachments into public right-of-way, safeguards during construction, existing structures and more. **359 pages, 8¹/₂ x 11, $39.95**

CD Estimator

If your computer has *Windows*™ and a CD-ROM drive, CD Estimator puts at your fingertips over 160,000 construction costs for new construction, remodeling, renovation & insurance repair, home improvement, electrical, concrete & masonry, painting, earthwork, and plumbing & HVAC. Monthly cost updates are available at no charge on the Internet. You'll also have the *National Estimator* program - a stand-alone estimating program for *Windows*™ that *Remodeling* magazine called a "computer wiz," and *Job Cost Wizard*, a program that lets you export your estimates to QuickBooks Pro for actual job costing. A 60-minute interactive video teaches you how to use this CD-ROM to estimate construction costs. And to top it off, to help you create professional-looking estimates, the disk includes over 40 construction estimating and bidding forms in a format that's perfect for nearly any *Windows*™ word processing or spreadsheet program. **CD Estimator is $78.50**

Steel-Frame House Construction

Framing with steel has obvious advantages over wood, yet building with steel requires new skills that can present challenges to the wood builder. This new book explains the secrets of steel framing techniques for building homes, whether pre engineered or built stick by stick. It shows you the techniques, the tools, the materials, and how you can make it happen. Includes hundreds of photos and illustrations, plus a CD-ROM with steel framing details, a database of steel materials and manhours, with an estimating program. **320 pages, 8¹/₂ x 11, $39.75**

Contractor's Guide to QuickBooks Pro 2007

This user-friendly manual walks you through QuickBooks Pro's detailed setup procedure and explains step-by-step how to create a first-rate accounting system. You'll learn in days, rather than weeks, how to use *QuickBooks Pro* to get your contracting business organized, with simple, fast accounting procedures. On the CD included with the book you'll find a *QuickBooks Pro* file for a construction company (You open it, enter your own company's data, and add info on your suppliers and subs.) You also get a complete estimating program, including a database, and a job costing program that lets you export your estimates to *QuickBooks Pro*. It even includes many useful construction forms to use in your business.
344 pages, 8¹/₂ x 11, $53.00
Also available: **Contractor's Guide to QuickBooks Pro 2001, $45.25**
 Contractor's Guide to QuickBooks Pro 2003, $47.75
 Contractor's Guide to QuickBooks Pro 2004, $48.50
 Contractor's Guide to QuickBooks Pro 2005, $49.75

Craftsman Book Company
6058 Corte del Cedro
P.O. Box 6500
Carlsbad, CA 92018

☎ 24 hour order line
1-800-829-8123
Fax (760) 438-0398

Name_____

e-mail address (for order tracking and special offers)

Company_____

Address_____

City/State/Zip   ◯ This is a residence

Total enclosed_____(In California add 7.25% tax)
We pay shipping when your check covers your order in full.

In A Hurry?

We accept phone orders charged to your

◯ Visa, ◯ MasterCard, ◯ Discover or ◯ American Express

Card#_____

Exp. date_____Initials_____

Tax Deductible: Treasury regulations make these references tax deductible when used in your work. Save the canceled check or charge card statement as your receipt.

Order online http://www.craftsman-book.com
Free on the Internet! Download any of Craftsman's estimating databases for a 30-day free trial! www.craftsman-book.com/downloads

10-Day Money Back Guarantee

◯ 36.50 Basic Engineering for Builders
◯ 78.50 CD Estimator
◯ 41.75 Construction Forms & Contracts with a CD-ROM for *Windows*™ and Macintosh.
◯ 53.00 Contractor's Guide to QuickBooks Pro 2007
◯ 45.25 Contractor's Guide to QuickBooks Pro 2001
◯ 47.75 Contractor's Guide to QuickBooks Pro 2003
◯ 48.50 Contractor's Guide to QuickBooks Pro 2004
◯ 49.75 Contractor's Guide to QuickBooks Pro 2005
◯ 49.50 Contractor's Plain-English Legal Guide
◯ 89.50 Estimating & Bidding for Builders & Remodelers
◯ 39.95 Estimating with Microsoft *Excel*
◯ 32.75 Handbook of Construction Contracting Volume 1
◯ 33.75 Handbook of Construction Contracting Volume 2
◯ 28.50 How to Succeed w/Your Own Construction Business
◯ 37.00 Illustrated Guide to the *Int'l Plumbing & Fuel Gas Codes*
◯ 32.50 Markup & Profit: A Contractor's Guide
◯ 42.00 Moving to Commercial Construction
◯ 57.50 National Construction Estimator with FREE *National Estimator* on a CD-ROM.
◯ 39.95 National Contractors Exam Study Guide
◯ 99.95 Peerless Inst. Contractor's Law & Bus. for Calif. Const. Exam
◯ 99.00 QuickPass CD-ROM for the General Building (B) Examination
◯ 26.50 Rough Framing Carpentry
◯ 39.75 Steel-Frame House Construction
◯ 35.00 Building Contractor's Exam Preparation Guide
◯ FREE Full Color Catalog
Prices subject to change without notice

||||||

NO POSTAGE
NECESSARY
IF MAILED
IN THE
UNITED STATES

BUSINESS REPLY MAIL
FIRST CLASS MAIL PERMIT NO. 271 CARLSBAD, CA

POSTAGE WILL BE PAID BY ADDRESSEE

 Craftsman Book Company
6058 Corte del Cedro
P.O. Box 6500
Carlsbad, CA 92018-9974

||||||

NO POSTAGE
NECESSARY
IF MAILED
IN THE
UNITED STATES

BUSINESS REPLY MAIL
FIRST CLASS MAIL PERMIT NO. 271 CARLSBAD, CA

POSTAGE WILL BE PAID BY ADDRESSEE

 Craftsman Book Company
6058 Corte del Cedro
P.O. Box 6500
Carlsbad, CA 92018-9974

||||||

NO POSTAGE
NECESSARY
IF MAILED
IN THE
UNITED STATES

BUSINESS REPLY MAIL
FIRST CLASS MAIL PERMIT NO. 271 CARLSBAD, CA

POSTAGE WILL BE PAID BY ADDRESSEE

 Craftsman Book Company
6058 Corte del Cedro
P.O. Box 6500
Carlsbad, CA 92018-9974